Bruculinu,

AMERICA

Bruculinu, AMERICA

Remembrances of Sicilian-American Brooklyn, Told in Stories and Recipes

Vincent Schiavelli

A Chapters Book

Houghton Mifflin Company

Boston   New York   1998

For information about permisson to reproduce selections from
this book, write to Permissions, Houghton Mifflin Company, 215
Park Avenue South, New York, New York 10003.

Library of Congress Cataloging-in-Publication Data is available.
ISBN 0-395-91374-8

Grateful acknowledgment is made for permission to reprint
the following recipes, which originally appeared in *Papa Andrea's
Sicilian Table* (Carol Publishing), copyright © 1993 by Vincent
Schiavelli: *Brudu 'i Gaddina* (Chicken Soup), *Tumala d'Andrea*
(Rice Bombe), *Cucciaddatu* (Christmas Pastry), *Limunata*
(Lemon Ice) and *Sfinci 'i San Giuseppi* (Filled Puffs).

"Christmas Eve in Bruculinu," "Lemon Ice to
the Heart, L.A.M.F." and a portion of "The Feast"
were originally printed in the *Los Angeles Times*.

Cover photograph courtesy of Culver Pictures, Inc.
Designed by Susan McClellan

Printed in the United States of America
QUM 10 9 8 7 6 5 4 3 2 1

For my family,
whose nurturing love and poetic song
created for me the heart of
Bruculinu, America

Contents

$\mathscr{I}$ntroduction

THE SPARK FOR MY WRITING THIS BOOK was ignited by an address. It is written on the envelope of a letter my grandmother received in 1905 from a cousin in Polizzi Generosa, Sicily. It simply reads:

Carolina Vilardi

Bruculinu, America

This address clearly illustrates our country cousin's charming naïveté regarding the size and population of Brooklyn. On the other hand, the letter did arrive.

In the early years of the twentieth century, Bruculinu, as the Sicilian immigrants called their Brooklyn neighborhood, was a remarkable place. The old three- and four-story frame tenements overflowed with new arrivals. Whole families, in some places practically the population of whole towns, were clustered in particular buildings and streets. It was not uncommon to see the latest arrivals, with their bundles, trying to find the residence of a cousin in

8

America, their only reference an address on a slip of paper held tightly in hand. The people they passed on the stoops and outside the shops certainly knew for whom they were searching, but in true Sicilian fashion would offer no information; the matter was none of their business.

If the weather was fair, the streets themselves would be teeming with life. Women would be haggling with pushcart vendors in Sicilian and broken English over prices of fruits and vegetables. Other vendors in horse-drawn wagons would be chanting their wares, amid the sound of the ragman's bell and the iceman's bellow. Butcher shops, live-poultry markets, bread bakeries, fishmongers and pastry shops all added to this theater of daily life.

During the dead of winter, these new immigrants might wonder why they left the brilliant sunshine of Sicily for this bleak foreign land, this *La Merica*, but in the end, most of them stayed.

They prospered, or not, but always strove for a better life while maintaining their ancient Sicilian culture. They married, had families and tried to rear their children according to these customs. Some traditions survived, but others, perhaps for the best, were left to the dust of time and memory.

The Bruculinu of my childhood, some 50 years later, was virtually unchanged, down to the horse-drawn carts. Growing up in this place was like having one foot in mid-twentieth-century United States and the other in mid-sixteenth-century Sicily. It was a straddle that seems more impossible as the years pass. Back then, however, this was our life.

Television was beginning to come into our homes to show us a glimpse of how "the Americans" lived in such TV towns as those of *Father Knows Best* or *Leave It to Beaver*. At the time, we simply did not believe that people lived in such places or behaved in such ways. (Maybe no one actually did.)

The harmony of life in the old Brooklyn neighborhood, and

9

the coda of this book, is based on Sicilian food. No matter what, one always had to eat. Specific dishes were used to mark seasons and events; others, according to traditional wisdom, had medicinal value and could restore health or well-being; still others were imported and adapted from the other immigrant cultures all around us, or from "the Americans," whose cuisine generally left us puzzled. We didn't know what they ate.

Supper, a daily ritual observed in every household, provided a forum for exchange among the generations of family members. The food was always the centerpiece of this ritual. In addition to providing sustenance, it served to nourish our heritage. Food is, after all, edible culture.

The 2,500-year-old culinary tradition of Sicily was very much in evidence in our apartment at 1264 Myrtle Avenue, between Cedar and Hart streets in the Bushwick section of Brooklyn. My grandfather, Papa Andrea, prior to his immigration in 1900, had been *monzù*, master chef, to the Baron Rampolla of Polizzi Generosa.

The culinary tradition of the *monzù* began in Sicily at the outset of the nineteenth century. It was then the fashion among the houses of the powerful aristocracy to import chefs from France. These great masters applied the French method to traditional Sicilian cuisine, creating a collection of dishes known for their subtle refinement. Throughout that century, this style of cuisine remained popular and grew, as native-born Sicilian apprentices learned from French masters. So, from these original *monsieurs* evolved the Sicilian *monzù*.

The 70 or so recipes that accompany these stories and embody these qualities are from the hand of Papa Andrea. They represent the everyday fare of our household, as well as the more elaborate dishes prepared for holidays and special occasions. Their magic still delights the senses and enriches the home hearth.

The stories themselves may not always contain the strict facts, but they certainly tell the truth of that place, of that time, of our Bru-culinu.

I.

Nana Caterina and the Miracle of the Carnations

THE SICILIANS of my grandparents' generation believed in miracles. The presence of the god force in their everyday lives was as palpable to them as bread. Their relationships with the saints were similar to those with the nobles of their native country, but far more personal and trusting. The saints were poor like themselves and, therefore, on their side. Heavenly intercession could cure the sick, prevent accidents and find lost objects.

Because of their devotion to a particular saint or an apparition of the Virgin, certain women in the neighborhood were believed to have a special pipeline to Heaven. They would offer prayers on someone's behalf as readily as the literate would write letters for those who were less educated. One of these women lived upstairs from my family on Ellery Street in Brooklyn during the twenties and thirties.

Nana Caterina was a widow of indeterminable age. She was short and round with thick, pure white hair tied up in a bun. She wore a black skirt over many spotless white petticoats, reaching to the floor. Her legs were covered in heavy black stockings, her feet in bedroom slippers. She always felt a chill and wore a large, black, woolen sweater in all seasons. Her head was often bound in a dish towel filled with peeled potatoes, a remedy she believed eased her constantly throbbing headache. Her pale face had a certain glow emanating from her gray eyes, the glow of someone who had peered into the eye of God.

The top-floor tenement apartment of Nana Caterina was more like a chapel than a residence. The rooms were filled with statues of various saints surrounded by candles. The centerpiece of these shrines was an actual altar, supporting a large statue of the Madonna of Fontanellato, to whom Nana Caterina was particularly devoted. She sincerely believed that the Virgin of this apparition spoke directly to her in dreams and signs.

If Sunday's weather was inclement, Nana Caterina would instruct all the children in the building not to go to church for Mass. "Come to me," she would say. "I will say Mass. God will understand."

Years earlier, in 1907, my grandmother Carolina gave birth to her first child, Salvatore Calogero Coco. My grandfather Andrea, thrilled to have a child and a son, gave the infant his first bath in champagne. Salvatore was not only the firstborn, he was an American.

As time passed, Salvatore grew into a fine young man, adored by his mother and idolized by his younger sisters and brother. He was industrious and hardworking, leaving school at 13 to work with my grandfather at the wholesale fruit market. He was quite handsome, and the impeccability of his clothing has become family legend. It is said that one of the neighborhood girls had to be hospitalized for "a nervous breakdown" after he refused her advances.

Sometime in his midteens, Salvatore changed his name to

Robert—Bob for short. His vision of the future would take him out of the neighborhood, and for this dream "Salvatore Calogero" just didn't work.

In 1925, tragedy befell the family. Bob, at the age of 18, was taken ill with pneumonia. In those days, a generation before the discovery of antibiotics, pneumonia meant almost certain death. Doctors had very few tools with which to combat the pernicious bacteria. The best they could hope for was a miracle cure.

Bob lay in bed in a darkened room. The household spoke in whispers, so as not to disturb him. Everyone's eyes were red from crying, with exhausted expressions from lack of sleep. Relatives and friends visited in a constant stream to learn the latest condition of the patient. The women joined my grandmother and her daughters around the bed in praying the Rosary. The men congregated in the kitchen with my grandfather, cursing all the saints in heaven for this betrayal of trust.

After days of frequent visits, the family doctor made his final pronouncement: "Within the next 24 hours, Bob will either pass his crisis or not. It is in God's hands now." The women and girls redoubled their prayers to Heaven, the men silenced their blasphemy.

Bob's condition grew more and more critical as his fever rose higher and higher. Life seemed to be leaving his young body. The vigil continued through the night and, by morning, the fever still raging, Bob fell into unconsciousness. A priest was called and the last rites administered. Everyone kissed Bob good-bye as he embarked on that final journey.

Early in the morning there was a knock at the door. It was Nana Caterina, breathless and holding a bunch of carnations. "Last night," she said to my grandmother, "the Madonna of Fontanellato appeared to me in a dream. She said to me, 'Caterina, my devoted servant, is there any favor you wish from me?' I said to her, 'Blessed Mother, Queen of Heaven, there is a fine young man downstairs dying of illness. Perhaps, my Lady, you could please help him?' The beautiful woman said, 'Bring him carnations in my name and remember me.' With that, I awoke and ran to the florist to buy these carnations, which I bring to your son in the name of the Virgin."

My grandmother brought the carnations to her dying son. She placed them in his listless hands, gently moving them up to his ashen face. After a moment, Bob became aware of their fragrance, and began to inhale it with the gusto of a starving man at a banquet. Suddenly he opened his eyes, his fever broken, his crisis passed. All present, including the men, knowing they had witnessed a miracle, fell to their knees, praising and thanking Heaven.

THE NEXT DAY, NANA CATERINA GAVE MY GRANDMOTHER a picture card of the Madonna with a prayer in Italian printed on the back:

Remember, O most compassionate Virgin Mary, that never was it known in the world that anyone who fled to your protection, implored your help or sought your patronage, was ever left unaided. Inspired by this confidence I, too, come to you, O Virgin of virgins, my Mother. To you I come with tears in my eyes, guilty of a thousand faults, prostrating myself at your feet, asking for pity. Please do not disdain my supplication, O Mother of the Word, but kindly listen and hear my plea.

Whatever the outcome, Our Lady of the Holy Rosary of Fontanellato, pray for us.

My grandmother, keeping her contract with the Virgin, remembered to say this prayer every day of her life.

Uncle Bob lived a long, rich, full life. He married and had three children and six grandchildren whom he watched grow to adulthood. He died at 85, from an illness complicated by pneumonia. Some might say that his death was postponed 67 years by Nana Caterina and the miracle of the carnations.

Recipes

IN OUR HOUSEHOLD, to celebrate the birthday of each of my grandmother's children, we ate the same food that she did before going into labor. Although most of these dishes were common everyday fare throughout the neighborhood, when served on these days, they magically took on special significance and flavor.

Fucurinia

rickly Pears

THE NOVEMBER 6 BIRTHDAY OF MY AUNT MAE, who was given the beautifully aristocratic name Gandolfa Francesca Paola, was always celebrated by eating prickly pears. Each year, this wonderfully sweet fruit found its way from the American Southwest to our table in Brooklyn. A more remarkable journey, however, is the one it took in the sixteenth century from America to Sicily.

At that time, Spain held a worldwide monopoly on cochineal, a red dye prepared from the bodies of an insect native to the New World. The prickly pear cactus is host to this insect, and the Spanish wished to bring production closer to their European markets. For that reason, they transplanted many cuttings from their colonial holdings in the Western Hemisphere to the Kingdom of the Two Sicilies, at that time also part of their empire. Based on the error of the day as to where these "new" lands were, the Sicilian name, *fucurinia*, derives from the Italian, *fichi d'India*, "figs of India."

To us, the fragrant deep red fruit with its many edible seeds found beneath the dangerously spiny skin was part of Sicily itself. As we ate them, my grandfather enjoyed making prickly pear jokes, which inevitably ended with some fool sitting on the thorny fruit.

Nowadays, prickly pears found in markets have had their spines removed. It is still best, however, to peel them using the traditional method, which helps to keep the soft, juicy fruit intact. Refrigerate prickly pears until slightly chilled. Carefully holding the fruit between the spines with your fingertips, cut off both ends. Slip a fork in one end and slit the fruit along its length. Using this slit as a starting place, peel the skin away in one piece with a knife. Pull the fruit off the fork and eat it with your fingers, seeds and all.

Pasta chi Fasoli

Macaroni with Beans

THIS WARMING DISH was served the evening before Aunt Bessie (short for Sebastiana) was born, December 21. Numerous versions of this peasant fare exist throughout Italy and across the sea to Sicily. This recipe is a very simple one of my grandfather's.

For 6 servings

1 pound dried pinto beans
  Pinch of cinnamon
¼ cup plus 2 tablespoons extra-virgin olive oil, plus more for drizzling over the beans
1 medium onion, chopped very fine
6 cups spring water, for cooking
2 tablespoons plus 1 teaspoon sea salt
1 tablespoon chopped leaves of wild fennel or bulb fennel
1 pound ditalini or other small tube pasta
  Black pepper

Put the beans in a colander and wash them under cold running water. Check for small stones and other debris. Transfer to a large bowl, add the cinnamon, cover with cold water and soak for 12 hours.

Drain the beans. Put the ¼ cup olive oil and the onion in a large pot over low heat. Sauté until the onion has turned a rich golden brown, about 10 minutes. Stir in the beans and add the spring water. Season with 1 teaspoon salt. Simmer gently, with the cover askew, for 1 hour. Add the fennel and continue to cook for 1 hour longer, or until the beans are tender. Puree about ½ cup of the beans in a blender or food processor. Stir the puree back into the rest of the beans.

Fill a large pot with 6 quarts water. Add the 2 tablespoons oil and the 2 tablespoons salt and bring to a boil. Add the pasta and cook until al dente. Drain the pasta and add it to the pot of beans. Let stand for a few minutes so the flavors mingle.

Serve from the pot, with a drizzle of olive oil and a grinding of black pepper.

Sosizza chi Patati

Sausage with Potatoes

THIS RECIPE FOR ITALIAN SAUSAGE brings out its hearty, rustic goodness. In our household, it was cooked for Uncle Bob's birthday, January 13.

For 6 servings

2 pounds russet, Yukon Gold or Yellow Finn potatoes
3 bell peppers, assorted colors
1 medium onion
2½ pounds thin or thick sweet (mild) Italian sausage, preferably in a coil rather than links
¼ cup extra-virgin olive oil
Sea salt
Black pepper
1½ cups dry red wine
¼ teaspoon dried oregano

Preheat oven to 450°F.

Peel the potatoes and cut them into strips about 3 inches long and ½ inch thick. Put them in a bowl with just enough cold water to cover and set them aside to soak.

Seed the peppers and cut them into pieces about 2 inches long and 1 inch wide. Peel the onion, slice it fairly thin and separate into rings.

Arrange the sausage in a coil in the center of a large roasting pan. Drain the potatoes and place them on either side of the sausage. Arrange the peppers and onion rings on top of the potatoes. Drizzle the olive oil over the vegetables. Season with salt and black pepper.

Roast for 20 minutes, then pour the wine over the sausage and vegetables. Turn the vegetables. Using a metal spatula, carefully loosen any potatoes that may have stuck to the bottom of the pan. Roast for 20 to 40 minutes more, depending on the thickness of the sausage, or until the sausage and potatoes are cooked through. Sprinkle with oregano and serve.

Brudu

$\mathcal{M}$eat Broth

WHEN GIUSEPPINA, AUNT JO, WAS BORN on March 2, the month must have come in like a lion. This broth, delicate, warming and delicious, alternated with chicken soup as Monday-night fare during the colder months in our household.

The key to making good broth is to simmer it very slowly so that all the flavors of the meat, bones and vegetables cook into the liquid. This recipe calls for short ribs, and by the time the broth is cooked, they have given their all to it. Nonetheless, there is a certain comfort in eating the meat with the broth.

For 6 servings

- 4 pounds short ribs
- 1 pound veal bones
- 4 quarts plus 1 cup spring water
  Sea salt
- 2 large carrots
- 2 celery ribs
- 2 small Roma tomatoes
- 2 medium onions
- 4 cloves
- 12 sprigs Italian parsley, chopped
- 2 tablespoons extra-virgin olive oil
- 1 pound orzo, pastina or little star pasta
  Grated imported pecorino cheese, preferably Locatelli
  Black pepper

Put the short ribs, veal bones, water and 1 tablespoon salt in a stockpot. Place the pot on the stove with the cover askew. Very slowly bring it to a boil over medium heat. Skim away the foam that rises to the top.

Meanwhile, prepare the vegetables. Scrape the carrots and cut them in half. Wash the celery and tomatoes, cutting them also in half. Peel the onions and push a clove in each end. When the broth comes to a boil, add the vegetables and reduce the heat to low. Simmer, with the cover askew, for 3 hours, removing foam as necessary. Check occasionally to make certain the simmer is maintained. Do not let the broth boil.

When the broth is ready, turn off the heat and let it settle for 5 minutes. Strain through a fine-mesh strainer into a large bowl. Discard the veal bones and vegetables. Transfer the short ribs to a small pot. Pour a little broth over the ribs, cover the pot and keep warm on low heat.

Remove the fat from the broth with a fat separator or large spoon. Return the broth to the pot, stir in the parsley and taste for salt, adding more if necessary. Cover and keep the broth hot over low heat.

Fill a large pot with water. Add the oil and 2 tablespoons salt and bring it to a boil. Add the pasta and cook until al dente. Lift out the pasta with a large perforated spoon, placing about ⅓ cup in the bottom of each soup bowl.

Ladle the broth into the bowls and serve with a sprinkling of grated cheese and a grinding of black pepper. Accompany it with good, crusty Italian bread. Serve the ribs on the side.

Refrigerate the leftover meat and broth together. Drain the leftover pasta and store it separately. To serve the leftovers, reheat the broth and ribs, then add the pasta for about 2 minutes.

Spaghetti e Purpetti

Spaghetti and Meatballs

IT IS WIDELY BELIEVED that this dish is completely American in origin. It has certainly become so, with versions that lack any of the subtlety of the original. Rest assured, however, that the dish does have Old World roots. To maintain authenticity, do not eat the spaghetti and meatballs at the same time, but rather eat the meatballs as a second course out of the same bowl. Drizzle a little tomato sauce over them and serve with good Italian bread.

My grandfather used to drain meatballs and other fried foods on brown paper bags. This method is perfectly safe, as the heat of the frying oil is so high it kills any bacteria. Paper towels can be substituted for this purpose, but I find brown paper still to be the best material for the job.

The flavors of this meal still lingered with my grandmother when she gave birth to Calogero, Uncle Charlie, on that April 20.

For 4 servings

FOR THE TOMATO SAUCE

2 28-ounce cans peeled Italian plum tomatoes
1 small onion, finely chopped
2 tablespoons extra-virgin olive oil
2 tablespoons tomato paste dissolved in ½ cup water
   Sea salt
   Black pepper
2 teaspoons sugar
¼ teaspoon dried basil

FOR THE MEATBALLS

¾ pound ground veal

4 ounces ground pork

2 1½-inch-thick slices Italian bread, crusts removed, soaked
   in milk and squeezed of excess liquid

2 large eggs

⅓ cup grated imported pecorino cheese, preferably Locatelli

¼ cup extra-virgin olive oil

1 garlic clove, peeled and left whole

FOR THE SPAGHETTI

2 tablespoons extra-virgin olive oil

2 tablespoons sea salt

1 pound spaghetti
   Grated imported pecorino cheese, preferably Locatelli

Prepare the tomato sauce: Place a food mill fitted with the smallest-holed (1/16 inch) disk over a bowl. Mill the tomatoes in order to remove the seeds, which can make the sauce bitter. Scrape the pulp from the bottom of the mill into the bowl. Put the onion in the olive oil in a heavy medium pot over medium heat and sauté the onion until it turns translucent, about 5 minutes. Stir in the dissolved tomato paste. Let the mixture thicken for about 1 minute and add the tomatoes. Season with salt and pepper and add the sugar and basil. Reduce the heat to low and simmer the sauce, uncovered, stirring from time to time, for 40 minutes. Do not let it boil.

Prepare the meatballs: Put the veal, pork, bread, eggs and cheese in a bowl. Knead the mixture with your hands until smooth. Form it into 10 oval meatballs about 2 inches long and 1 inch thick.

Heat the oil and garlic in a heavy medium skillet over medium-high heat. When the garlic begins to color, remove and discard it. Brown the meatballs, turning them, until they are a rich color, 2 to

2½ minutes on each side. Drain them on brown paper or paper towels and put them in the sauce. Simmer gently for 1 hour.

Prepare the spaghetti: While the meatballs are cooking, fill a large pot with 6 quarts water, add the oil and salt and bring to a boil. When the meatballs are ready, cook the pasta until al dente. Drain well.

Place portions of the spaghetti in pasta bowls and top lightly with a few spoonfuls of sauce and grated cheese. Serve the meatballs as a second course.

CHAPTER I.

Cunserva 'i Fraguli

Strawberry Jam

WHEN MY GRANDMOTHER was about to give birth to my mother, she mysteriously had the taste of strawberries in her mouth, although she had not eaten any. Baby Carmella, known as Katie, had a small, delicate strawberry mark behind her left ear, so we ate strawberries for my mother's birthday, August 10.

In that place and time, strawberry jam was the only way to taste that summer fruit in all seasons. We always had it in the house. This recipe produces a jam that is sure to relieve a craving for the flavor and texture of fresh strawberries. The ingredients and process are not intended for canning, but rather to make a small batch quickly and easily.

For about 1 pint jam

1 pound strawberries, deep red and perfectly ripe
2 cups sugar
½ cup spring water
2 teaspoons lemon juice
Pinch of cinnamon

Wash, hull and halve the strawberries.

Place the sugar and water in a heavy medium pot over very low heat. Stirring constantly with a wooden spoon, dissolve the sugar. Stop stirring, increase the heat to low and let the mixture boil for 3 minutes. Add the strawberries, lemon juice and cinnamon and continue to boil for about 10 minutes. When the mixture bubbles up in the pot, stir it down.

27

Fill the sink with a few inches of cold water to cool the pot when the jam is ready. When the mixture no longer bubbles up, immediately remove it from the heat and place it in the sink to stop the cooking process.

Pour the jam into a hot sterilized pint jar, cool, cover and refrigerate. The jam will keep for about 2 weeks.

II.

U Clubbu

NOWADAYS IN AMERICA, the men's club barely exists. In
the mid-fifties in Bruculinu, however, these institutions
dotted the old neighborhood. I am not speaking of
great granite structures where men in stodgy suits,
seated in tufted leather armchairs, met to read the *Wall Street Journal*.
Our clubs were housed in storefronts; here the journals most often
read were the *New York Daily News* and the *Racing Form*.

We had several types of men's clubs. Most of them had the ini-
tials S.A.C., for Social-Athletic Club, following their names. The
men of these clubs played ball or bowled on the amateur circuit.
On occasion, the clubs sponsored dances or other social events, but
their main function was as a meeting place where the workingman
could find a bit of relief from the pressures of family life.

Some of the S.A.C.s were the clubhouses of street gangs. Their
social-athletic activity took the form of street fighting with their ri-
vals. A few of the other clubs had blackened windows, and their serious, dark-suited members maintained a low profile. These were the
meeting places of "da wise guys, da boys." We all knew who they
were and what they did, but no one ever even spoke of them. They
could rely on the respect of our silence, and in return they kept the
neighborhood quiet and safe.

The progenitor of all the men's clubs in our neighborhood was La Società di Polizzi Generosa, the Polizzi Generosa Society. It was established by immigrants from that Sicilian town at the turn of the twentieth century. Its purpose was to provide a safe haven in this hostile new world. The club supported the men and their families in maintaining their ancient Sicilian traditions *'a via vecchia,* "in the old way," against encroaching Americanism. It sponsored lectures and forums and social functions. The annual Polizzi Generosa Society Ball was the most important social event of the community.

Another important aspect of the club was its function as a kind of savings and loan, offering short-term credit to members on the collateral of their integrity and a handshake. Many a neighborhood business was originally financed by these good-faith loans.

The club was also a strong political force, endorsing candidates for city government and furnishing advocacy against prejudicial injustice. To the "American" Brooklynites, the Sicilian immigrants were spaghetti benders, greaseballs, dirty guineas, wops and dago bastards, to name but a handful of the common ethnic slurs of the day. Their ungrounded fear of a culture they didn't understand, a continuing American tradition of bigotry, made it difficult for the Sicilians to move forward. Many decades would pass before Sicilian names like Joe DiMaggio, Antonin Scalia and Martin Scorsese would become important pieces of the American patchwork quilt.

WHEN I WAS A BOY IN BRUCULINU, the charter members of the *clubbu,* the patriarchs of the community, met at the clubhouse every afternoon to smoke cigars and play cards. Many of these men had known one another before their arrival in America, having grown up together in one of the seven sections of Polizzi Generosa, or in nearby villages. In some cases, these relationships had spanned more than 70 years. To call them old friends doesn't quite express the depth of experience they had shared. Even so, they never used the intimate form in conversation, always prefacing one another's names with *Don,* or *Professuri,* or *Mastru,* titles of mutual respect and the education of a lifetime.

Most days, my grandfather Papa Andrea joined his cronies at the *clubbu* for the afternoon's activities. During this time he was incommunicado. Only for the rarest of emergencies would one of the ladies of the household consider going to this male bastion to see him, or even telephone him there. If the family matter at hand was of lesser importance, it simply had to wait until he returned home. This protocol changed when I was eight, for then I could be sent as messenger without offending propriety.

I remember my first clubhouse visit. My grandmother Carolina wrote a note in her exquisite handwriting, which said, in Sicilian, that her brother and his wife were unexpectedly coming for dinner that night. "Perhaps, Andrea, you should stop at the poultry market on the way home for a larger chicken."

My grandmother told me that I should say none of this to my grandfather, I was only to show him the note. What went on in our household, she reminded me, was no affair of the men at the club. It was private family business.

I walked the six long blocks down Hart Street in the direction of the club, the note secure in my pocket. As I reached Wyckoff Avenue, I could see the club across the street a few doors in from the corner. The large gold-lettered sign stenciled along the double storefront windows glinted in the afternoon sunlight. Below it, spanning the width of the windows, were baize curtains, pressed and neatly gathered. They hung from wooden rings on polished brass poles.

I crossed Wyckoff and entered, standing in the doorway. My eyes began to burn from the acrid, pungent fog created by the smoke of skinny, twisted Italian cigars, nicknamed "guinea stinkers." The large dark room was filled with old round and square card tables and a collection of well-worn bentwood chairs. Along one wall was a coffee bar. Every place was filled with mustached old men in virtually identical cardigan sweaters. They puffed away as they played intense games of pinochle or *briscola,* a Sicilian game of trumps. No one spoke. There were only the occasional grumble and the snap of cards as they hit the table.

As I scanned the room for Papa Andrea, no one acknowledged my presence. I found him seated deep in the room facing the door, an old Sicilian precaution. I silently moved toward him, stopping short of his table, careful not to interrupt the game. When the hand was over, he nodded in my direction. I came closer, and, in an almost whisper, explained in Sicilian that I had a note from home.

He read the note with a poker face that revealed nothing of its contents. Refolding it, he placed it in his sweater pocket, with the gesture of an international spy having just learned his latest assignment.

I stood there for a moment not knowing what to do next. Papa Andrea gave a slight nod at the door. I picked up the cue and backed away, bidding a low, respectful good afternoon to the other men at the table, all of whom had been surreptitiously following the exchange out of the corners of their eyes. They solemnly returned the greeting as cards were dealt for a new hand.

Later that afternoon Papa Andrea returned home. He proudly strode through the door with a freshly killed plump chicken under his arm and a huge smile on his face. He sat down next to me at the kitchen table where I was doing my homework. Taking my face in his hands, he said, *"Figghiu miu, ha fattu bravu."* "My son, you did good."

ONE AFTERNOON, A COUPLE OF YEARS LATER, Papa Andrea was late in getting home from the club. My mother and aunts, who held jobs as secretaries or bookkeepers in offices in downtown Brooklyn or Manhattan, returned home, but still he had not appeared. They phoned the club, but there was no answer. We all speculated on where he might be, avoiding the worst-case scenario for a missing 86-year-old man.

Aunt Jo decided to go to the club—maybe there was a note on the door for us. She took me with her in case a male presence was needed. We walked quickly along the route in silence, holding hands for support. Upon reaching our destination, we found the door unlocked and the lights blazing. Hands of cards were laid in each place. Cigar smoke curled up from ashtrays. Everything was as it should have been, except there were no people.

Aunt Jo sent me inside to explore. Even under these circumstances, she would go no farther than the doorway: propriety always takes precedence.

I didn't realize how deep the building was. Behind the card room was a large darkened room that I supposed was used for the famous annual ball. A bit of light seeped into its far end from around a corner. I moved toward it, my footsteps echoing through the empty ballroom. As I approached the turn, an old man popped out. He raised a finger to his lips, whispering as if in church. "Shhh! The maestro is cooking."

In the bright light of a small kitchen, I saw my grandfather, Papa Andrea, in front of the stove, standing beside a large platter of breaded veal cutlets. He was in the middle of giving a cooking lesson to the other old men gathered around him, transfixed. As the last cutlet was ready, they could wait no longer and rushed the platter, grabbing cutlets, eating them off paper napkins with their fingers. They made sounds of enjoyment as bits of the delicate breading caught in their mustaches.

I told Papa Andrea that Aunt Jo was waiting at the door. He said good-bye to his appreciative friends and hurriedly went out the door to mitigate his daughter's fears. Relieved at seeing him, she let out a heartfelt thank you to Heaven.

Looking at her with a smile in his eyes, he said, "My dear child, don't worry. If I die, I'll phone you."

ONE SPRING DAY WHEN I WAS 12, Papa Andrea and I were out food shopping. As we passed the club, he suggested we go inside for something to drink. He had an espresso, I had a Coca-Cola. Standing at the coffee bar, he was introduced to a neighbor of one of the members, brought along for an afternoon of card playing. The man presented himself as Nicolò Cavallo. He spoke a language I had never heard before, Florentine Italian.

My grandfather returned the introduction in this same strange language. This set the whole room atwitter. When Papa Andrea said that he, too, was from the north, all the other men wandered silently back to the tables to resume their card games, keeping an ear up to hear what would happen next. Following their lead of feigned indifference, I slid down the bar and corralled my Coke, staring into the glass.

Nicolò Cavallo and Papa Andrea had a lengthy conversation in that mysterious dialect about the beauty of Florence and the refinement of its culture. In this clubhouse, filled with Sicilians, the exchange took on the same kind of coded inference two bigots might use in a room filled with African-Americans. At one point Nicolò leaned close to Andrea, and whispered, "It is unfortunate, *paisano,* that we are forced to live here among these stupid Sicilian pigs, but such is our fate." At this, Papa Andrea looked the man squarely in the eye, and with a loud voice in beautifully clear Sicilian, he said, "Don't you recognize me, Nicola Cavaddu?" The man grew flustered, pretending not to understand. "Your father was a *carbúnaiu,* he made charcoal. Your family lived in a filthy shack on the outskirts of town. We came over together from Sicily on the same ship. You still don't remember me, huh? I'm Andrea Coco."

The man tried to cover his embarrassment with laughter, pretending that it was just a joke, that he had recognized Andrea all along. No one bought it. They all refocused on their games, the cards now snapping down with the force of their anger at this betrayal by Nicola, one of their own.

Over the next few minutes, Nicola Cavaddu became more and more nervous, like a crab louse. On some stuttering pretext or other, he left the club, never to return.

The feelings of anger in the room subsided, replaced with a sudden burst of laughter. Everyone gathered around Papa Andrea, complimenting him on the way in which he exposed this pathetic fool. The event was comically reenacted, with someone dramatizing Nicola's ignoble exit in broad strokes, eliciting more laughter and calls for encore. Over time, the story of Mastru Andrea and Don Piducchiusu (Mr. Crab Louse), a.k.a. Nicola Cavaddu, became part of the oral tradition of the *clubbu*. The scene was acted out for many years, the players becoming as renowned as the real people.

A LTHOUGH THE CLUBHOUSE has moved to a different location, the Polizzi Generosa Society still exists. Afternoons there are quiet now, the patriarchs and their card games long gone. In time, perhaps, its younger, more American members will take the places of their grandfathers and great-grandfathers, but the world has changed and the sagacity of years seems to no longer have a place in it.

Cutuletti

Veal Cutlets

HERE IS THE RECIPE that so enthralled the members of Papa Andrea's club. At home, we would always have these cutlets with a mixed green salad. If there had not been a first course of soup or pasta, potatoes like the baked, mashed ones on page 140 would also be served.

For 4 servings

8 thin veal cutlets (about 1½ pounds)
2 tablespoons milk, plus more for soaking
  Pinch of cinnamon
2 large eggs
  Unflavored fine dry bread crumbs, for dredging
8 tablespoons (1 stick) unsalted butter
¼ cup olive oil
  Sprigs Italian parsley, for garnish
  Lemon wedges
  Sea salt

To pound the veal to a thickness of ⅛ inch, place each cutlet between sheets of waxed paper and use a meat pounder to gently hit the cutlet with glancing blows. Continue in a circular pattern, moving from the center to the edge, until the desired thickness is achieved. If the cutlets were cut very thick in the first place, it may be necessary to make small cuts along the edge to prevent them from curling. If they are very large after pounding, cut them in half.

Place the pounded cutlets in a bowl with enough milk to cover and the cinnamon. Cover and refrigerate for at least 4 hours.

Remove the cutlets from the milk and pat dry. Beat the eggs and 2 tablespoons milk together in a medium bowl. Put the bread crumbs on a plate or piece of waxed paper next to the bowl. Dip the cutlets in the egg wash, letting the excess drip off, and dredge in bread crumbs, being sure to coat completely.

When ready to fry, preheat the oven to 300°F and put in an empty roasting pan.

Heat the butter and olive oil in a large skillet over medium-high heat. When the foam subsides, slip in as many cutlets as will fit comfortably. Fry until the bottoms are golden and crisp, about 3 minutes. Turn with a spatula and cook the other side until golden and crisp. Note that the second side will take less time. Drain the cutlets on brown paper or paper towels and place them in the roasting pan while cooking the next batch.

When all the cutlets are ready, arrange them on a warmed platter circled with parsley and lemon wedges. Season with salt and serve.

III.

*C*afé Niuru

BEFORE ICED DOUBLE CAPPUCCINOS TO GO, before
home espresso machines and automatic-drip coffee-
makers, before automobiles and telephones, perhaps before the wheel, there was my grandmother's coffee.

The Sicilians called their coffee *café niuru,* black coffee, not because it was served without cream but because it was brewed from
dark-roasted, oily, rich beans. In former times, my grandmother Carolina roasted beans at home in the oven of her coal stove on Ellery
Street.

Many immigrants did the same because the available beans, more
lightly roasted, did not produce coffee black and bitter enough for
their taste. The Italian-American custom of serving lemon peel with
espresso to heighten the bitter flavor began at this time.

By the time I was a boy, in the 1950s, Carolina no longer roasted
her own beans because the proper product was now readily available in markets. She still, however, ground the coffee in an old hand-
cranked coffee grinder. She held the box between her knees,
cranking with her right hand as she added just the right amount of
beans with her left.

The method my grandmother used to make her coffee is as old

as the beverage itself. She'd put the grinds directly into boiling water and return the mixture to a boil. She'd then pour it through a fine-mesh strainer into a large cup. The resulting beverage was black, thick and robust, with a golden layer on top. Moments after pouring, the gold would turn into tiny rainbow bubbles and then disappear into the blackness, as if by magic.

At breakfast, the strained coffee was heated with an equal amount of milk and a little sugar, turning it into *café francisi,* French coffee. It accompanied slices of Italian bread, left over from the previous night's dinner, toasted and served with butter and strawberry jam. As a boy, my usual breakfast beverage was a cup of hot milk, with a little sugar, and *na macchia*—"a stain"—of my grandmother's robust black coffee.

Growing up, the aroma of *café niuru* was the first thing I smelled in the morning. Its glorious aroma gently roused me from sleep, providing me with a sense of security and well-being; it let me know that all was as it should be.

That smell still brings me back to our kitchen on Myrtle Avenue, to snowy mornings when we'd huddle around the radio to learn if school was closed. On hot, sunny summer mornings, it conjured images of Africa, the place I'd learned in school where coffee originates.

E VERY AFTERNOON, my grandmother had women friends and relatives in for a cup of her delicious brew. Over the years, the coffee had become the *raison d'être* for a daily event far more profound than a coffee klatch. Gossip had its place, but more importantly, my grandmother's kitchen was a meeting place where women of the neighborhood shared their lives. It provided a forum for medical and marital advice and information about pregnancy, birthing and child care. It was the first place to visit after a honeymoon and the first outing for mothers with new babies.

It was also the place where women whose entire families were illiterate took their letters from Sicily to be read. It was here that they learned the happy news of the intended emigration of a loved one or the tragedy of the death of a close relative across the sea. The other women shared in their joy and comforted them in their sorrow, and Carolina wrote out the dictated responses.

When my mother, aunts and uncles were children, teachers from the grade school across the street from their home on Ellery Street would stop for a cup of *café niuru*. Although these women were mostly "American" and didn't speak or understand the language that was spoken, they understood the camaraderie and compassion of this sisterhood.

B Y THE TIME I WAS A BOY, this meeting had been in session for more than 50 years. In the afternoons, when my grandfather was at the *clubbu*, the women, now older, gathered around our oil-cloth-covered kitchen table. They shared news, gossiped or just sat quietly enjoying their coffee, thankful for the break in their still busy household schedules.

In the year or so before I entered the first grade, I enjoyed being a silent party to these afternoon gatherings. I would play with some mechanical toy or other on the kitchen floor, seemingly uninterested, but attentive to every word and gesture. As far as the women were concerned, I was still a baby, and they felt no need to censor their activity.

I marked the delicacy with which the ladies drank their coffee and ate their biscotti. One of them had a most remarkable dunking technique. She'd hold the cookie over the cup, spooning the coffee over a section of it until it reached the desired saturation. Using her teaspoon as a sort of safety net to prevent the fragile moistened cookie from falling, she would carefully lift it to her mouth.

Sometimes I would position myself under the table, a great vantage point to see under the ladies' dresses. My interest was by no means sexual. It was mechanical. To me, the tangle of garter clips, straps and girdles was as wondrous an architecture as that of the Brooklyn Bridge.

The regulars numbered about eight, including my grandmother's cousin Angelina Termini, her friend Nana Rosa, and our next-door neighbor Minnie. Angelina, the daughter of my grandmother's first cousin, was considerably younger than Carolina, but she bore the old-fashioned manner of a peer. Her broad smile and steady goodness inspired reassurance. To this day, Angelina maintains the family's oral history. She always brought news of family members on both sides of the Atlantic, as well as a large bakery bag of Sicilian ladyfingers, called *taralli,* my grandmother's favorite cookie.

Nana Rosa was a woman of advanced years. A widow for a long time by then, she wore the blackest of dresses. Rosa stood four feet eight and was endowed with enormous breasts. She'd arrive a bit winded from climbing the two flights of stairs to our apartment. As she sat down, she'd lift her breasts with a sigh and rest them on the kitchen table in front of her.

Minnie was much younger than the other women. She was a bit underweight with a pale complexion and dark hair. Having grown up in the neighborhood, she spoke fluent Sicilian with a Minsk accent. Everyone marveled at this result of cross-culturalism in immigrant Brooklyn.

She and her husband, Maxie, lived next door on the ground floor in the apartment behind the shop. It had been Maxie's kosher butcher shop until the untimely death of his mother had thrown him into a deep depression. As a result, he had tried to commit suicide with one of his butcher knives. To avoid further tragedy, the shop was closed, and Maxie found employment as a clerk, away from sharp objects.

Minnie was as devoted to her observance of Judaism as the other women were to Roman Catholicism. In a profound effort to overcome the disappointments created by her husband's recurring condition, Minnie always found the humor in any situation, no matter how grim, and we all admired her ability to sift nonsense from what was truly important.

NEITHER THE COLD OF WINTER NOR THE SWELTER OF SUMMER ever prevented the women from meeting in our kitchen. One particularly bitter winter's day, the women could speak of nothing but the weather. They turned over their sleeves and hems to show the number of layers they had worn against the chill. Minnie displayed her protection, her husband's fire-engine red long johns. Everyone laughed at this particularly unfeminine attire. When Minnie hitched one side of her full woolen skirt to her belt and posed in her baggy red flannels with her arms over her head, like a Spanish dancer, everyone laughed even louder.

My grandmother began to grind the coffee. The sound of the old cast-iron mechanism scraping against the coffee beans set up a Moorish rhythm. To this accompaniment and in that costume, Minnie began prancing around the kitchen like Carmen. She hummed her way through the habanera. When she reached the chorus of "Amour, Amour," the only words of the aria she knew, she nearly sent the other women off their chairs.

Soon most of the other women had joined Minnie on the kitchen dance floor, prancing about and warbling out the tune. My grandmother and Angelina had all they could do to keep old Nana Rosa from getting up with the others, but she finally agreed to stay with them on the sidelines and clap out the rhythm. The room was afire with the sheer rapture of a dozen Carmens strutting their stuff.

Suddenly the door opened and my grandfather, his hatted head still down against the cold, stepped into the kitchen. He lifted his eyes just in time to catch the last moments of this spectacle, as the women, acutely aware of his presence, hurried back to the table and their coffee.

Papa Andrea bid everyone a good afternoon and made his way to the living room to sit down and read his paper, as if he had witnessed nothing. The women took up the same pretense, firmly assuring one another that there was nothing to be embarrassed about. During this whispered discussion, Minnie shrugged her shoulders, as if to say, "So what!"

Later on, after the other women had left, I overheard a conversation between my grandparents. Innocently, but at the same time with a wry smile on his face, Papa Andrea inquired, "Carolina, my dear, is this what you and these other women have been doing in the afternoon for all these years?"

It was 1953, and my grandparents had been married 47 years. Carolina had given birth to 11 children, including two sets of twins, on the kitchen table, the hardness of that surface making it easier for her to push. Five of these children had tragically died in infancy. The other six had been raised in very close quarters on a shoestring budget. Carolina had nursed their illnesses, made their clothes, done the wash and maintained an immaculate household. She had found time to instruct her children in religion and instill in them a strong sense of morality, charity and generosity.

Even after all those years and all those shared experiences, Carolina and Andrea maintained an ignorance concerning what went on in meetings of the opposite sex. They took great pleasure in sustaining this mystery, an integral part of their nineteenth-century social code.

Carolina responded to Andrea with the same wry smile and feigned innocence. "Of course, my dear Andrea, only *this,* and a cup of *café niuru.*"

43

Taralli

Ladyfingers

THESE COOKIES WERE THE FAVORITE of my grandmother and her friends. Their delicate flavor and light, airy texture make them perfect for dunking in coffee or milk. Don't hold them in the liquid too long, though, or pieces will break off and fall in. *Taralli* are what these cookies are called in Polizzi Generosa. Throughout the rest of Sicily and Italy, they are called *savoiardi*.

For centuries powdered eggshell was the secret ingredient of pastry chefs for keeping beaten egg whites from collapsing. I first learned this secret from my grandfather. To prepare an eggshell for this purpose, peel away and discard the inner lining of the shell, wash it with warm water and let it dry thoroughly. Keep it in a small jar, and pulverize a small piece as needed with a mortar and pestle or between two spoons. The shell will keep for many years, and one egg's worth is enough for many batches. This recipe may be doubled, but it's best to try the single recipe first to become familiar with the process and with the texture of the batter.

For about a dozen cookies

Butter, for greasing the baking sheet
½ cup bleached all-purpose flour, plus more
for dusting the baking sheet
3 large eggs, separated
½ cup sugar
½ teaspoon vanilla extract
⅛ teaspoon powdered eggshell or a pinch of cream of tartar
Confectioners' sugar

Preheat the oven to 350°F, with the rack positioned in the upper third. Lightly grease and flour the baking sheet.

Double-sift the ½ cup flour. Set aside.

Using an electric mixer or by hand, beat the egg yolks with the sugar until the mixture is pale yellow and forms ribbons. Mix in the vanilla. While continuing to beat, add a small amount of flour. When it is absorbed, add more. Continue in this manner until all of the flour has been beaten in and absorbed.

In a clean, grease-free bowl, copper if possible, begin to beat the egg whites. When they are frothy, add the powdered eggshell. Continue to beat until the whites are stiff and form high peaks but are not dry. Vigorously beat about a third of the stiffened egg whites into the egg yolk mixture, to loosen it. Quickly but gently fold the remaining egg whites into the yolk mixture with a rubber spatula. If the frothy structure of the batter begins to collapse, stop folding.

Put the batter in a pastry bag fitted with a 1-inch plain round tip. Pipe the batter onto the baking sheet in 5-inch-long cookies, separated by a distance equal to their width. Thoroughly dust each cookie with a thin layer of confectioners' sugar. Wait until the sugar has been absorbed, about 5 minutes, and dust them again. When the second sugar coating has been absorbed, bake the cookies until pale golden on top, 10 to 12 minutes.

Remove the cookies with a metal spatula and transfer to a rack to cool and harden for several hours.

Café Niuru

Black Coffee

THE WOMEN OF MY GRANDMOTHER'S CIRCLE drank their "black magic" out of large coffee cups. Demitasse cups were far too fussy for them. These delicate little china cups sometimes did leave their high cupboard for more formal occasions, but usually just for routine cleaning.

To make *café francisi*—French coffee—reheat the strained coffee with an equal amount of milk and 2 teaspoons sugar.

For each 6-ounce cup of coffee

7   ounces plus 2 teaspoons spring water
2   rounded tablespoons regular-grind espresso
    or decaf espresso
    Sugar

Bring the 7 ounces water to a boil, turn off the heat and stir in the coffee. Bring the coffee to a boil over low heat. Turn it off just before it overflows the pot.

Add the 2 teaspoons cold water. This will cause the grinds to fall to the bottom of the pot. Pour the coffee through a small fine-mesh strainer into a cup. Serve with sugar to taste.

IV.

*A*unt Mary
and Uncle John

I N BRUCULINU, LOVE STORIES OFTEN SURPASSED Holly-
wood's best tearjerkers, with more interesting plots, livelier
characters, and real credibility. One of the greater romances
was the one between my grandmother Carolina's brother,
Uncle John, and his spouse, Aunt Mary.

Uncle John was born Giovanninu Vilardi in Polizzi Generosa
in 1893. Having little interest in school, at the age of 10 he was ap-
prenticed to his uncle, a barber. At 12, he immigrated to America,
sponsored by his newlywed sister, Carolina, and her husband, Andrea.

Once in the New World, he sought a more skilled occupation—
one not permitted him in the old country. He endeavored to become
a tailor. Eventually he learned pattern making. Most of his working
career was spent in a clothing factory, cutting fabric for men's
trousers. This position offered him job security and, eventually, a
pension.

In keeping with his profession, Uncle John was dapperly dressed,
but, at the same time, never loud or showy. His suits, needless to

say, were always well tailored. His shirts were bright white and well starched. The widest part of his necktie exactly matched the width of his lapel, a true sign of the well-dressed man. From the sharp creases in his trousers to his perfectly shaped fedora, Uncle John always looked as if he had just stepped out of a bandbox.

For John, as for many Sicilian immigrants living in Bruculinu, learning English was not a high priority. Women at home with their children didn't need it. All the transactions needed for their household business could be conducted in Sicilian. The men learned just enough to get them through work. Although John had come over as a boy, he never lost his strong "watsa-matta-you" accent.

S EVERAL YEARS AFTER HIS ARRIVAL, the family moved to an apartment at 319 Ellery Street, between Broadway and Beaver Street, in the Williamsburg section of Brooklyn. Two doors down was an Italian grocery store. The proprietors had a daughter named Mary, three years younger than John.

Mary's refined, delicate manner and industrious, serious nature caught John's eye, but he was unable to approach her, except to ask for a box of salt or a can of tomatoes. For John had an inferiority complex due to a minor genetic problem: from the time he was 15, the hair on his head had begun to thin at an alarming rate.

When John learned of Mary's engagement to an attorney from the wealthy suburb of Port Chester, he understood that she was moving out of his league. Realizing that he couldn't keep her in the grand style of his unknown, rich American rival, he gave up hope.

One morning, just weeks before her wedding day in 1914, Mary awoke with blurry vision. Over the course of the next few days, her condition grew worse. Incomprehensibly, after five days, Mary was profoundly blind.

The family doctor was consulted, but because there had been no illness, no trauma, he was unable to find a cause or a cure. He recommended a specialist, who recommended another and then yet another. They were all stumped, and Mary began to despair of ever regaining her sight.

Through this ordeal, John was always nearby, ready to accompany her on endless bus and subway trips to the various doctors, providing pep talks. He managed to speak of things other than groceries. Mary was growing quite fond of this tailor with the soft, kind voice. John was finding it easier to share his thoughts and allow his spirit to shine, knowing that his balding head was of no matter to a blind woman.

At last, one of the specialists' findings was extremely hopeful. He was certain that he could effect a cure, but it would involve surgery. In those days, eye surgery was filled with hazard. Sterile, surgical gloves, thin enough for the delicate work, had not yet been developed. Surgeons scrubbed their hands as well as possible, but, even so, infection was almost inevitable.

Recovery was slow and extremely uncomfortable. Because there were no sutures fine enough to stitch the eye, the patient had to lie still, flat on her back for two weeks with a sandbag on either side of her head. The boredom became unbearable.

Mary agreed to undergo the surgery, but when the bandages were removed, there was no change; she was still blind.

As THE MONTHS PASSED, and the hope of a cure for Mary's mysterious blindness became more and more remote, the lawyer from Port Chester broke the engagement. A blind wife didn't fit his life's plan.

Mary despaired, certain that she would spend a lonely life as a spinster. John, however, had other plans, and was beginning to be more secure in expressing them. Whenever he did, Mary would change the subject, she believed, for his own good.

That summer, John could no longer tolerate his hair loss.

"Wenn-a my Mar-ee sees-a," he thought, "betta she-a don-na look-a such-a ugly ting." Remembering the folk wisdom he had learned years earlier as a barber's apprentice, he shaved his head, believing the hair would grow back thicker.

The next day, he went to Coney Island with his pals. The weather was overcast, and John, thinking the sea air would be good for his seeding head, took off his skimmer. Unfortunately, his recently cleared field burned to a blister. Save for a two-inch fringe around the edge, not one hair ever grew back.

B Y HER TWENTY-FIRST BIRTHDAY, Mary had spent three long years in darkness. John kept her hope alive as best he could, keeping correspondence with doctors, exploring every lead. One day, a letter arrived from a surgeon on the staff of the New York Eye and Ear Hospital. In it, he said that he had discussed Mary's case with a world-renowned Swiss eye surgeon, recently added to the hospital's staff, who wished to examine her.

Reluctantly, Mary allowed John to take her to the hospital on Second Avenue in Manhattan. After the examination, the doctor saw a glimmer of hope in a new, experimental procedure. The learned Swiss physician, assessing the situation, said, "My dear girl, the outcome could change your life." But Mary remained hesitant. Another disappointment, she thought, would be too much to bear.

Each night, she knelt at the foot of her bed and prayed fervently to Heaven for guidance, imploring the intercession of Santa Lucia, patron saint of the eyes. The good doctor's words echoed in her ears; he was right. Finally, she entered the hospital to undergo the ordeal of eye surgery for the second time.

During the weeks of waiting after the surgery, John visited Mary every evening. He'd read to her to help pass the time. The minutes ticked into hours, then into days and weeks. At last, the time for the bandages to be removed was at hand.

John spent the entire morning getting ready. He put on a new suit and tie and his best white shirt and collar. Not wishing to shock Mary on what he hoped would be the first day of her new life, he debated about whether to wear his hat. Then he laughed off this foolish notion. How could he, a gentleman, keep on his hat in the presence of a lady?

Mary's parents, John and all the doctors assembled in Mary's darkened hospital room. They formed a semicircle around Mary, who was seated in a sparkling white metal hospital chair. The Swiss surgeon carefully snipped the bandages wrapped around her head and gently removed the pads from her eyes. In a calm, reassuring voice, he said, "All right, Mary, when I count to three, slowly open your eyes." Everybody in the room held his breath.

Mary, ever so slowly, opened her eyes. John was looking at her, a glowing smile on his face. When their eyes met, and Mary smiled back, everyone else's eyes filled with tears of joy. The darkness had been lifted. Mary could see, and what she saw, bald head and all, pleased her greatly. Two years later, on July 15, 1918, John and Mary were married.

In praise of Santa Lucia for the restoration of her sight, each year, from then on, Mary observed the saint's day by cooking the traditional, devotional dish for the occasion, a porridge made of wheat berries called *cuccia*. Wheat berries are dried, whole, unprocessed wheat kernels, and *cuccia* is the ancient staple of the poorest Sicilian peasants' diet. In this century, in America, it is eaten only for Santa Lucia's Day, December 13.

Devotees of the saint each cooked a mighty cauldron of this porridge, distributing it to an odd number of households to commemorate the date. Uncle John, in later years assisted by one of his sons, Donald, spent the afternoon bringing jars of *cuccia* to 51 families around the neighborhood. Many other men and boys could be seen coursing the streets, laden with shopping bags, on the same mission. On this feast day, no one in Bruculinu ever ate bread, only *cuccia*.

Some ate their *cuccia* as a savory dish, with salt, pepper and olive oil; others, as a sweet, with cornstarch pudding and *vinucuottu*, a type of wine jelly. To accommodate all, the grain was cooked without salt. This aspect of the cooking process, too, became ritualized. To cook *cuccia* with salt was considered sacrilege, certainly not pleasing to Santa Lucia, thereby "defeating its own purpose."

IN THEIR OLDER YEARS, Aunt Mary and Uncle John came to our house for dinner without fail every Thursday night. At exactly six o'clock, they left their apartment at Bushwick and Suydam, and slowly walked the four blocks to our place, arm in arm.

Aunt Mary wore a hat and pristine white gloves. Uncle John, also hatted, was always impeccably attired in a suit and a freshly starched white shirt. Depending on the season, he carried a crumb cake from Duggins Bakery or hand-packed vanilla ice cream from Eli and Terry's candy store.

After dessert and coffee, the adults would gather around the kitchen table to play cards. Their favorite game was Michigan rummy. Bets were a penny, and an evening's gains or losses never exceeded a dollar or two. Even so, the high drama in the room might have led an outsider to believe that the stakes were in the hundreds.

To play Michigan rummy, several cards from another deck, called money cards, are laid in the center of the table. At the beginning of each hand, each player drops a penny on each money card. Cards are played in suit and number order, and whoever holds a money card collects the pennies on it as it is played. When a player runs out of cards, the hand is over. The pennies on any money card not played are left, and the sums grow with each succeeding hand.

Aunt Mary and Uncle John sat next to each other for these games. In a stage whisper that could be heard "all away out in Canarsie," she urged him to play certain suits. He, embarrassed by her obvious coaching, became more and more oblivious with each poke and prod. She, believing her behavior to be highly discreet, prodded and poked and whispered all the more.

Everyone else, wishing not to be disrespectful, tried to ignore the scene. At times, these antics became so hilarious that the other players would bury their heads in their hands, biting their tongues to suppress the laughter. These goings-on were far more entertaining than the card game itself, well worth the possible loss of a buck.

IN 1963, AUNT MARY UNEXPECTEDLY DIED of complications from routine gallbladder surgery. After nearly 46 years of marriage, Uncle John was lost. He put on his black tie and armband and moved in with his daughter and her family, in faraway Queens Village. The era of Thursday-night card games and crumb cake abruptly came to an end.

Uncle John went on as best he could. He watched his grandchildren grow to adulthood, marry and start families of their own. The happier the occasion, the more he wished Mary was at his side to share in the joy. Eleven years later, he came to the end of his life.

I went to visit him in the hospital. He was heavily sedated, moving in and out of consciousness. Opening his eyes, he saw me standing there and pulled me close. "Vinzí," he whispered in his broken English, "I gotta tell-a ya soma-ting. I-a read-a in-a da papers-a, dat dey gotta noo ting. Dey teach-a ya 'ow ta fly! I'm-a learn-a now, an' wen I-a finish-a, I'm-a gunna fly-a up ta Heavena, an'-a see-a Aunt-a Mar-ee."

A few days later, his lessons completed, Uncle John began his final journey to the stars and Aunt Mary's side.

Cuccia

Wheat Berry and Chickpea Porridge

YOU CAN FIND WHEAT BERRIES and dried chickpeas in health food markets. The porridge is always eaten by Sicilians in honor of Santa Lucia on December 13. In Bruculinu, all we ate for dinner on that day was *cuccia*. As my cousin Donald says, "Maybe you're a little hungry by bedtime, but it's only once a year." The yield given in the recipe is for such a meal, but if the devotees are less orthodox and eat *cuccia* as a first course or side dish, this quantity will feed many more.

For 8 to 10 servings

4 cups (2 pounds) wheat berries
2 cups (1 pound) dried chickpeas
5 quarts spring water, for cooking
Sea salt
Extra-virgin olive oil
Black pepper

Place the wheat berries in a strainer, rinse under cold running water and put them in a large pot. Cover with cold water and soak for 12 hours.

Meanwhile, put the chickpeas in a colander and wash them under cold running water. Check for small stones and other debris. Transfer to another large bowl, cover with cold water and soak for 12 hours.

Drain the wheat berries and put them in a large pot with the 5 quarts spring water. Cover and simmer, stirring occasionally, for 4½ to 5 hours, adding the drained chickpeas after the first 45 minutes. During the last hour, place the cover askew so the water evaporates and the liquid thickens.

Serve hot with salt, olive oil and pepper.

Manicuotti

Filled Crepes

EVERYONE IN THE FAMILY AGREES that Aunt Mary's *manicuotti* were sublime. A covered dish with a sample arrived at our house whenever she prepared them. The word *manicuotti* derives from *manichi cuotti*, cooked sleeves. Traditionally, the wrappers are made not of pasta, but of a delicate crepe. *Manicuotti* are served as a first course.

For 6 servings (24 crepes)

FOR THE CREPES
2   cups all-purpose flour
2   cups spring water
½   teaspoon sea salt
3   large eggs
2   tablespoons extra-virgin olive oil, for greasing the pan
    Grated imported pecorino cheese, preferably Locatelli,
     for serving

FOR THE TOMATO SAUCE
1   recipe tomato sauce for Spaghetti and Meatballs (page 24)

FOR THE FILLING
2   pounds good-quality ricotta
2   large eggs, beaten
1   cup grated imported pecorino cheese, preferably Locatelli
4   sprigs Italian parsley, finely chopped
    Black pepper

Prepare the crepes: Beat the flour and water into a smooth batter. Beat in the salt and eggs.

Preheat the broiler, with a rack positioned in the middle. Leave the door open. Line a work surface with sheets of waxed paper, waxy side up.

Pour the oil into a well-seasoned 5½-to-6-inch skillet or one with a nonstick surface, and heat it over very low heat until hot. When the oil is hot, pour it into a small bowl and wipe out the skillet with wadded paper towels until only a very light coating remains. Place the paper towels in the bowl of oil and save them for regreasing the skillet.

Fill a ¼-cup measure or small glass with 3 tablespoons water and note or mark the water level. Empty the container and use it to measure the batter for each crepe.

Pour 3 tablespoons batter into the pan and quickly swirl it to cover the bottom evenly. After a few seconds, when the edges dry, place the skillet under the broiler for a few seconds longer, to dry the top. The crepes should not brown in the slightest on either side. Turn the crepe out onto its own sheet of waxed paper.

After you have made 6 crepes, regrease the skillet with the oiled paper towels. When all of the crepes are cooked and cooled, the sheets of waxed paper may be stacked, with an additional sheet between layers, waxy side facing the crepes.

Prepare the tomato sauce: Simmer for 20 minutes and set aside.

Prepare the filling: Place a food mill fitted with a large-holed disk over a medium bowl. Mill the ricotta to break it up. Using a rubber spatula, thoroughly mix in the eggs, pecorino, parsley and several grindings of black pepper. Do not use an electric mixer.

Preheat the oven to 400°F. Very lightly coat a baking sheet with tomato sauce.

Using the rubber spatula, spread 2 tablespoonfuls of filling down the center of a crepe. Fold over the edges and place it, seam side

down, on the baking sheet. Fill all the crepes in this manner, placing them close together on the sheet so they cannot spread or open
during baking. Drizzle a line of tomato sauce down the center of
each row of *manicuotti*.

Bake for 20 minutes.

Serve each person 3 *manicuotti* with a small amount of tomato
sauce and grated cheese on top. This is the standard serving size.
Rest assured, seconds will be called for.

V.

Johnny

MY FATHER WAS BORN Pasquale Giovanni Schiavelli, but everyone called him Johnny. People say that he was the kindest, gentlest, funniest man they had ever met. He was so loved and respected that in the old neighborhood, businesses served by his garbage truck closed in mourning on the day of his funeral.

His sudden, untimely passing came in 1951; he was only 37 years old, and I was three. Everyone seemed to have a tale about my father, and he took a place in my mind and heart next to all the other mythological heroes of boyhood.

Johnny was born in 1914, the only child of his father's second marriage. Vincenzo Schiavelli, a junk man by trade, was a giant of a man. A widower for many years, at 63 he got it into his head to re-marry. To this end, he sent to Naples for a mail-order bride. His grown children, although shocked and scandalized by his choice, knew that there was no chance of dissuading him. Vincenzo was from Calabria, a region of Italy whose inhabitants are renowned for being thickheaded.

Several months later, Anna arrived. She was 40 years younger than Vincenzo, and stood a diminutive four feet six. My father's half brother, Paul, told me that the first time he saw her he was sitting on the seat of his father's horse-drawn junk wagon. Unable to contain his laughter, he pretended to lose his balance and fell backward into a pile of junk to cover his disrespect. In spite of their ridiculous appearance, there must have been something between the Calabrian giant and the Neapolitan spitfire. Within two years of their marriage, Anna gave birth to a son.

J OHNNY GREW UP IN THE SECOND-FLOOR APARTMENT of a rear house on Skillman Street. It was small and crumbling, consisting of a main room and two tiny bedrooms. One of the bedrooms was used as a kind of cold pantry, with cheeses and salamis hanging from the ceiling. Johnny slept in a corner of the main room near a coal stove used for cooking and heating the place in winter. As an added misery, the old man contracted polio, leaving him paralyzed. Anna became his nurse. How she managed to move her massive husband into bed or lift him into the bathtub next to the coal stove remains a mystery to this day.

Life for Anna in America was not as she had planned. She turned to alcohol for relief. Her favorite drink was a liqueur she made from tangerine peels and pure neutral spirits, cut with sugar syrup. On a Christmas visit to Skillman Street when I was 12, over my mother's protests, my grandmother Anna insisted on my having some. I can still remember the burn as the sip went down, along with the feeling that my socks had curled.

In an effort to keep her son close to her, Anna, misguided by the drink, told Johnny elaborate scary stories about a ghostly white horse. It came out after dark, she said, to carry children off to hell. These tales of the nightmare made a strong, fearful impression on the child, and he endeavored never to be out after dark.

As a boy, Johnny worked part-time as a chicken plucker. One bleak winter's evening, he hurried home to beat the encroaching darkness. The wind howled and gushed through the desolate streets on his way. Clutching a freshly killed chicken in one arm and a dozen eggs in the other (his week's wages), he whistled to allay his fear. By the time he'd reached his house, the darkness of night had fallen.

He entered the pitch-black hallway and climbed the creaky, winding, wooden stairs to his apartment. Upon entering, he was surprised to find the place in complete darkness. He called out, "Ma, Ma, I'm home," but there was no response. His eyes adjusting, he perceived the large white form of something in the room. His worst fear had come true: it was the white horse, come to snatch him! He screamed in terror, his arms flailing the air, the dead chicken flying once more, the eggs exploding on the floor. Suddenly the lights snapped on to reveal his mother pulling off a white bedsheet, convulsed in uncontrollable laughter.

By 16, Johnny had grown into a gangly young man. His long, thin face framed dark, sloping eyes with thick lids and a dreamy, sad expression. He was by no means movie-star handsome, but his smile was so infectious that the whole world couldn't help smiling back.

Johnny was employed full-time on the truck of a small, private garbage-collection company. The work was strenuous and dirty, emptying heavy steel garbage cans into the top of the open dump truck. But Johnny had dreams of one day opening a business of his own. After all, this was America.

It was during this time that my parents met. At 16, my mother, then Katie Coco, stood five foot one and weighed 99 pounds. Her long, braided hair wound around her head, framing her pretty, china-doll face. Her brown eyes held an expression serious beyond her years. Having graduated from secretarial school, she was now working for the Golub Insurance Company, located in the bank building on Broadway and Ellery Street, down the street from where she lived. Mr. Golub, her fatherly boss, concerned that such a skinny girl would never find a husband, decreed, "Katie, I'm gonna bring ya ev'ry day a nice chop-liva sanvich mit chicken fat." But Katie was focused on

61

learning the insurance business, and marriage was not on her mind.

Katie and Johnny first met at the birthday party of a mutual friend. She could see that he was attracted to her, but the feeling wasn't mutual. "Oh, dear God!" she asked herself. "What does this long drink o' water want with me?" A year later, however, when she accidentally ran into him at the ticket booth of a local movie theater, her opinion changed. "Der was some-tin' about his smile," she said, "an' dat was it!"

Katie and Johnny saw each other often, going on dates to the movies or to the ice cream parlor for a soda. In Bruculinu in those days, a girl didn't bring a boy home to meet her parents until she was contemplating something serious. Moreover, a boy didn't bring home a girl until they were engaged. There was no such thing as a casual relationship. It implied a frivolous nature and could lead only to "no damn good." Not yet knowing what their intentions were, Johnny and Katie took a more American approach: he picked her up in front of the corner candy store.

In the old neighborhood filled with relatives, it was difficult to maintain something like "keeping company" secret for long. The very evening Uncle John saw them for the first time walking arm in arm to the movies, he made an emergency visit to my grandmother. "My dear-a sista," he said to her. "I gotta tell-a you soma-ting you ain-a gonna like-a too-much-a." Drawing close for dramatic emphasis, he whispered, "I seen-a Ka-tie a-walk-a wid a fella, an'-a no only dis-a, but he-a wear a cap-pa!"

In the 1930s in Bruculinu, no man was seen in public without a hat of some kind. To go hatless was never even considered. To the older Sicilian immigrants, with their nineteenth-century sense of propriety, caps could be worn by men only during the day. In the evening, especially when out with a lady, gentility and respect designated brimmed hats as appropriate headgear. Men in caps were ruffians and wise guys.

Tears welled up in my grandmother's eyes as she began to sob, repeating over and over her brother's words, "He wear a cap-pa! A cap-pa! A *cap-pa!*" Attracted by the commotion, my grandfather came over. He cursed Heaven, for the bad news, "By the filthy thighs of the Madonna! He wear a cap-pa!"

My grandmother and grandfather waited in silence at the kitchen table for Katie's return. Her sisters remained out of sight but within earshot. This confrontation was not to be missed. At about 10 o'-clock, Katie came through the door. The serious expressions on her parents' faces led her to believe there had been a tragic death in the family. "What happened?" she demanded, steeling herself for the worst. My grandmother did the talking in Sicilian. Katie, easily brought to tears, began to cry because she was so relieved to learn that her family was still whole.

"Mama, Papa, he's not a bad man because he wears a cap. He works hard all day and sometimes he doesn't go home before he meets me, and that's all," she explained in Sicilian. My grandfather chimed in, "Then what is there to be ashamed of? Bring this man in a cap here. We want to meet him."

The next evening at eight, Johnny knocked at the door. He nervously smiled his way through introductions to the whole family. My grandmother invited him to sit down for a coffee, while my grandfather conducted the interview. Johnny's gentle, respectful manner made him easy to like. It was clear, too, that he was hardworking and intelligent. What pleased them most of all were his honorable intentions toward their daughter. "What a nice fellow," they agreed. "But why doesn't he buy a fedora?"

J OHNNY VISITED THE COCOS OFTEN, soon becoming part of the family, who thought of him more as a son than a suitor. It was not uncommon for him to take Katie's sisters with them to the movies. Sometimes, late at night, he and Katie's kid sister, Jo, would go to the Jewish bakery on Broadway for hot bagels. As they walked the four blocks to the bakery, he tightly clutched the girl's hand, fearing, no doubt, the possibility of an encounter with the white horse.

Katie and Johnny had a 10-year engagement. Whenever they had saved the money necessary to start a household of their own, one Depression-era financial crisis or another delayed their plans. In April 1941, they were at long last wed.

Their first apartment was in a fairly modern building at the corner of Bushwick Avenue and Suydam Street. Their neighbors were mostly other young married couples, also struggling along. Life-long friendships developed among them. The Second World War began, but still they managed to have as good a time as was appropriate. Pooling their war rations into potluck dinners, they made the most of it for the duration.

At these gatherings, Johnny had a kind of antenna for anyone feeling sad or low. His charm and sense of humor always brought a smile to the face of a neighbor concerned for a husband or brother overseas.

A year after his marriage, Johnny, too, received one of those letters from Washington beginning with the well-known salutation "Greetings." Johnny had been drafted. Much to his disappointment, he failed the physical. As the result of a badly set childhood fracture, his left ankle was slightly deformed. Nevertheless, Johnny continued his efforts to boost morale on the home front.

Once, he was sent to a warehouse to cart away the debris of a serious fire. A portion of it was a large quantity of water-damaged new diapers. Knowing how difficult diapers were to find because of wartime cotton rationing, Johnny convinced one of his regular customers, a commercial laundry, that it would be a grand show of patriotism to wash the diapers gratis. Then he happily gave away the stacks of freshly laundered diapers to all the new mothers in the neighborhood.

J UST AFTER THE WAR, Johnny's boss decided to sell the carting business and retire. Although the truck was old and needed to be replaced, the route was profitable and the area was booming. Johnny saw his opportunity "ta get ahead." Although most of the private carting companies in Bruculinu were owned by "da boys," Johnny was permitted to operate one out of respect for his father the junk man; he was, in a sense, grandfathered in.

Johnny couldn't manage the financial outlay on his own so he found a silent partner. Mr. Fini would put up most of the purchase funds, and Johnny would do the work. After seven years, Johnny would gain full partnership through sweat equity. As was commonplace in Bruculinu, Mr. Fini and Johnny shook on it, and the deal was sealed.

A second man was needed to work on the truck. Johnny's brother-in-law, Dominic Di Gangi, nicknamed Duffy, had been recently laid off from the Brooklyn Navy Yard, due to a postwar slowdown. It was strange that this dark, squarely built Sicilian had acquired such an obviously Irish moniker, but there it was. Johnny hired him as the second man. Duffy was married to Katie's sister Bessie, and he and Johnny were like brothers.

Duffy had a family reputation for being tight with his money. Johnny was the only one who ever tried to rib him. When the two couples would go to nightclubs in "the City," Johnny would shame Duffy into picking up every check. "Dis round's on Duffy," Johnny would say, or, "Tanks fa da drinks, Duff." At the end of the evening, Johnny would say, "OK now, all kiddin' aside, wat do I owe ya?" Without dropping a beat, Duffy would have the accounting ready, halved to the exact penny. Johnny howled, and Duffy laughed too, in spite of himself.

One time, Duffy told me, they were given two bushels of squid and octopus by one of their restaurant customers. He was closing for summer vacation, and the fresh seafood would not keep until his return. The bushels were packed with ice, covered, and placed in the cab. All morning, as the men made their rounds, Johnny kept repeating, "Hey, Duffy, you eat dat stuff? Not me, it turns my stomach just ta look at it . . . disgustin'."

It being Saturday, the men knocked off at noon. Duffy took home the goods and spent the whole afternoon engaged in the task of cleaning the octopus and squid, an arduous job for such a large quantity. Just as Bessie, Duffy and their guests were about to sit down to eat, the doorbell rang. There, at the bottom of the stairs, were Katie and Johnny. With a big smile, Johnny yelled up, "Are we on time?" Duffy responded, "I thought ya didn't like dis stuff."

"Watta ya talkin' 'bout?" Johnny answered. "It's my favorite ting." Duffy gave a little smile, saying, "Uh-huh, so it's just the cleanin' ya don't like. Anyways, Bessie an' me was expectin' yous all 'long."

"Oh, sure," Johnny answered, believing that Duffy was trying to cover being conned. But when Johnny saw the two extra place settings, he realized that the con had failed, and laughed all the louder.

JOHNNY AND DUFFY WORKED HARD. Once, Johnny misjudged the weight of a garbage can and it flew over the truck, hitting Duffy square on the head. He was unhurt, but the trash can made a loud bong on impact, sending Johnny into spasms of laughter. "Boy, Duffy, dat's some hard head ya got der." Although Duffy knew this was all an accident, he waited for a chance to get even.

One of their clients on Broadway was a Chinese restaurant, which opened only for dinner. For the very early morning garbage collection, Johnny was given a key to the cellar. Going into that darkened space terrified him, for this was a perfect hiding place for the evil white horse. On some flimsy pretext, he always managed to send Duffy in alone while he waited at the bottom of the stairs. Duffy would bring the garbage pails to this point, and Johnny would carry them up to the truck. It was here that Duffy found his opportunity.

One day, Duffy found a pair of dead rats lying on top of one of the pails. He knew that Johnny feared rats almost as much as white horses. He brought that can nearly to the entrance, still cloaked in the darkness of the cellar. Telling Johnny that this one was very heavy, he lifted it from behind onto Johnny's shoulder and stepped back. Johnny put one arm around the garbage can, and the other over the top of his head to grab the rim. When his fingers felt the fur of the dead rodents, he let out a mighty yell, sending the pail skyward, releasing a torrent of old bok choy and shrimp shells. Now it was Duffy's turn to laugh.

A FTER A FEW YEARS, as America began to tool up for the cold war, Uncle Duffy went back to work at the navy yard, and my father found other helpers for the carting business. On November 30, 1951, there was to be a strike meeting of the private sanitation workers of New York. At six P.M., Johnny's two helpers, one of whom had a car, came to pick up their boss. The men joked about how their mean boss was going to get his at the meeting. In reality, they were already being paid more than the minimum rate the union was demanding. My mother recalls them saying, "If dey was all like Johnny, we'd be stayin' home ta-nite."

The fix being already in, management capitulated quickly and the meeting turned into a sort of party. Johnny laughed and joked with men from both sides of the aisle as they came up to the bosses' tables for mutual congratulations. Cigars were passed around, and everyone lit up. Johnny couldn't find an ashtray, and when the man beside him turned his back, he flicked his ashes inside his hat. At this, everyone roared with laughter. Johnny's laughter was so extreme that the others laughed all the more. Then they noticed that he was clutching his chest. Trying to stand, he keeled over, falling to the floor. Johnny was dead.

THE DAY AFTER THE FUNERAL, my mother received a surprise visit from Mr. Fini, the silent partner. Grief-stricken at the sudden loss of her husband, my mother was in shock. Fini used this to his advantage. He presented her with a check for $675. The sum, he claimed, was Johnny's share of the business. This was, of course, not true, there being less than nine months left on the original handshake deal. But there were no written records, leaving my mother with no legal grounds on which to pursue the matter.

Within the week, Mr. Fini, too, received a surprise visit. The owners of the larger private garbage companies got wind of his deed and sent several serious men in black suits "ta give 'im a good talkin' to." They reminded Fini that the only reason he was allowed into that business in the first place was because of Johnny's father. "Ya tink ya' can do just like ya want?" they said. "Fa tryin' ta gyp Johnny's widda an' da kid, ya gonna sell us da truck, an' you, an' ya whole family, down ta da grandkids, can fa-get 'bout bein' in da gar-bitch business, from here ta' Hoboken." The next part of the decree was given with special emphasis: "So now, ya' rat bas-did, ya betta do da right ting by Katie an' da kid." Fini, of course, did, and that was the end of that.

OVER THE YEARS, many, many other people have had stories to tell me about my father. I, too, have a memory of him.

I am nearly three, sitting on the living room floor of our apartment on Bushwick Avenue. All around and above me in chairs, adults are talking. I can hear their voices, but from my point of view, I can see them only from the knees down.

I'm playing with a small battery-operated truck. In a moment the truck stops working. I begin to fuss, and a large, steady hand enters the frame. It snatches the truck up and out of sight. Seconds later, the hand returns, replacing the fixed toy in front of me. I know that this hand, loving, helpful and strong, filled with the power to fix anything, can only be the hand of my father, Johnny.

Calamari Fritti

*F*ried Squid

ONE OF THE APPETIZERS THAT UNCLE DUFFY served at his seafood dinner was fried squid. He prepared it in the most basic way, to emphasize its fresh, ocean flavor.

Cleaning squid is a simple process. Unlike the squid in Duffy's bushel basket, the five pounds called for in this recipe can be cleaned in less than an hour.

For 8 servings

5 pounds squid, about 5 inches long
2 garlic cloves, peeled and left whole
Olive oil, for frying
All-purpose flour, for dusting
Sea salt
Lemon wedges

Place 2 bowls with cold water, a small cutting board and a sharp knife next to the sink. Keep the cold water tap running gently.

Separate the tentacles from the body of each squid by pulling them away with a slight twist. Most of the viscera will come away with them. Cut off the tentacles just in front of the eyes. Discard everything except the tentacles and the body. In the center of the ring of tentacles, there is a hard, round object containing the beak. Push it through and discard it. Rinse the tentacles and place them in one of the bowls.

Working under the running water, squeeze the body to remove any remaining jelly. Be sure to remove the bone, which resembles a strip of cellophane and is attached at the top of the body. Tear off the fins and remove the skin from them by rubbing it under running water and then peeling it away. Remove the skin on the body in the same way and place both parts in the other bowl.

When all the squid are cleaned, change the water in both bowls. Cut the bodies into rings about 1½ inches wide. Place them in the same bowl as the tentacles. Leave the fins whole. Change the water in the bowl 1 or 2 more times until it runs clear. Drain the squid thoroughly and pat dry.

Put the garlic and ½ inch of oil in a heavy skillet. Heat until nearly smoking. When the garlic is golden, remove and discard it. Lightly dust the squid with flour. To prevent the rings from sticking together, place them in the skillet in small batches. Fry for 1 to 2 minutes, or until the squid are light golden. Drain on brown paper or paper towels. Salt the squid and serve hot with lemon wedges.

Calamari Chini 'o Furnu

$\mathcal{B}$aked Stuffed Squid

ANOTHER OF UNCLE DUFFY'S APPETIZERS was stuffed and baked squid. When choosing squid for stuffing, it is better to use the females, those with thicker bodies.

For 8 servings

 2 sun-dried tomatoes
18 thick-fleshed squid, about 5 inches long
¼ cup chopped fresh Italian parsley
 1 tablespoon finely chopped golden raisins
 1 small garlic clove, finely chopped
    Pinch of crushed red pepper
    Sea salt
    Black pepper
½ cup unflavored fine dry bread crumbs
 3 tablespoons extra-virgin olive oil
    Oil-cured black olives, for garnish

Put the sun-dried tomatoes in a small bowl, cover with boiling water and soak for 5 minutes to rehydrate them. Drain and finely chop the tomatoes. Set aside.

Clean the squid using the method described on page 70, but leave the fins in place and do not cut the bodies. Put the squid in a bowlful of cold water. Change the water 1 or 2 times until it runs clear.

Finely chop the tentacles and put them in a medium bowl. Add the tomatoes, parsley, raisins, garlic and red pepper. Season with salt and black pepper. Add the bread crumbs. Slowly stir in just enough of the oil to create a soft paste.

Preheat the oven to 375°F.

Drain the squid bodies and pat them dry. Stuff them loosely with the bread-crumb mixture, about three-quarters full. To do this easily, hold the end of the squid open with a sausage stuffing nozzle or a tube of sturdy paper. Be certain that the sacs are not stuffed too tightly since they will shrink while baking. Close the opening of each sac with a toothpick. Rub each stuffed squid with olive oil and put on a baking sheet.

Bake for 15 minutes. Remove the toothpicks and arrange the squid on a serving platter circled with oil-cured olives. Serve warm.

Purpu ca Sarsa

*O*ctopus in Tomato Sauce

W HEN PROPERLY COOKED, octopus has a soft, melting texture and a delicate flavor. The secret is slow simmering. Cooked slowly, octopus is never rubbery.

The sauce is used to dress a first course of thin linguine. Then the octopus is served in the same bowl as a second course, covered with more sauce and accompanied by crusty bread. Refrigerate any leftover octopus separately from the sauce and serve chilled with a squeeze of lemon.

For 8 servings

2	tablespoons golden raisins plumped in white wine
3	2-pound octopuses (1½ pounds each), cleaned
2	28-ounce cans peeled Italian plum tomatoes
⅓	cup plus 3 tablespoons extra-virgin olive oil
3	garlic cloves, peeled and left whole
	Sea salt
2	teaspoons sugar
	Scant ¼ teaspoon crushed red pepper
	Black pepper
24	oil-cured black olives, pitted
¼	cup chopped fresh Italian parsley, plus ¾ cup more for sprinkling
2	pounds thin linguine

If the octopus has not been cleaned, do so while the raisins plump: cut off and discard the mouth, turn the octopus inside out and empty the contents. Rinse under cold running water and turn right side out.

Put the octopus in a bowl and soak it in several changes of cold water until the water runs clear. Make sure the sink is clean and dry. Put the stopper in place to prevent the octopus from sliding down the drain and tenderize it by wadding it in your hand and throwing it against the bottom of the sink about 10 times. Tweak off as much skin as will easily come away and place the octopus on a plate to drain.

Place a food mill fitted with the smallest-holed (1/16 inch) disk over a bowl. Mill the tomatoes in order to remove the seeds, which can make the sauce bitter. Scrape the pulp from the bottom of the mill into the bowl.

Pour the 1/3 cup oil into a heavy, medium nonreactive pot with a tight-fitting lid. Add the garlic and sauté over low heat until light golden. Remove and discard. Turn off the heat to avoid splattering and stir in the milled tomatoes. Season to taste with salt and add the raisins, sugar, red pepper and black pepper. Stir well. Slip the octopus into the pot, cover and bring slowly to a boil. Immediately reduce the heat and simmer very gently for 1½ hours.

Shortly before the octopus is done, fill a large pot with water, add the 3 tablespoons oil and 2 tablespoons salt and bring to a boil.

After 1½ hours, add the olives and ¼ cup of the parsley to the octopus. Check the salt and cover again.

Add the linguine to the boiling water and cook until al dente. Drain thoroughly. Divide it among 8 pasta bowls, spoon some sauce on top and sprinkle with the rest of the chopped parsley. Include a couple of the olives with each serving.

Cut the octopus at the table and serve as a second course, with more sauce.

Mannarina

*T*angerine Liqueur

THIS TANGERINE LIQUEUR will not curl your socks as did that of my grandmother Anna Schiavelli. Nonetheless, it is approximately 68 proof.

In order to properly macerate the orange zest, high-grade pure neutral spirits, rated at 190 proof (95 percent by volume), are required. A common national brand distilled from corn is Everclear. (The company does make alcohol at a lower proof, but it is not suitable for this purpose.)

Unfortunately, pure neutral spirits are not legal in all states. Although state alcoholic beverage control laws change constantly, at this time the product is not sold in California, New York, Florida and parts of Illinois and Nevada. *Do not experiment with alcohols not intended for human consumption. They can cause serious, or even fatal, illness.*

It is best to use tangerines that have not been waxed. The alcohol will emulsify this wax, tainting the flavor and color of the liqueur.

You can substitute lemon or orange zest in this recipe. In Sicilian, these liqueurs are called *limunedda* and *arancedda,* respectively. *Mannarina* and the other citrus-flavored liqueurs are marvelously refreshing. They are best served cold from the freezer.

For about 5½ bottles (750 ml each)

12   medium tangerines, unwaxed and bright orange
2   750-ml bottles 190-proof alcohol
11   cups spring water
8¼   cups sugar

Wash and dry the tangerines. Using a zester or very sharp paring knife, peel off the thin layer of orange-colored zest. Leave behind the white pith beneath it, as it will cause the liqueur to become cloudy and interfere with the tangerine flavor.

Place the zest in a clean 2-quart canning jar. Pour in the alcohol, close the lid tightly and macerate for 4 days.

The evening before the maceration is complete, prepare the syrup. Place the spring water in a saucepan, cover and bring to a boil. Turn off the heat, remove the cover and let cool for 2 minutes.

Stir in the sugar, letting it fall in a slow, constant stream. Stir over low heat just until the sugar is dissolved and the liquid turns clear. This method will prevent the syrup from turning cloudy when mixed with the alcohol. Cool slightly and transfer to a clean jar to finish cooling.

The day the maceration is complete, sterilize the bottles by placing them in the sink and filling them with boiling water. After a few minutes, drain the bottles and let them cool.

Filter the alcohol through a clean gold coffee filter set in a glass or stainless steel funnel into a large, clean jar or stainless steel bowl. Use a new filter since it is difficult to remove the coffee flavor from a filter that has been used to make coffee. As an alternative, a paper coffee filter may be used, but only the kind marked "natural brown" or "unbleached." Do not taste the alcohol before adding syrup.

Add 11½ cups of the syrup. Taste the liqueur, bearing in mind that chilling it in the freezer before serving will reduce the alcohol flavor. If, however, you prefer a weaker liqueur, add more syrup. Add ¼ cup or less at a time, mixing it in well and tasting after each addition.

Pour the liqueur into bottles and prepare the corks by boiling them in water for 5 minutes. Let the air bubbles escape from the bottles before corking by letting the bottles stand for a few minutes.

If you wish to label the bottles, be sure to use waterproof ink. Glue the labels to the bottles with white glue.

Store the bottles in a cool place. Before serving, chill a bottle in the freezer for at least 8 hours. Return the opened bottle to the freezer for storage.

VI.

*C*hristmas Eve
in Bruculinu

T HE MYRTLE AVENUE EL TRAIN that rattled in front of
our flat eventually crossed the Williamsburg Bridge,
descended underground and ended up in Manhattan—
"New York," as we called it. You might say we were
"only 45 minutes from Broadway," but our neighborhood was in a
different direction from the bucolic suburb of the George M. Cohan
tune. In Bruculinu, you imagined that if you could ride the subway
a little bit longer, you'd be in Palermo.

In our household, we were Sicilians first, Brooklynites second
and Americans only in matters of national allegiance. At Christmastime, this Sicilian identity was most in evidence. Its means of expression centered around the table.

In our house, my grandfather did all the cooking. In Bruculinu
his cooking skills were legend. Once, during my childhood, a restaurant owned by a *paisanu* of his had fallen into financial difficulty. A
series of bad chefs and unreliable kitchen staff were the cause. Papa
Andrea offered to help. He introduced a new menu and attracted
better staff. He spent long days preparing, cooking and training people on the line. Word spread throughout the neighborhood of his

wonderful food. Within two weeks, the queue for dinner circled the block, and the restaurant was stabilized. Papa Andrea was 82 at that time. It's no wonder his cronies called him *mastru*.

AFTER THE FEAST DAY OF SANTA LUCIA, December 13, the Christmas season officially began. In the kitchens of my Brooklyn neighborhood, the first order of business was to prepare the traditional Christmas pastry, *cucciaddatu*. In the Madonie Mountains of Sicily, the source of this pastry, the poor prepare its filling with dried figs, the rich with raisins. In these Sicilian mountains, fig trees are plentiful, and one can always find figs to dry. But to have raisins, one must own a vineyard.

The figs or raisins are chopped together with an equal combined weight of blanched almonds, filberts (hazelnuts) and whole pine nuts. All of the nuts are then added to a mixture of honey, sugar, cinnamon, cocoa powder and cognac, heated until the syrup spins a gossamer thread when a bit is dropped from a spoon. After it is cooled, the filling is wrapped in *pasta frolla,* a soft pastry made with eggs and shortening.

As a boy, it seemed to me that the shelling of nuts for *cucciaddatu* would never come to an end. Everybody in the household did his part. The "shooting" of warm blanched almonds out of their skins into a bowl did offer some diversion from the repetitive task, but it seemed as if Christmas would come and go, and we would still be at the kitchen table with the nuts.

Finally, this work completed, the candy for the filling was prepared. The house would fill with the wonderful aroma of boiling sugar and cinnamon. At just the right moment, my grandfather would add the chopped nuts and raisins and the whole pine nuts. He then set about the task of preparing a mountain of pastry dough. He formed *cucciaddatu* in long logs, short logs and small turnovers. This work was being mirrored by the women of Polizzi Generosa, who at the same time of year, now as then, gather in small groups to bake their *cucciaddatu* in wood-burning ovens.

When ours were baked and cooled, the small turnovers were stored in tins, the logs wrapped in dishcloths and stashed in drawers all over the house. For some reason, the drawers of choice were those containing bed or table linens. Anyone who visited in this season left with *cucciaddatu* in one form or another. One year, my grandfather noticed my apprehension at this generosity. He led me to a remote hiding place, and unwrapped a particularly perfect plump log-shaped pastry. With a twinkle in his eye, he said to me in Sicilian, "This one, my boy, is for you and me." As a boy of seven, the concept of a plentiful universe was beyond me, but I still understood the lesson, and remembered it.

The week before Christmas, a crate of oranges would arrive, a gift from my grandfather's former employer at the wholesale fruit market. These weren't ordinary oranges, but giant sugary sweet navels. As we sat after dinner slurping at sections of these beauties, my mother would recall that when she was a little girl, Papa Andrea would bring home crates of oranges and bushels of apples and pears from that same employer to share with all the neighbors. She remembered her mother placing a piece of orange peel in the kitchen coal stove, producing a lovely perfume throughout the house. My grandparents and aunts were enraptured by the memory of this simple pleasure and of a simpler time.

I N THE DAYS BEFORE CHRISTMAS, reports flowed in from relatives and friends as to the prices of essential items needed for the Yuletide feasts. The news that certain vegetables were unavailable or that their prices were "outta dis world" precipitated great discussion and concern. Eventually, things would look brighter. Although some items remained "too high," we managed. Good news about the prices of baby artichokes or eggplant sent my grandfather and me

81

on special missions to fruit stores throughout the neighborhood. We kept warm by singing Sicilian songs as we walked; we survived the jostling from hundreds of women in black by being gentlemen.

My eldest aunt, Bessie, brought the best news of all. The fruit store at Knickerbocker and Troutman had *baccalaru* for only "49 a pound!" *Baccalaru* is dried salted codfish, and no Sicilian Christmas Eve dinner would be complete without it. The salting process had been taught to the Sicilians by the Normans during their occupation of the island in the Middle Ages. The families from Polizzi Generosa prepared their special version of Christmas Eve salt cod, called *cunigghiu*—Sicilian for rabbit. In centuries past, while the rich aristocrats did indeed eat rabbit stew at Christmastime, the only rabbit the peasants saw on their tables was salt cod.

Baccalaru is dried in two forms, one slightly softer and moister than the other. Both, however, are remarkably stiff, resembling a petrified fish fillet. The word *baccalaru* is also a vulgar Sicilian name for a part of the male anatomy in a particular state. "Stop standin' der like a *baccalaru!*" or "Dat guy was a real *baccalaru!*" were common phrases of derision. *Baccalaru* never entered our house without one of the ladies giggling a reference to this theme. The favorite story came from Zia (Aunt) Valentina.

In her youth, Zia Valentina was a beautiful, full-figured woman with a flawless complexion. One year she went to the fruit seller to buy *baccalaru* for Christmas Eve. It was sold exclusively from outdoor fruit stands, I suspect, because no one wanted the profound fish odor in his shop. Zia asked the fruit seller if his *baccalaru* was stiff and dry, or soft and moist. He replied that his was always stiff and moist. "Stiff and moist?" she innocently inquired, being unfamiliar with the vulgar meaning. He chuckled licentiously. She caught his meaning, turned scarlet and stormed off in indignation. Later in life, she laughed at her youthful naïveté, the blush returning to her still beautiful face.

T HE CODFISH needed to be soaked for three days before cooking in order to rehydrate it and remove the salt. This was accomplished in a large, lidded stockpot. Mercifully, the strong aroma filled the house only twice a day, when the water was renewed.

One year a relative gave us such a large quantity of *baccalaru* that the only place to soak it was in the bathtub! My mother swore she could smell it from three blocks away. All the strong odors were gone, however, when my grandfather set his sublime *cunigghiu*, Christmas Eve Salt Cod, on the Christmas Eve dinner table.

The traditional Christmas Eve dinner in southern Italy and Sicily is composed of an assortment of fried fish and vegetables. The tradition has existed since the sixteenth century, when the sumptuary laws of the Church called for purification before the celebration of great holidays. These meals were truly spectacular. While following the letter of the law, they successfully avoided its spirit. In our house, these historical facts were unknown. People came to eat.

P REPARATION BEGAN EARLY in the morning of the Eve. After the *cunigghiu* was cooked and shredded and a salad composed, attention was turned to the vegetables. The eggplant was peeled, sliced, salted and pressed to remove its bitter liquid. Baby artichokes were cleaned and parboiled, as were the cardoons and cauliflower. If asparagus could be found, it, too, needed preparation. Rice was boiled and formed into *arancini*, Sicilian rice balls.

The fresh fish included fillet of sole and fresh sardines, smelts or whiting, blowfish, squid and shrimp. These needed cleaning as well, with special attention paid to the blowfish, making certain that the fishmonger had properly removed the poisonous sac.

As a boy, I sat at the far end of the kitchen table and watched. Sometimes, I was given a small task, like peeling asparagus or removing the tough outer leaves from artichokes, but mostly I watched. My grandfather wore a dish towel tucked into his high-waisted trousers, like a great chef's uniform. The sleeves of his flannel shirt were rolled up, revealing his long underwear. But what held my attention was his measured, methodical technique. He would form *arancini,* each one perfectly round, and line them up in neat rows like soldiers, on waxed paper. He would then take them one at a time, pass them through beaten egg whites, then bread crumbs, and return them to the ranks. I loved to watch the columns slowly change color from white to beige. As he continued dusting and breading, he treated each tiny artichoke heart or cauliflower floret as if it were a small masterpiece—as if it were the last morsel of food on earth.

A CROSS THIS VAST COUNTRY, the Americans were also preparing their Christmas feasts. Great turkeys and hams were being roasted, large casseroles were being arranged and baked. It was, perhaps, inconceivable to them to prepare a dinner for 20 or more in bite-sized pieces. Then again, in our Bruculinu, in our flat under the Myrtle Avenue el, we were not in that America.

All at once, it seemed, preparation was complete; the food on the sideboard at parade rest. Folding tables were set up and joined to the kitchen table. Together, they nearly filled the length and breadth of the room. The tables were set under the discerning eye of Aunt Mae, who quickly remedied a wrinkled tablecloth or spotted glass. My grandfather placed the *cunigghiu* in the center, flanked by a large platter of green and black olives and a giant bowl of mixed green salad. Aunt Jo came into the kitchen dressed in "something Christmasy," her beautiful spirit shining. My grandfather, my mother and Aunt Bessie tended to the pots of olive oil, heating for the onslaught. Uncle Duffy, Aunt Bessie's husband, and I sneaked olives off the platter. Aunt Jo joined us. We giggled as we avoided capture by the real adults. My grandmother watched, quietly praising God for this bounty.

The doorbell rang, and, in short order, my grandmother's brother, Ziu Giovanninu (Uncle John), and his family and their families filled our already full kitchen. Ziu carried an enormous brown bag, filled with bread from the Giangrasso Bakery. The loaves were covered in sesame seeds, and were still warm. The guests shed their coats and hats, and soon all 22 of us were at the table.

We started with the *cunigghiu,* everyone marveling at the sweetness and delicacy of Papa Andrea's recipe. Next, from the stove, not more than two feet away, came the *arancini,* creamy and flavorful inside their golden brown coating. The furious activity of my grandfather and his assistants resulted in a constant flow of fish and vegetables to the table. The vinegary dressing on the salad was an excellent accompaniment to the fried foods. The wine flowed, but no one ever drank to excess. To become drunk would have shown a lack of respect, self-control and common sense. Wine was viewed as a healthful beverage. We children were offered a splash of it in our glasses, which were kept filled with seltzer water from one of the Good Health Company's siphon bottles that always sat on our table.

The conversation grew livelier and livelier. Gales of laughter filled the house. At times it became difficult to hear one of the cooks announcing the presence of some new dish. "Da blowfish is ready!" one of them might scream. My mother might say, "Who's gonna eat da last piece o' cauliflower? It looks so lonely der on da plate." Understanding her meaning, someone would respond, "Why don't you eat it. Gaw-head." At some point during the meal, some of the diners would insist on changing places with the cooks so that they too could have a chance to sit down and eat. In a room full of Sicilians, everybody's a cook.

The meal wound down with oranges, *cucciaddatu* and coffee. My grandfather cut the peel off the oranges in the shape of eyeglasses for us children. We all looked very scholarly eating our giant oranges.

Around this time, a party began to form to go to Midnight Mass. In my memory, it always snowed on Christmas Eve. Aunt Jo and the rest of us would start out for the church at about ten-thirty in order to get a good seat. As we neared St. Joseph's Church on Suydam Street three blocks away, we would encounter the throngs of merry Christmas churchgoers.

THE CHURCH ITSELF WAS ABLAZE WITH CANDLES, the altar decorated with a multitude of potted poinsettias, red and white. The crèche, which filled an entire side chapel, housed life-sized statues. The cradle still lay empty. In the choir loft, the organist played Christmas carols and the choir prepared. The organist struck the opening chords of the High Mass, and the service began. It was very grand, filled with the old-style pomp and spectacle. When the choir sang the "Alleluia," Heaven rocked.

To this accompaniment, the priests and altar boys formed a procession, carrying the statue of the baby Jesus throughout the church and resting it in its cradle. As the congregation grew excited by the high drama, their breath quickened, and the air, heavy with frankincense, mingled with the rising aroma of *baccalaru,* fried fish and vegetables.

As my Aunt Jo and I walked home from church in the middle of the night on those bitterly cold Christmas Eves, our feet crunching on the new snow, the quiet stillness in our small world echoed the sincerest wish of the larger world—Peace on Earth.

When we arrived home, my grandmother had hot cocoa and buttered Uneeda Biscuits waiting for us. My grandfather was preparing for Christmas Day. Everyone else, having cleaned up the house, was busily wrapping Christmas presents. I tried, in vain, to catch a glimpse of the boxes as they whizzed by.

My mother, noticing the hour, would say to me, "Go ta sleep now, honey. Tomorra is an-oter busy day." Her motherly tone made me realize the extent of my tiredness. As I climbed into bed, I knew that Christmas Day would bring my aunts and uncles and cousins and presents; that we would sit down at that same improvised table, renewed with fresh linens, and eat one of Papa Andrea's meals fit for a baron. I knew that I would wake up to the smell of onions sautéing in olive oil; to the aroma of roasting capons, covered with pancetta and stuffed with chestnuts. There would be the taste of hot milk flavored with coffee and sugar, and buttered Italian toast for breakfast. My eyes would be filled with the sight of Papa Andrea's magnificent rice bombe that he called a *tumala*.

As I lay in my bed, dreaming of all these things, wondering how much snow we'd get, wondering if it was snowing all over the world, even in Sicily . . . where exactly is Sicily? . . . my mother's words came back to me, "Go ta sleep now, honey. Go ta sleep. Merry Christmas."

Recipes

A CASUAL FAMILY SETTING IS BEST for this Sicilian Christmas Eve dinner. As you cook each dish, bring it to the table, rather than serving entire courses all at once. Traditionally, *cunigghiu* is served only at Christmas. At other times of the year, *arancini* are served as an antipasto. Individual fishes are served as a second course, and the vegetables appear as either accompaniments or as antipasto.

Cunigghiu

Christmas Eve Salt Cod

THE VIKINGS FIRST SALTED CODFISH, and the Normans later adopted the practice. They taught it to the Sicilians, who in turn taught the Portuguese. These explorers took the technique with them to the Caribbean, from where it spread throughout Central and South America. Today salt cod is still eaten in various preparations in all of these places, as well as in France, Spain and Italy. In the United States, it is available in specialty or ethnic stores and in some supermarkets.

The traditional recipe for *cunigghiu* calls for salted, sun-dried *cucuzza*, a long, light green, Sicilian squash. Some women in Bruculinu did preserve squash in this manner during the summer, and the women of Polizzi Generosa do it to this day. Replacing the dried *cucuzza* with zucchini cooked in heavily salted water brings an approximation of the ancient flavor to the dish.

For a smaller party, this recipe may be halved, keeping the same concentration of salt in the water for cooking the zucchini and the same amount of lemon-water for soaking the artichokes.

For 12 servings

2 pounds salt cod
6 medium artichokes, about 5 inches long and
   3½ inches in diameter
2 lemons, halved
1 pound russet, Yukon Gold or Yellow Finn potatoes
   Sea salt
1 pound zucchini, about 6 inches long

89

  1 small head cauliflower (1¼ to 1½ pounds)
 12 celery ribs
     Extra-virgin olive oil, for frying
  2 medium onions
  1 cup white wine vinegar
  2 tablespoons sugar
 24 large green olives, pitted and quartered
  3 tablespoons capers, rinsed and drained
     Black pepper

Soak the salt cod in a large covered pot of cold water for 3 days.
Change the water twice a day. It is not necessary to refrigerate it,
but keep it in a cool place. The soaking will reconstitute the fish
and wash away the salt.

Prepare the other ingredients on the day the dish is to be served.
Boil or steam them separately as follows.

Pour water into the bottom of a steamer. Cut off 1½ inches from
the top of each artichoke and trim the stems short. Rub the artichokes with lemon and place them upside down on a steamer rack.
Squeeze the lemons and add the lemon juice and rind to the water in
the steamer. When the water boils, lower the rack into the steamer.
Cook the artichokes for about 30 minutes, or until tender. When the
artichokes are cool enough to handle, peel away the tough outer
leaves until you get to the ones that are completely edible. Quarter
the artichokes, remove and discard the spiny chokes and purple
leaves with a small knife or a spoon and cut the quarters in half. Set
aside.

Peel the potatoes and cook them in lightly salted boiling water
until tender, about 30 minutes. Drain them and put them back in the
pot under cold running water until cool. Quarter the potatoes, cut
them into ¼-inch-thick slices and set aside.

Peel and cut the ends off the zucchini. Halve them and cook in

1 quart boiling water with ¼ cup salt, with the cover askew, for 5 minutes. Drain and cool under running water. Cut into ¾-inch-thick pieces and set aside.

Cook the whole cauliflower, with the leaves attached, in lightly salted boiling water, covered, until tender but firm, about 12 minutes. Cool under running water. Cut away the leaves and break the head into small florets. Set aside.

Cook the celery in lightly salted boiling water, covered, until tender but firm, about 12 minutes. Drain, cool and thinly slice. Set aside.

Sauté each vegetable separately in a small amount of oil until the pieces gain a bit of color, about 3 minutes. Clean the pan between vegetables so that each one maintains its individual flavor. Drain on brown paper or paper towels.

Drain the salt cod, rinse it and pat it dry. Remove the skin and bones and cut it into strips ¾ inch thick, 1 inch wide and 1½ inches long. Sauté the fish in hot oil over a medium-high heat for 5 minutes. Remove all the pieces with a slotted spoon, including small ones that have flaked away. Drain on brown paper or paper towels.

Peel the onions, cut them in half and thinly slice them. Heat 2 tablespoons olive oil in a heavy pot large enough to accommodate all the ingredients. Sauté the onions over medium-low heat until pale golden, 10 to 15 minutes. Add the vinegar and the sugar. Cook for 1 minute and reduce the heat to low. Add the artichokes, potatoes, zucchini, cauliflower, celery, onions, fish, olives and capers. Very gently fold everything together. Let the flavors mingle for 3 minutes.

Spoon the *cunigghiu* into a shallow serving bowl and add several grindings of black pepper. Serve at room temperature.

A r a n c i n i   a l   B u r r u

*R*ice Balls with Butter

THE WORD *ARANCINI* means dear little oranges. Saffron gives the inside an appropriate yellowish color. Cheese is added to the rice, the kind depending on the region of Sicily. At the center, representing the orange's seeds, is a flavoring. The most familiar version uses a meat *ragù* and peas. The lighter, meatless *arancini* in this recipe have a small piece of buttered mozzarella in the middle. *Arancini* are best eaten with the hands, a napkin nearby.

This recipe may be divided or multiplied as desired, but use eight cups of olive oil for frying any number of balls.

For 18 rice balls

FOR THE FLAVORING
4 tablespoons (½ stick) unsalted butter, melted
¼ pound mozzarella cheese

FOR THE RICE BALLS
5½ cups (2¼ pounds or 1 kilo) Arborio rice
1 tablespoon sea salt, for the cooking water
8 tablespoons (1 stick) unsalted butter, melted
3 pinches of saffron
6 large eggs, separated
1¼ cups grated imported pecorino cheese, preferably Locatelli
Black pepper
8 cups olive oil, for deep-frying
Unflavored fine dry bread crumbs, for dredging

92

Prepare the flavoring: Melt the butter and set it aside to cool.

Cut the mozzarella into twenty ½-inch dice. (You will not use all of the cheese, but it is easier to cut from a larger piece.) Put the cubes in a shallow bowl. When the butter is cool enough not to melt the cheese, pour it over. Refrigerate to set until needed.

Prepare the rice balls: Boil the rice in abundant, lightly salted water, as for pasta, until it is slightly underdone. Run cold water into the pot to stop the cooking process. Drain thoroughly and put the rice in a large mixing bowl. Combine the melted butter with the saffron and mix it evenly into the rice. Beat the egg yolks, and when the rice has cooled enough not to cook them, mix them in well. Mix in the grated cheese and a few grindings of black pepper. Spread in a shallow layer and let cool to room temperature, uncovered.

Cover a work surface with waxed paper. Using your hands, gently form some of the rice mixture into a ball about the size of a Valencia orange. With your finger, poke a hole in it to the center and insert a piece of buttered cheese. Fill the hole and set the ball on the waxed paper.

When all of the balls are formed, pour the oil into a 6-quart pot, filling it to a depth of about 2 inches. Heat it over medium heat to 350°F. Test by dropping in a small square of bread. It should brown quickly but not burn.

Lightly beat the egg whites in a shallow bowl. Place the bread crumbs in a deep bowl.

Dip the *arancini* one by one into the egg whites, lifting to let the excess drip off, and roll in the bread crumbs. Return each ball to the waxed paper. When the oil is hot, gently lower the *arancini*, two or three at a time, into the pot. Fry until they are a rich golden brown. Remove with a slotted spoon and drain on brown paper or paper towels. The *arancini* may be kept hot in a 300°F oven, uncovered, until all of them have been cooked. Serve hot.

Cacuocciuli Fritti

*F*ried Artichokes

PROTECTED INSIDE A LIGHT COATING of fried bread crumbs, artichoke hearts have a wonderful silky quality. They were served not only at Christmas but throughout the year as an accompaniment to fish or as part of an antipasto.

When doubling this recipe, do not change the number of lemons. The artichokes may be fried in the same pot of olive oil after the *arancini*.

For 6 servings

       4 lemons
      12 baby artichokes, about 3 inches long
       2 large eggs
       2 tablespoons milk
       1 cup all-purpose flour, for dusting
    1½ cups unflavored fine dry bread crumbs
       8 cups olive oil, for deep-frying
          Sea salt

To prepare for trimming the artichokes, pour cold water into a large bowl. Juice one of the lemons and add the juice and rind to the water. Keep another lemon nearby so you can pass your knife through it as you trim the artichokes, which will keep them from turning black.

Working with 1 artichoke at a time, cut off ½ inch from the top. Remove the outer leaves, stopping where the leaves are thin and pale green. Cut off and discard the stem. Cut the artichoke in half

94

and place it in the bowl of lemon and water. Add the juice and rind of another lemon to the bowl and let the artichokes soak for 15 minutes.

Fill a large pot with water, add the juice and rinds of the remaining 2 lemons and bring to a boil. Drain the artichokes and add them. Cover and cook for 10 minutes, or until tender but firm. Drain and run under cold water to stop the cooking process. Drain the artichokes thoroughly and pat them dry.

Cover a work surface with waxed paper. Beat the eggs and milk together in a shallow bowl. Line up the flour in a deep bowl, the bowl with the egg wash, and the bread crumbs in another deep bowl. Dust the artichokes with flour, coat with the egg wash, letting the excess drip off, and dredge in the bread crumbs, being sure to coat completely. Place on the waxed paper and set aside until ready to fry.

Pour the oil into a 6-quart pot, filling it to a depth of about 2 inches. Heat it over medium heat to 350°F. Test by dropping in a small square of bread. It should brown quickly but not burn.

Gently lower the artichokes into the pot in two or three batches and fry until a rich golden brown, about 4 minutes. Remove the artichokes with a slotted spoon and drain on brown paper or paper towels. The artichokes may be kept hot in a 300°F oven, uncovered, until all of them have been cooked. Serve hot with salt.

Sparaci Fritti

ℱ ried Asparagus

FRIED ASPARAGUS is a common Sicilian preparation. For this rather prodigious meal, allow two or three asparagus per serving. As an accompaniment or antipasto to a different meal, the amount should be doubled. Asparagus may be fried in the same pot of oil after the artichokes.

For 6 servings

12-18 medium-thick asparagus
2 large eggs
2 tablespoons milk
1 cup all-purpose flour, for dusting
1½ cups unflavored fine dry bread crumbs
8 cups olive oil, for deep-frying
Sea salt

Cut away the thick, fibrous ends of the asparagus and peel the thickest part. Tie them with kitchen string in 2 or 3 bundles. Bring a large pot of water to a boil. Add the asparagus and blanch for 4 minutes. Run under cold water until cooled. Open the bundles and spread out the asparagus on a kitchen towel to dry.

Line a work surface with waxed paper. Beat the eggs and milk together in a shallow bowl. Line up the flour on a plate or piece of waxed paper, the bowl with the egg wash, and the bread crumbs on another piece of waxed paper. Dust the asparagus with flour, coat with the egg wash, letting the excess drip off, and dredge in the bread crumbs, being sure to coat completely. Place on the waxed paper and set aside until ready to fry.

Pour the oil into a 6-quart pot, filling it to a depth of about 2 inches. Heat it over medium heat to 350°F. Test by dropping in a small square of bread. It should brown quickly but not burn. Gently slip the asparagus into the oil four or six at a time and fry until a rich golden brown. Remove and drain on brown paper or paper towels. The asparagus may be kept hot in a 300°F oven until all of them have been cooked. Serve hot with salt.

Vruacculu Frittu

$\mathcal{F}$ried Cauliflower

CAULIFLOWER PREPARED IN THIS WAY gains a remarkably sweet flavor and a texture similar to crab. Fried cauliflower can be served as an accompaniment to grilled, baked or fried fish.

For 6 servings

1 medium head cauliflower
  Sea salt
  Freshly grated nutmeg
2 large eggs
2 tablespoons milk
1 cup all-purpose flour, for dusting
  Olive oil, for frying

Cut away and discard the stalk and green leaves of the cauliflower. Cut the cauliflower in half and cut the florets away from the inner core. Soak the florets in salted cold water for 15 minutes.

Place a steamer on the stove with several scrapings of nutmeg in the steaming water. When it comes to a boil, drain the cauliflower and steam it, covered, for 10 minutes or until tender but firm. Drain and run under cold water to stop the cooking process. Drain the florets thoroughly and pat them dry.

Line a work surface with waxed paper. Beat the eggs and milk together in a shallow bowl. Next to it, line up the flour on a plate or piece of waxed paper. Coat the florets with the egg mixture, letting the excess drip off, and dredge in flour. Place on the waxed paper and set aside until ready to fry.

When all the florets are coated, pour about 1 inch oil into a 9-inch skillet over medium heat and heat until nearly smoking. Pan-fry the cauliflower quickly at a high heat until a light golden color. Remove with a slotted spoon, drain on brown paper or paper towels and serve.

Sardi all'Antica

*A*ncient-Style Sardines

FRESH SARDINES HAVE A DELICATE yet rich flavor. In this traditional recipe, they are marinated in vinegar for 24 hours before
cooking, which gives them a rather sweet-and-sour taste. You can
buy the sardines already cleaned, but it is not difficult to clean them
yourself.

If fresh sardines cannot be found, fresh-frozen ones may be substituted. Defrost them, well covered, in the refrigerator, never in
water or at room temperature. For this dinner, allow two sardines per
serving.

For 6 servings

12   sardines
     Sea salt
     About 2 cups red wine vinegar
     All-purpose flour, for dusting
     Olive oil, for frying

Scale the sardines, if necessary, and rinse them under cold running water. Working with 1 fish at a time, snap off the head by twisting it away from the body. Holding the fish in one hand, slit the belly
with the thumbnail of your other hand. Remove and discard the
guts. Continue the slit down the fish. Laying it flat on a work surface covered in waxed paper, open the fish like a book. Slip a thumbnail under the spine and remove it with all the bones. Cut off the
tail and the dorsal fin, but do not separate the 2 fillets or remove
the skin. Rinse the fish under cold running water. As each sardine is

cleaned, place it on a platter, slightly tilted so that the liquid drains away from the fish.

Lightly salt the fish and pour on enough red wine vinegar to nearly cover them. Cover the platter with plastic wrap and refrigerate for 24 hours.

When ready to fry the sardines, pat them dry and dust with flour. Pour about ½ inch oil into a 9-inch skillet over medium heat and heat until very hot. Pan-fry the sardines for about 2 minutes on each side, or until light golden and crisp. Remove and drain on brown paper or paper towels. Serve very hot.

Pisci Fritti

ried Fish

I N ADDITION TO THE SALT COD, sardines and shrimp, four other kinds of fish were served at our Christmas Eve dinner. Smelts, which might be one of the types served, are left whole, dusted with flour and pan-fried like the sardines; allow two per person. Other kinds of fish—use any locally available fillets and steaks—should be either breaded or simply dusted with flour before frying. For this dinner, allow half a fillet and about three ounces of fish steak per person.

For 6 servings

2	large eggs
¼	cup milk
½	cup all-purpose flour, for dusting
1	cup unflavored fine dry bread crumbs, for dredging
1½	pounds sole, red snapper or orange roughy fillets, cut into 6 pieces
1½	pounds shark, swordfish or tuna steaks, about ½ inch thick, cut into 6 pieces
	Olive oil, for frying
	Lemon wedges
	Sea salt

Cover a work surface with waxed paper. Beat the eggs and milk together in a medium bowl. Line up the flour on a plate or piece of waxed paper, the bowl with the egg wash, and the bread crumbs on another plate or piece of waxed paper.

Prepare the fillets: Dust each one with flour, coat with the egg wash, letting the excess drip off, and dredge in bread crumbs, being sure to coat completely. Place on the waxed paper and set aside until ready to fry.

Pour about ½ inch oil into a 9-inch skillet over medium heat and heat until very hot. Pan-fry the fillets, without crowding the pan, for about 2 minutes on each side, or until light golden. Remove and drain on brown paper or paper towels.

Prepare the steaks: Dust each one thoroughly with flour just before frying.

Wipe the skillet clean, pour another ½ inch oil into it and heat until very hot. Pan-fry the steaks, without crowding the pan, for about 3 minutes on each side, or until light golden. Remove and drain on brown paper or paper towels.

Serve very hot with lemon and salt.

Ammari 'n Pastedda

$\mathscr{B}$atter-Fried Shrimp

A LTHOUGH BATTER-FRIED SHRIMP is a common preparation in this country, the turning-tastes of orange zest and black pepper give it a uniquely Sicilian flavor.

The yield given is tailored for this dinner. When served as a second course in a more usual format, the recipe should be doubled for 6 servings. The shrimp may be deep-fried in the same oil as the other dishes, provided that they are done last.

For 6 servings

28	shrimp without heads (about 1 pound)
2	large eggs
½	cup milk
⅓ -½	cup all-purpose flour
8	cups olive oil, for deep-frying
	Grated zest of ½ large orange
	Black pepper

Shell and devein the shrimp. Leave the tail attached as a handle. Beat the eggs and milk together. Whisk in enough flour to achieve the consistency of thin yogurt.

CHAPTER VI.

Pour the oil into a 6-quart pot, filling it to a depth of about 2 inches. Heat it over medium heat to 350°F. Test by dropping in a small square of bread. It should brown quickly but not burn.

Dip each shrimp into the batter and slip it into the pot, without crowding. Fry until light golden, about 3 minutes. Remove and drain on brown paper or paper towels.

Sprinkle the shrimp with orange zest and a grinding of black pepper. Serve very hot.

Cucciaddatu

Christmas Pastry

THE PASTRY FOR THIS DESSERT is called *pasta frolla*. Versions of this soft, short dough are used in many Sicilian pastries, both sweet and savory. The use of cognac in the filling is from the tradition of the *monzù*.

This recipe may be multiplied or divided.

For 2 logs or about 5 dozen turnovers

FOR THE FILLING

1¾ cups (½ pound) hazelnuts (filberts)
1½ cups (½ pound) blanched almonds
3½ cups (about 18 ounces) dark raisins
¾ cup honey
¼ cup water
¼ cup sugar
2 teaspoons ground cinnamon
2 teaspoons unsweetened European-process cocoa powder
2 tablespoons cognac or nut liqueur, such as Fra Angelico
½ cup (3 ounces) pine nuts

FOR THE PASTRY

8 cups bleached all-purpose flour
1 cup confectioners' sugar
⅛ teaspoon salt
1 pound (4 sticks) unsalted butter, cut into small pieces
8 large whole eggs
2 large egg yolks

3 tablespoons cognac
2 large egg whites, beaten, for brushing the log
   Nonpareils, for decoration

Prepare the filling: Preheat the oven to 450°F. Toast the hazelnuts for about 10 minutes. Take care that they do not burn. When they are cool enough to handle, rub them together to remove as much of the brown skin as possible.

Chop together the hazelnuts, almonds and raisins. Combine the honey, water, sugar, cinnamon, cocoa and cognac in a 4-quart saucepan over low heat and bring the mixture slowly to a boil. Let it boil for 5 minutes. Stir in the chopped nuts and raisins and the pine nuts until well coated. Remove the pot from the heat and let cool.

Prepare the pastry: Sift together the flour, confectioners' sugar and salt into a large bowl. Using an electric mixer or by hand, cut in the butter until the flour has the consistency of cornmeal. Beat together the eggs and egg yolks. Work the eggs into the dough with the mixer or a spatula. Mix in the cognac.

Turn out the dough onto a lightly floured surface and knead just enough to form a soft, smooth and elastic dough. Remember that overkneading pastry dough will make it tough. Form the dough into a ball, cover and let it rest at room temperature for 15 minutes.

Preheat the oven to 350°F, with a rack positioned in the upper third.

If you are preparing logs, divide the dough in half and roll each half into a rectangle, 16 by 9½ by ¼ inch thick. Place half the filling on each rectangle and roll it up into a log shape. Close the ends and seal the seam very well. Each log should be about 12 inches long, 4½ inches wide and 2 inches high. Place the logs, seam side down, on a baking sheet. Lightly beat the egg whites and brush the logs. Decorate with nonpareils. Bake for 1 hour, or until pale golden brown. Cool for 10 minutes on the baking sheet, then transfer to a cooling rack. When the logs are completely cooled, wrap them in plastic wrap.

If you are making turnovers, roll out the dough 1/16 inch thick. Cut out 4-inch circles. For each turnover, place a small mound of the filling on the bottom half of the circle, about 1/4 inch from the edge. Lightly beat the egg whites and brush the edges with some. Fold over the top half of the dough and pinch or crimp the seam together to form a tight seal. Place the turnover on a baking sheet. (You will need 3 baking sheets, but bake them one at a time.) Brush the tops with egg white and decorate with nonpareils.

Bake for about 20 minutes, or until barely golden on top. Transfer the turnovers to a rack and cool to room temperature. Store in an airtight container.

Struffuli

*Y*uletide Wreath

ALTHOUGH THIS CHRISTMAS TREAT is Neapolitan in origin, we adopted it for our own holiday tables. In some homes, a candle in the wreath's middle transformed it into an edible centerpiece.

The word *struffuli* derives from the Italian verb *strofinare*, to rub. To make this dessert, you rub bits of soft dough into little balls between your hands. Then you fry the balls, coat them in a honey glaze, and form them into a wreath and decorate.

For a 12-inch wreath

FOR THE BALLS

4 cups bleached all-purpose flour
½ cup confectioners' sugar
   Pinch of baking powder
2 tablespoons cold unsalted butter
   Zest of 1 lemon, finely chopped
   Zest of 1 orange, finely chopped
4 large eggs, beaten
3 tablespoons orange liqueur, such as Curaçao,
      Grand Marnier or Cointreau
3 cups corn oil, for frying

FOR THE GLAZE

1   cup honey
½   cup sugar
3   tablespoons water
⅓   cup chopped candied fruit

FOR THE DECORATION

¼   cup sliced almonds
Nonpareils

Prepare the balls: Sift together the flour, confectioners' sugar and baking powder twice into a large bowl. Using an electric mixer or by hand, cut in the butter. Stir in the zest and then work in the eggs. Mix in the liqueur. Knead in the bowl or on a lightly floured surface, just enough to form a soft, elastic dough. Cover with a cloth and let it rest for 15 minutes at room temperature.

Line a work surface with waxed paper. Form the dough into balls about the size of a hazelnut and place them on the waxed paper. When all the balls are formed, heat the oil in a 9-inch skillet. Place one of the balls in the oil. It has reached the proper temperature, 350°F, when the oil around the ball starts to gently sizzle. Discard the ball. Fry the balls in small batches until they are a rich golden color, 1 to 2 minutes. Remove them with a slotted spoon and drain on brown paper or paper towels.

Prepare the glaze: Have ready a wet 14-inch serving platter. Heat the honey, sugar and water in a medium pot, stirring until the sugar dissolves. Stop stirring and boil until the liquid and froth turn clear.

Immediately add the balls and candied fruit to the pot. Be careful not to splash the hot syrup, which can give a painful burn. Turn off the heat and coat the balls well with the glaze. Turn the entire contents of the pot onto the platter. Using two wooden spoons,

110

form the *struffuli* into a wreath. Hold one spoon against the balls at the outer edge of the platter. Hold the other in the center and move the balls toward the edge. Continue this process around the platter until the wreath is round and even. Decorate with the almonds and nonpareils. Cool before serving.

If *struffuli* is not to be served within several hours, cover it tightly with plastic wrap when it is completely cooled and store at room temperature. It will lose its freshness after a few days.

VII.

Malucchiu

IN ADDITION TO ALL THE OTHER DANGERS of inner-city life, in Bruculinu there were dangers unseen, dangers not of this earth. They were conjured by the depraved minds and black hearts of the envious, of the resentful. We called their sinister practices by many names, sometimes silly ones like "da coochies," in an effort to dispel their ascribed power. But their invisible talons could strike anyone at any moment, without warning.

Whenever someone suffered a mysterious illness or fell upon a particularly devastating streak of bad luck, everyone had the same thought. Some of the more religious or pragmatic people in the neighborhood might not say the word aloud, but they thought it nonetheless: *malucchiu,* the evil eye.

We took precautions to ward off the evil eye in a vast variety of situations. For example, a giant red bow always adorned the rearview mirror of a new car. Sometimes the ribbon hung there until the sun faded it to pink, rotting it until it fell off by itself. By this time, the car was no longer new, and the danger of *malucchiu* had passed.

Before moving into a new home, we sprinkled the corners of the rooms with salt to cast out any evil residue from the previous tenant. If a loaf of bread went moldy or a bottle of wine turned, it was a sure sign that a curse had passed through the house. People crossed themselves and prayed as they threw out the tainted food.

Babies were particularly vulnerable to malediction. Their parents always dressed them in red, the protective color. A small medal of the Madonna or a crucifix was pinned to their undershirts. Older babies and children wore a discreet gold medallion on a thin chain around their necks. The best protection of all, it was believed, was a red coral amulet of a twisted horn. Called a *cornu,* its attributed powers date back to the ancient Greeks.

Just 10 years ago, after seeing my then six-month-old child for the first time, a cousin of my mother's took me aside, whispering, "Ya got a medal on dat kid? Ya know, a nice boy like dat, y'outta put a medal on 'im."

One could never be sure if praise or compliment from a casual acquaintance was in earnest or a *maladittu,* a curse. At these moments, the complimented would make the hand sign for the horns: a fist with the index finger and pinkie extended. When pointed at a suspected maledictor, it would turn their evil intentions back at them.

When we were schoolchildren, the nuns taught us that superstition was a mortal sin. We didn't believe them, and we really didn't believe in *malucchiu* either. It held the same place in our beliefs as the sandman or black cats. But we liked the scariness surrounding it all.

ONE OF MY GRANDMOTHER'S SISTERS, ZIA GANUFA, was our family's expert on *malucchiu.* She knew many fables on the subject. As children, my cousins and I enjoyed hearing them as much as she enjoyed telling them. She spoke only Sicilian, and as she told a story, those of us who understood, simultaneously translated for the others.

Zia Ganufa had a nephew who married an "American girl" and moved far away, to Ohio. One August, he took his family back to Bruculinu to see relatives. On the hottest day of the year, they visited

Zia Ganufa. She welcomed them with a grand, multicourse dinner, in spite of the heat.

After dinner, she asked if they had enjoyed the meal. "Yes," said the nephew, "but I wish I had a slice of your *cucciaddatu* to top it off." He was, of course, joking, it being so far from Yuletide.

Zia Ganufa suddenly remembered that there might still be a pastry from the previous Christmas stored among her linens. She went into the chest in her bedroom. Slipping her hand between the layers of pressed, white sheets, her fingers nudged the forgotten pastry. It had been neatly wrapped in waxed paper and covered in a dishcloth.

Moments later, she reappeared in the dining room with a plate of the sliced pastry. The nephew's eyes widened. "But how could it be, Auntie," he said in wonder, "how could you have made this fresh *cucciaddatu* so quickly?"

"You see, my children," Zia Ganufa told us in a low, sure voice, "we are good, clean people. We always pray to God and he protects us from *malucchiu*. Our food never spoils, we are in His grace. Even my *cucciaddatu* stayed fresh for eight months."

WHEN I WAS NINE, I had my own experience with the evil eye. For no apparent reason, over the course of a week, I became alarmingly thin. One Saturday, my mother took me to the doctor. After hearing my symptoms, he concluded that I had contracted pinworms.

My mother's face took on a horrified expression. In an effort to put her at ease, the doctor explained that it was not uncommon for children, especially boys, to get these parasites. "Children play in the streets," he continued, "and their hands get quite dirty. They often visit the candy store to buy unwrapped penny candy from open bins. Along with the candy," he concluded, "their filthy fingers bring God-knows-what-else to their stomachs."

To support his diagnosis, the good doctor needed concrete proof. Perhaps darkness could coax an appearance. He told me to undress from the waist down and lie on my stomach. He turned out the light, saying he would return in a few minutes.

The paper that covered the hard, leather examining table crackled with my every squirm in the darkened room. Frightened, I asked my mother what he was going to do to me. She said not to worry, all he was going to do was look for worms. I didn't know what she meant.

As promised, the good doctor returned, holding a flashlight. As he turned it on, it finally dawned on me why I was in this odd position, and from where the worms would present themselves. After the most embarrassing few minutes of my young life, the doctor excitedly exclaimed, "Look, Mrs. Schiavelli! Look! There they are! Worms!"

I dressed quickly, trying to put distance between the event and myself. Medicine was prescribed, my mother paid the $4 office fee and we left. My mother suggested that we visit my grandmother Anna, who lived close to the doctor's office. Although we often visited her on Saturdays, what with the newly found creatures and all, it seemed an odd choice. My mother insisted.

We climbed the winding, wooden stairway of the old rear house on Skillman Street to my grandmother's apartment. We sat in the main room of the cold-water flat, near the coal stove. My mother told her about my illness. The four-foot-six-inch toothless old woman in black listened attentively and then croaked out a single word: *malucchiu*.

My mother protested, saying there was no such nonsense, but Grandmother insisted that the only thing to do was to go see a *strega*, a witch, just to be sure. She reminded my mother that if I had been a victim of evil doing, no amount of medicine could cure my illness without first removing the curse.

I wasn't too keen on undergoing a second worm hunt that day, but Grandma Anna assured me that wouldn't happen. The witch would look for cause, not effect. I saw that my mother, while still voicing protest, was the first one of us ready to leave for the witch's house.

A seemingly modern woman, my mother was covering all bases to protect me. She knew that in Bruculinu children could get worms for reasons far outside the reach of medical science. To that end, she had taken me on this oddly timed visit, knowing full well that Anna would insist on sending me to a *strega*. At the same time, she didn't want to bind me with the fear of her own ancient superstitions by letting on that the idea had come from her.

We walked the three blocks to the witch's house and knocked on the door. An old woman in black with a black shawl over her head admitted us. Perceiving our reasons for coming, she led us through a maze of dark, incense-smoked rooms, filled with other old women similarly attired, buzzing a chorus of incantation. As the murmuration of old women grew denser and louder, we found ourselves face to face with the witch herself.

She was a woman of about 50. Except for a ring on every finger and a number of necklaces, she looked surprisingly ordinary. Without being briefed, she told me in Sicilian that she was sorry I had worms, and then she asked if she could touch me.

Tentatively, I said yes. She placed one hand on the back of my neck, and the other over my stomach. The witch had a mother's touch, gentle and sure. She closed her eyes, and the murmur hushed. I felt a strange sort of tingle flow through my body between the two points of her touch. After a few minutes, she opened her eyes, and the chanting resumed. Turning to my mother and grandmother, she gave a slow, certain nod.

With her arm around my shoulder, we walked to another room followed by all present. On the way, the witch asked about my schoolwork, wanting to know if I had been a good boy, respectful to my elders. It was a very ordinary conversation, one I might have had with any number of adults in the neighborhood.

We entered the room, which was foggy with incense. At its center was a small, round table covered in an old embroidered piano shawl. On it sat a large glass bowl, flanked by two pitchers. She asked me to put my hands on the outside of the bowl. Whispering something in a language I'd never heard before, she poured water from one of the pitchers into the bowl. Then, from the other pitcher, she poured olive oil in a spiral pattern. The oil immediately floated to the center, forming a circle. The witch whispered with great drama, "Look, ladies! Look! There it is! *Malucchiu!*"

The witch then took a small bottle out of her pocket and sprinkled me with fragrant water. In a strong, commanding voice, she ordered the evil spirit to leave my body. Afterward, she led me back to my mother, saying, "*Tutti cosi, ora, sunnu a postu, grazii Diu.* Everything is now in place, thank God." The whole assembly let out a sigh to Heaven.

My mother happily dropped $3 into a basket near the front door. I remember thinking at the time that it was a better deal than the doctor, far more entertaining, and there were no flashlights to boot.

Over the next week, I took the doctor's medicine, ate my grandfather's hearty, restorative food and was a very, very good boy. The worms went away and never came back.

NOWADAYS, IN NEW AGE AMERICA, *malucchiu* and the *strega* have been transmuted into karma and the psychic, superstition into alternative belief structures. It is the same song with a different voice. My mother was right not to want me bound by it, and I am not. Even so, I automatically cross myself whenever throwing out a piece of moldy bread. I tell myself it is only a habit.

Recipes

THE BEST CURE OF ALL was Papa Andrea's hearty, nour- ishing food. He provided menus designed to restore me to health and keep away the evil eye.

Aneddi cu l'Ovu e Tumazzu

Anellini with Eggs
and Cheese

PASTA WITH EGGS AND CHEESE was our ultimate comfort food. It nourished me through childhood illnesses, providing physical as well as spiritual well-being. As an adult, I find it to be the best cure for rainy Mondays and general malaise. The fact that you can prepare this dish in minutes, even when there is "nothing" in the house to eat, only enhances its curative power.

Peas, not always available in Bruculinu, were a welcome surprise in this dish. Everyone was amused to find them inside anellini, the little pasta rings.

Today in this country, raw eggs can be contaminated with salmonella, a problem unheard of in Bruculinu. Because of this, it is best to buy eggs from small, local farms rather than large producers. Health food stores are also a good source for fresh, clean eggs.

For 4 servings

2   tablespoons extra-virgin olive oil, for the pasta water
2   tablespoons sea salt
1   pound anellini or small-shell pasta
¾   cup fresh or frozen peas
2   tablespoons unsalted butter
3   large eggs, beaten
¾   cup grated imported pecorino cheese, preferably Locatelli
    Black pepper

Bring 6 quarts water, the oil and the salt to a boil in a large pot. Add the pasta. After 2 minutes, add the peas. Cook until the pasta is al dente. Drain thoroughly and return it to the pasta pot. Toss with the butter, eggs and cheese.

Divide among 4 pasta bowls and serve with a grinding of black pepper.

CHAPTER VII.

Ficatu e Cipuddi

Calf's Liver and Onions

FRESH CALF'S LIVER is the most exquisite of organ meats. The traditional pairing with onions enhances its sweetness and delicacy. Unfortunately, calf's liver is often overcooked, turning it into something more suitable for the cobbler's bench than for the dinner table. This quick treatment, however, has the power to turn liver's most adamant opponents into ardent fans.

For 4 servings

2   pounds calf's liver, cut into ½-inch-wide strips
     Milk, for soaking
4   medium onions
3   tablespoons unsalted butter
1   tablespoon extra-virgin olive oil
     Sea salt
     Black pepper
1-2 tablespoons lard
6   sprigs Italian parsley, chopped

Place the liver in a bowl and cover it with milk. Cover and refrigerate for at least 3 hours.

When the liver is in its last 30 minutes of soaking, preheat the oven to 300°F. Peel the onions, cut them in half and thinly slice them. Separate the rings.

Put the butter and oil in a heavy skillet over low heat. When the butter stops foaming, add the onions and slowly sauté until soft, stirring from time to time, about 12 minutes. Be careful not to burn

121

them. Turn up the heat to medium-high, season with salt and continue to sauté until the onions are pale golden, about 4 minutes. Season with pepper and transfer to the oven to keep hot while the liver cooks.

Grease a large skillet generously with lard and heat it over high heat until very hot. Remove the liver from the milk and pat it dry. Cook for 2 minutes on each side, until it is pink throughout. Remember that it will continue to cook on its way to the table.

Quickly place the liver on a warmed serving platter and lightly season with salt. Place the onions on top and sprinkle with parsley. Serve immediately.

Caroti chi Chiovi 'i Garufunu

*C*arrots with Cloves

THE SWEETNESS OF STEAMED CARROTS perfumed with cloves makes this dish an unlikely but excellent accompaniment to Calf's Liver and Onions.

For 4 servings

12 whole cloves
6 large carrots
2 tablespoons extra-virgin olive oil
   Black pepper

Place a steamer over high heat with the cloves in the water. While the water comes to a boil, scrape the carrots and slice them on the diagonal ¼ inch thick. Steam the carrots for 10 minutes, or until they offer no resistance when pierced with a fork.

Place the carrots in a serving bowl and toss with the olive oil and several grindings of black pepper.

Budinu 'i Ancili

$\mathscr{P}$udding of the Angels

I N OUR HOUSEHOLD, as well as in all of Bruculinu, the belief in egg yolks as a restorative was universal. They were fed in various sweet concoctions to anyone in need of fortification. Candidates included sickly children, anemic older persons and grooms on their wedding night.

One part of this dessert is chilled zabaglione, a custard of egg yolks, sugar and sweet Marsala. It is best cooked in a shallow double boiler. If you don't have one, you can improvise by placing a stainless steel or copper mixing bowl on top of a pot. The water in the pot should not touch the bottom of the bowl.

Because this dessert contains raw egg whites, use only the freshest eggs from small producers.

For 6 servings

2 large egg whites
7 tablespoons sugar
1 cup heavy whipping cream
1 tablespoon cognac
8 large egg yolks
½ cup sweet Marsala wine
½ cup orange liqueur, such as Curaçao, Grand Marnier or
    Cointreau
    Sliced almonds, for decoration

Beat the egg whites in a large bowl until they form high peaks that are stiff but not dry. While continuing to beat, slowly add 4 tablespoons of the sugar, 1 tablespoonful at a time. To prevent the meringue from collapsing, do not add the next spoonful of sugar until the previous one has been absorbed. Refrigerate until needed.

Combine the cream and cognac in a medium bowl and whip it until very stiff. Fold it into the meringue and return it to the refrigerator.

Bring the water in the lower pot of a double boiler to a boil, without the top bowl in place. In preparation for chilling the zabaglione, fill a bowl with ice.

Put the egg yolks and the remaining 3 tablespoons sugar in the top bowl of the double boiler. Whisk together until the yolks are pale yellow and frothy. Whisk in the Marsala and orange liqueur.

When the water comes to a boil, put the top bowl in place and, whisking vigorously, cook the mixture to the consistency of thick paint, about 4 minutes. Do not let it boil, as that would cause the zabaglione to collapse.

Immediately thrust the bowl of zabaglione into the ice. Continue to whisk for 1 to 2 minutes, or until it has cooled somewhat and is no longer in danger of collapse.

When the ice has chilled the zabaglione a bit, place equal amounts of the meringue mixture in 6 small stemmed wine glasses. Spoon equal amounts of the zabaglione on top. Using a small, thin knife, ribbon the two parts together.

Decorate the center of each glass with a cluster of sliced almonds. Cover with plastic wrap and refrigerate to set for at least 3 or up to 12 hours.

VIII.

$\mathcal{T}$he Americans

THOSE IN OUR NEIGHBORHOOD who weren't Sicilian, Italian, Jewish, African-American or Puerto Rican were *i mericani*, "The Americans." They were considered to be dirty, drunk and slow, with strange barbaric customs. I'm sure that they held the same opinion of us.

In Bruculinu, social and ethnic groups were defined by strict criteria. First and foremost there was the family, the most important social group to which anyone could belong. No matter what sort of internal discord or feuding existed within these huge blood branches, the family always presented a unified face. In return, being part of a family respected by the community provided members of all ages with favor and consideration.

Next came the bonds of being *paisani*, that is, having roots in the same Sicilian town. Most of my parents' and my generation were born in this country and had never even visited Sicily. Nonetheless, we carried the banner of our grandparents' town as if it were the home team.

Larger groups defined themselves as being from Sicily or from one of the various provinces of the Italian peninsula. The unification of Italy, nearly 100 years in the past, was not recognized as an ethnic unity by the country of Bruculinu. Inside the neighborhood, we were

126

Polizzani, or Palermitani, or Calabrisi or Napolitani, to name just four of hundreds of microethnic identities. But when asked our nationality by outsiders, we said Italian-American, simplifying the issue.

We felt kindred to certain groups of outsiders, most notably the Jews. We recognized their strong commitment to family, God and food as similar to ours. We understood their way of doing business. Their style of bargaining was not unlike that of the Sicilian shopkeepers, although the Jewish merchants had better prices.

Everyone in the neighborhood knew that the best prices on goods, ranging from buttons to window fans, were at King Solomon's Variety Store on Knickerbocker Avenue. At Christmastime, King Solomon's goods filled five-foot-high bleachers cascading down to the street in front of the shop. The owner, who we all called Mr. King Solomon, stood in judgment on a platform above his wares, entertaining all price offers. At times, he would turn a deaf ear to an absurd offer, and the other party would walk away with great resolve. After perhaps several go-rounds of this show, complete with arm gestures and waving, the deal for tinsel or crèches always worked out to each party's satisfaction.

WITH THE AMERICANS, IT WAS A DIFFERENT STORY. On our block, they all lived in the same building. "The American building," we called it, not only because of its tenants, but also because of its renovated modern postwar style. The undisputed leaders of this enclave were Pete and Peggy. They had lived in the neighborhood their whole lives, from the time when it was predominantly German. Pete had gone off to fight the war as an older enlistee, managing to return in one piece. Both he and Peggy had jobs in the same light industrial factory in Long Island City. But their real work was the continuing celebration of V-J Day, now approaching its fourteenth anniversary.

Every evening during the warmer months of the year, they sat on beach chairs in front of their building, drinking highballs under the shadow of the Myrtle Avenue el. The tall glass tumblers were decorated with badly painted orange sailboats and were set on a turquoise folding snack table.

As they drank, Pete and Peggy chain-smoked, flipping their ashes into a dirty, chipped ceramic ashtray shaped like a swimming pool. At one edge was the figure of a bathing beauty, reclining, with her legs raised. The legs were held in place inside the torso with a hook, held in the air by means of a counterweight. When an el train passed, the vibration caused the legs to wiggle.

On hot summer evenings, Pete sported a dingy white athletic undershirt, Peggy a yellowed summer dress. Pete liked to sit with his hands clasped behind his head. Although the hair on his head was thinning and of indeterminable color, under his arms it was abundant and deep red. It flashed like a fire engine.

If my mother or one of my aunts walked by and saw him posing this way, the first thing they would say upon entering the house was, "I just saw ya know. Isn't he embarrassed?"

The Zwickey family also lived in the American building. No one knew exactly how many children they had, but the family was so large that they occupied two apartments. We never saw Mr. or Mrs. Zwickey. The joke around the neighborhood was that they were too busy upstairs.

Each one of the Zwickeys was more blond than the next. It was odd to see so many towheads in our neighborhood. The girls were thin and plain. Their dresses were worn hand-me-downs. The older girls looked after their younger siblings. They rarely smiled.

The Zwickey boys were tough guys, involved in petty crime. They weren't too bright and always got caught. Each one of them held a J.D. card, an identity card issued by the cops to juvenile delinquents with police records. Among young hoods, the J.D. card was considered a status symbol.

As a younger boy, I watched as the Zwickeys hung out in a wad in front of their building. They wore tight black "continental" trousers, hemmed four inches above their pointy black shoes. This high-water style was designed to show off bright orange or green socks. They rolled a pack of cigarettes into the sleeves of their black or white T-shirts. To top off the look, their hair was styled in a "*Dee*-troit," with sides long and swept back, top buzzed and greased to stand up two inches high.

They joked and laughed, giving each other "skin." Sometimes they were visited by tough-looking girls with Marie Antoinette hair-dos and tight sweaters. The girls popped their gum in awe when the boys whipped out their J.D. cards. It proved they were the *vrais choses*. Pete and Peggy watched, smiling and nodding between slugs and puffs, as if to say, "Ah, youtt!"

Often sharing the ashtray with Pete and Peggy, but without a beach chair, was Elaine. She didn't want to sit because, as she often said, "I bin sittin' all day at work." Elaine was a skinny woman with dark, messy hair, sharp features and rhinestone cat's-eye glasses.

The work that kept her "sittin' all day" was in an olive-packing plant down on Flushing Avenue. After the olives had been pitted and stuffed with pimientos, they were deposited at Elaine's station. Sitting on a high stool, she arranged them in slim bottles with long tweezers.

Elaine was very proud of her position in the olive plant, taking it as seriously as if she were assembling the H-bomb. "Very delicate work," she called it. "It's all in da foist four olives," she explained. "If ya get dem in nice 'n tight, den da only ting ya gotta worry about is da twistin'."

Explaining her work in minute detail, she made it clear that she was under great pressure; mistakes were not tolerated by the management. "If da olives toyns out twisted, dey docks ya. An' at da end o' da week, alls ya get ta take home is olives. Me, I don't even like olives."

Elaine was divorced and lived with her son, Leonard, who was a year older than I. He was a large, quiet boy with a passion for "customized" cars. If his nose wasn't in an auto magazine, he was carefully painting plastic models with lacquer finishes or applying miniature flame decals. Leonard had inherited his mother's talent for detail and perfection.

For a brief period of time when I was 11, Leonard and I became good friends. One day, he invited me up to see his collection of model custom cars. Unfortunately, Elaine's penchant for order did not extend to housework. The place looked as if someone had just moved in or had just moved out. It was impossible to distinguish between garbage and salvage.

Everyone else I knew had neat, ordered households. If the floor wasn't clean enough to eat off, it was considered dirty. Here, one couldn't find a plate clean enough to eat off, let alone the floor. The only other American households I had seen were on TV, but this one wasn't brought to us by Procter and Gamble.

Leonard did have quite a collection of beautifully finished model cars. He roamed through the disorder, fishing them out, explaining every fender detail, every hood modification. He supported his choices by comparing them to photos in the stacks of auto magazines that adorned every flat surface.

One Saturday, during Leonard's lecture on flared wheel wells, Elaine said, "Did ya show Vince ya art books? Go an' get 'em." Leonard produced a tattered gift box from under his bed, gleefully handing it to his mother.

By way of introduction, Elaine said, "Like I always says ta Leonard, da 'uman body is a beautiful ting. Der ain't notin' ta be ashamed about it. When yous boys get older, yous gonna get certain urges. Dese tings are natural and come from God. OK?"

With that she handed Leonard the box, and he led me to his room. With a sweeping gesture, he cleared a place for us to sit on his bed. As he opened the box, I realized that the so-called art books weren't books at all, nor did they contain art like my *World Book Encyclopedia*. Instead, they were tawdry magazines filled with photos of nude men and women, provocatively posed. They weren't exactly Botticellis.

Leonard, in a maniacally obsessed manner, began explaining each photo to me as if he were describing customized headlights or tail fins. I had seen engaged or newlywed couples kissing and cuddling, and I could sense the sparks flying between them, but this was something different, and it made me feel uncomfortable. Even now, I can only speculate as to why Elaine had thought it a good idea to sexualize her preadolescent son. On that Saturday, all I knew was that I wanted no part of whatever this was. Making some excuse, I left.

Passing the Zwickey boys at their post, holding up the front of the building, I overheard one of the older ones say to another, "Leonard musta showed 'im his art books. Dat's some art!"

Ultimately, Leonard's parent-approved pursuit of fast cars and loose women was not one I shared. I had other interests, more appropriate for an 11-year-old. After that Saturday, I didn't see much of Elaine and Leonard; they were too weird for me.

ONE YEAR, Pete sponsored a Fourth of July fireworks display. The Fourth was the American holiday we understood the least in Bruculinu. We all knew, of course, what the celebration commemorated, but the form it took was strange to us.

In the first place, we knew of no special food associated with it. We could relate to Thanksgiving turkey, but for the Fourth, all we saw the Americans do was drink too much and make noise. To our eyes, they lacked respect for the founding fathers and the country in general. Out of our own sense of respect, however, we held our tongues, trying to feel American, in spite of ourselves.

From the beginning of June, the Zwickey boys clustered around 131

Pete in his outdoor living room. They listened in hushed silence as he explained and reexplained safety procedures for handling fireworks. Pete wanted to eliminate the possibility of anyone losing a finger or putting out an eye, which would have definitely soured the celebration.

All fireworks were illegal in the five boroughs of New York, but that had little effect on their availability. About two weeks before the event, Pete put on a Hawaiian print shirt and climbed into his old Chevy with the oldest Zwickey riding shotgun. They drove into the City, to Chinatown, in search of the contraband.

Hours later, Pete signaled their return with two toots of his horn. All of the Zwickeys appeared to help unload the trunk, now filled with packages and bundles of fireworks. Smuggled from Hong Kong, their thin paper wrappers were decorated with beautiful red Chinese characters.

Pete, proud of the success of his mission, said, "Der da good ones, nice an' fresh." How he could tell, I have no idea, and I'm sure no one else did either, but he was the expert and no one questioned it. The Zwickey who had accompanied him chimed in, "Yeah, an' we had egg foo yung, too," as if this information somehow related to fireworks.

A S DUSK GATHERED ON THE FOURTH OF JULY, the fireworks were brought down from Pete and Peggy's apartment, stacked and covered with a blanket. For the occasion, he wore a particularly fresh undershirt, she modeled a new cotton dress. Since it had been a work holiday, by this time of day, they were pretty well oiled.

At nine, the festivities began. Pete lit a short length of rope for each Zwickey, the glowing end to be used to ignite the fuses. "OK, boys," he proclaimed, assuming his hands-behind-head position, "go an' do it."

The sound of the first cherry bomb summoned my family to

our second-floor living room windows. Not knowing what to expect, we preferred the safety of the indoors, just below the level of the el tracks, to joining the Americans on the street. We couldn't believe our eyes as we realized where Pete was sending the boys. In his drunken exuberance, the staging area Pete had chosen was the gas station across Myrtle Avenue. Wondering what sort of grand finale he was actually planning, we took a step back, just in case. With our hands wrapped tightly around cold glasses of lemon ice, we spooned the sweet-tart slush into our mouths to ease the tension.

The Zwickey boys, hair helmets greased in place, swaggered through the gas station like some strange, blond army. From his "bunker" across the street, Pete shouted out orders, commanding his troops to move right or left so the display wouldn't be blocked from his view by an el post.

There were strings of "ladyfingers," two-inch firecrackers fused together in a strand. When ignited, they sounded like bursts of machine gun fire. "Ash cans" made the most resonant explosions. Even at our distance we could feel the concussion in our chests. Twenty-packs of regular firecrackers provided the most drama, as they jumped and banged all over the gas station, critically close to the pumps. We ate the ice even faster to soothe our nerves.

Throughout the display, the younger Zwickeys popped "torpedoes," which exploded on impact. And as the Zwickeys swirled sparklers, their bright blue eyes and fair hair sparkled brighter than the burning bits of iron they held out in front of them.

My favorite fireworks were called "screamy meemies," rockets that trailed along the ground, emitting red and white light and whistling. Set off in all directions, they pierced the night with their sound, demanding right of way with their fire. Sometimes the boys sent them off in the wrong direction, forcing themselves into a comical hopscotch, to the amusement of all.

When a device failed to explode, tensions mounted. A Zwickey

133

would carefully move in to investigate, eliciting sharp orders from General Pete: "Get ya face outta-der!"

We waited for the grand finale, planned or accidental, but there was no rockets' red glare or bombs bursting in air. Pete didn't get those kinds of fireworks, only the kind that blow up with a great noise. There was no climax, only a cease-fire, and miraculously, no casualties.

As the intense smell of gunpowder was carried away on a breeze created by a passing el train, we readied for bed, unsatisfied and restless. Not that we wanted the gas station to blow up, but we longed for something lovely to help us form a connection to the second half of our hyphenated culture.

We knew that TV America was out there somewhere, its tree-lined streets filled with white clapboard houses and opportunity. The Americans on our block seemed to have forgotten this American dream. Their actions were not of a people who had established great freedom across a great sea. Paradoxically, these Americans no longer understood America.

ecipes

THE THING ABOUT THE AMERICANS we could never figure out was what they ate. Hot dogs and hamburgers we
knew, but we couldn't imagine tuna casserole. As far as the
strange dishes we saw on TV were concerned, they didn't
help at all to unravel the mystery. We didn't believe people
ate such things.

Sometimes, Papa Andrea would announce a meal as *roba
mericani*, American stuff. In the end it turned out to be as
American as their attempts at our food were Sicilian.

Purpettunu

Sicilian-Style Meat Loaf

THE WORD *PURPETTUNU* translates as large meatball. Using veal and pork instead of beef, and rice instead of bread crumbs, elevates this humble dish from the dry, sawdustlike fare of dreaded school lunches to something far more sublime. The mushroom gravy, from Papa Andrea, suits this meat loaf far better than the usual tomato sauce.

Refrigerate leftover meat loaf and gravy separately. Cold meat loaf makes great sandwiches, with or without hot gravy.

For 6 to 8 servings

FOR THE MEAT LOAF
- 2 teaspoons sea salt
- ¾ cup Arborio rice
- 2½ pounds ground veal
- 8 ounces ground pork
- 1 medium onion, finely chopped
- 6 large eggs
- 6 slices pancetta
- Black pepper

FOR THE MUSHROOM GRAVY
- 8 ounces crimini or Italian brown mushrooms
- 2 tablespoons extra-virgin olive oil
- Sea salt
- 3 tablespoons unsalted butter
- ¼ cup all-purpose flour

2 cups Meat Broth (page 22) or canned beef broth,
  at room temperature
½ cup dry white wine
  Black pepper
2 tablespoons milk

Prepare the meat loaf: Fill a 4-quart pot with water. Add 2 teaspoons salt and bring to a boil. Add the rice and cook until slightly underdone. Drain in a colander and rinse under running cold water to stop the cooking process. Cool to room temperature.

Preheat the oven to 375°F.

Place the veal, pork, rice, onion and eggs in a large mixing bowl. Knead together by hand, squeezing the mixture through your fingers. Turn it out into a 13-by-9-inch baking pan.

Shape the mixture into a giant oval meatball with squared corners, about 11 inches long, 7 inches wide and 3 inches high at the center. Cover the top with the pancetta and generously sprinkle with black pepper. Bake for 1½ hours.

Prepare the mushroom gravy: Wipe the mushrooms clean, using as little cold water as possible to remove dirt. Trim the stems, discarding any that are dried out. Slice the caps and remaining stems.

Pour the oil into a large, nonreactive skillet, and heat almost to smoking. Add the mushrooms, sprinkle with salt and sauté until they gain some color but before they shrink, about 2 minutes. Transfer to a plate to stop the cooking process. Set aside.

Melt the butter over low heat in a heavy medium skillet. When it stops foaming, whisk in the flour to make a roux. While continuing to whisk, cook it quite slowly until it is rust-colored. Bear in mind that the roux can burn quite easily. The moment it reaches the desired color, whisk in about ¼ cup of the broth. When it has been absorbed, add another small amount. Proceed in this manner until all of the stock has been absorbed by the roux. Pour the gravy into a saucepan. Add the white wine and the pepper. Continue to cook, stirring from time to time, until the gravy nearly boils. Add the mushrooms, along with any liquid that may have separated from them. Simmer the gravy for about 15 minutes to thicken it. To test the consistency, swirl a small amount on a saucer. The gravy should cover it like a veil. Taste for salt, adding more if necessary. If the gravy is ready before the meat loaf, keep it hot, covered, over low heat.

When the meat loaf is ready, carefully transfer it to a serving platter. Stir the pan drippings and milk into the gravy. Cut the meat loaf into ¾-inch-thick slices and serve with the gravy.

Giri al Agru

Cooked Chard Salad

COOKED GREENS were commonly found on our dinner tables. In their season, everything from spinach to wild dandelions growing in backyards and vacant lots was cooked, dressed and served hot or cold.

Chard is a member of the beet family and is cultivated for its leaf rather than its root. Red and green chard are the most commonly available varieties. There is also a variety of white chard with flat leaves that have a stronger flavor. Green or white chard is most suitable for this recipe.

For 6 servings

3   pounds green or white chard
    Sea salt
¼   cup extra-virgin olive oil
1   lemon, cut into wedges

Clean the chard and cut it into pieces about 2 inches long. Bring a large pot of water to a boil. Add the chard and cook until tender but firm, 3 to 5 minutes. Immediately add cold water to stop the cooking process. Drain and plunge the chard into ice water to maintain the bright green color. When the chard has cooled, drain thoroughly. Season with salt and toss with the oil. Serve with lemon wedges.

Purè 'i Patati Infurnatu

Baked Mashed Potatoes

BAKING MASHED POTATOES WITH EGGS and grated cheese into a kind of pie gives them remarkable fluffiness and intensity of flavor. Peas add sweetness. Another advantage to this dish is that it avoids the mad dash to mash the potatoes at the moment when the rest of the dinner is ready.

For 6 servings

2½ pounds russet, Yukon Gold or Yellow Finn potatoes
  Sea salt
1 cup fresh or frozen peas
4 tablespoons (½ stick) unsalted butter, plus more
  for greasing the pan
  Black pepper
3 large eggs
1 cup grated imported pecorino cheese, preferably Locatelli
3 tablespoons unflavored fine dry bread crumbs,
  plus more for dusting the pan

Peel the potatoes and cut them into large pieces of equal size. Put them in a pot of lightly salted cold water over medium-high heat. Bring to a boil, and cook until tender, 20 to 30 minutes, depending on the size of the pieces.

Meanwhile, parboil the peas for 2 minutes, drain and rinse under cold running water.

Drain the potatoes, put them in a large bowl and mash with the 4 tablespoons butter and a few grindings of pepper. Cool to room temperature.

Preheat the oven to 375°F. Generously grease a 9-by-5-inch loaf pan with butter and coat with bread crumbs.

Beat 2 of the eggs in a small bowl and mix them into the mashed potatoes. Mix in the cheese. Gently mix in the peas, being careful not to smash them. Turn the mixture into the loaf pan. Smooth the top with a rubber spatula. Beat the remaining egg in a small bowl and pour it over the top. Sprinkle with the 3 tablespoons bread crumbs.

Bake for 50 minutes to 1 hour, or until the top is golden brown. Let it stand for 5 minutes. Cut the loaf into slices and serve.

IX.

*T*he Duke

THE DUKE WAS THE PRESIDENT OF THE ELLERY BOPS, a street gang in the old neighborhood. He lived at 523 Flushing Avenue, near the brewery, at the far edge of our community. For the most part, our section was built with rows of two- and three-story shingled structures. The front doors had long glass panels dressed with white shades, but at 523 Flushing, there were no shades.

A great deal of myth surrounded the Duke. Some said that he was a veteran of the Korean War, greatly decorated, who afterward had taken a wrong turn in civilian life. Others said that he was just a bum, a bad boy whose gang life reflected his shiftless nature.

To us kids of seven or eight, he was a kind of antihero. We couldn't decide whether he was a "right guy" or a "bad guy." On the one hand, he and his gang were turning the streets into a battleground; on the other, they were protecting us from an evil we couldn't name and didn't understand. Whatever else we thought, we knew for certain that the Duke was boss.

One of my classmates, Vito, claimed that his brother, a lieutenant in the Ellery Bops, had taken him to the Duke's apartment. He said that "it was really weird," describing a place that was empty of furniture, save a small bed and a little table with two chairs.

The weirdest part of all, he said, was that in this large railroad flat, the Duke lived alone. This, to us, was unbelievable, and we doubted the truthfulness of Vito's story. We all lived in similar flats, filled with parents and brothers and sisters, or aunts and uncles and grandparents. No one in the neighborhood lived alone; no one "had nobody." Maybe that's why the Duke had his gang.

I HAD FIRST BECOME AWARE OF THE DUKE and the Ellery Bops when I was in the second grade, the first year that I was allowed to go to school without an adult. My friend Michael Tesarari and I generally walked together, although we were not yet permitted to cross the wider avenues on our own.

For the busiest one, Myrtle Avenue, we climbed up the stairs of the el station, passed through and descended the stairs on the other side of the street. If there was no crossing guard at Central Avenue and Suydam Street, we'd ask someone to shepherd us. "Lady, could you please cross me?" The women were always pleased to give us safe passage through the moving traffic.

In Bruculinu, all adults were surrogate parents, and we were taught to treat them with respect. There was never any question that they had our best interests in mind and would keep us safe. As Michael and I walked together, we spoke of many things, including schoolwork, planned summer vacations, Lionel electric trains, stickball and which sodas had the best bottle caps for the street game scullsy. At least once a morning, the topic was gangs.

We were still too young to be considered gang members, so we could proceed down the street unmolested. We couldn't comprehend why our neighborhood had turned into a battle zone. Our territorial street games were all make-believe. When the game was over, no one was hurt, and we were all still friends. But the gangs weren't playing. Their turf wars were for keeps. Their punches were hard; their bruises, blood and broken bones real.

We saw the gang members bopping down the street in large groups, dressed in gang jackets, their long hair slicked into duck's ass sweep-backs. Gloved hands clenched lengths of chain or car aerials. Along with brass knuckles, these were the weapons of choice. Practicing for the rumble ahead, they looked fierce, and we cleared the way.

Sometimes late at night, we'd be roused by war cries, made more intense by the sound of swinging chain, and the scurrying of many feet. At other times, the quiet of the night was broken by the harmonies of the Ellery Bops singing, a cappella. No matter how quickly I got up and ran to the window, I could find no one on the street, only the fading sound of the doo-wop.

ONE SPRING MORNING IN 1956, Michael met me in a dramatically dark mood. "Din-cha hear?" he asked, trembling. "Da Baldies are commin'!" These words filled me with such terror that I nearly dropped my books. The Baldies were a gang of dreaded ferocity; their heads were clean shaven and they dressed in black from head to toe. They looked frightening, like the Grim Reaper. We had all heard the stories in which they had terrorized whole neighborhoods.

It seems that that afternoon the Baldies were going to settle an old score with the Duke. Apparently, he had once been a member, and his departure remained unresolved. Michael went on, with a quiver in his voice. The Baldies were coming to the schoolyard after lunch, to scalp everyone. "Da nuns too?" I asked incredulously. "Yep," Michael said emphatically. "Everybody, even da ol' guy who sells da pretzels."

All morning I asked myself why this was happening to us. We were little kids—we "neva did notin' ta nobody." I hoped that at any moment our teacher would call our mothers, and we would be escorted back to the safety of our homes. As the clock ticked and the lunch bell threatened to chime, the whole class became more ter-rified. Sister Mary Immaculate phoned no one. The ringing of the bell sent us reluctantly home for lunch, dreading the bloody recess to follow.

One boy said he was going to tell his mother. The all-knowing Vito explained, "It's too late. If yous tell ya muddhas now, der gonna get scalped too." At that moment, this logic made sense, and we all vowed, like little anti-Communist patriots or crusaders for Christ, to protect our loved ones. "Ain't nobody gonna get it 'cause we was chicken."

We all went home and picked at our lunches, pretending that all was fine. The walk back to school was like a death march. Some of our classmates didn't return for the afternoon session, and we knew what *they* were.

The whole school clustered in the yard in small groups. No one played the usual games of tag or potsy. No one bought the old pret-zel man's goods, in preparation for the near uncertain future when he wouldn't be there. We waited, hoping that the bell would ring be-fore the Baldies arrived.

Quietly, an army of teens and young men dressed in orange satin zippered jackets assembled on the other side of the schoolyard fence. The bold white script letters sewn on the back let us all know that the marines had arrived. It was the Ellery Bops to the rescue. On the far corner stood an imposing figure, arms folded in front of him. His head was clean shaven, and he wore a large gold hoop ear-ring. A white satin jacket with orange letters was draped over his mas-sive shoulders. He was flanked by two lieutenants, one of whom was Vito's brother, brandishing car aerials. Although most of us had never seen him before, we all knew at once that this was the Duke.

All eyes, including those of the nuns, were fixed in his direc-tion. He seemed not to take notice, maintaining his serious, regal

145

pose. At one point he turned to one of his lieutenants, whispering something that brought a brief smile to both of their faces. We in the yard stood there transfixed, as the midday spring sun beat down, warm enough to toast the old man's full pushcart of pretzels.

Suddenly, with resounding fury, the school bell rang. Its certain finality declared the round over. The Baldies never showed: "Dey was chicken."

We lined up by class in half the usual time and silently marched into the safety of the schoolhouse. I turned to see the Duke one last time. He was facing us, with a serious expression and a hand raised in a gesture between a hail and a wave.

THE DUKE'S REIGN OF GLORY WAS SHORT-LIVED. The Ellery Bops, victors of every rumble, spent a little too much time celebrating. At first it was beer and booze, but soon they graduated to cough medicine with codeine and then to barbiturates, called "downs" on the street. In the end, most of them became junkies.

They hung out in Knickerbocker Park, doing their drugs, staggering from bench to bench. Many were arrested for petty crimes, like mugging old ladies. They lost respect among their peers, and we kids outgrew our fascination with them. As "boss" turned to "cool," the 1950s street-gang era of Bruculinu was coming to a close.

After a couple of years, both the Duke and the Ellery Bops disappeared. Occasionally, we'd raise their names in conversation, remembering in a child's miniature sense of time as if from long ago. By 1961, they were all but forgotten, replaced by the more wholesome heroes of the New Frontier. By mid-decade, these new charismatic leaders would involve not only Bruculinu, but the entire country in a different kind of conflict, the turf wars of peace and equality.

I N NOVEMBER 1963, we heard the news. The Duke, depressed over the loss of his gang to drugs and death, felt that he had no future. One day he took out his earring, and jumped off the roof of his building at 523 Flushing Avenue. The street took him, cracking his head on its pavement. It was a sad end to a wasted life, but by this time we had outgrown his legend and mystery. At the end, no one cared much about him. His time had passed.

Gaddina Aggrassata

Potted Chicken

I DOUBT THAT THE SOLITARY DUKE ever felt the comfort of home and hearth while this simple chicken stew bubbled on the back of the stove, as it often did in our house on a cold day.

Gaddina Aggrassata, a common country favorite, takes on exceptional flavor when cooked by the layered method of this century-old recipe brought over from Polizzi Generosa. To accentuate the rustic nature of this dish, bring it to the table in the pot in which it was cooked. Have the chicken cut into 2 legs, 2 thighs, 2 wings and 2 half-breasts; halve the back as well.

For 4 servings

1   3½-pound chicken, preferably free-range,
         cut into 10 pieces
3   tablespoons extra-virgin olive oil
1½   pounds russet or Yukon Gold or Yellow Finn potatoes
2   medium onions
½   cup dry white wine
     Sea salt
     Black pepper
     About 4 cups boiling water
3   sprigs rosemary

Wash the chicken under cold running water and pat it dry. Heat the oil over medium heat in a large heavy pot that will hold the chicken in a single layer. When the oil is nearly smoking, sauté the chicken, turning the pieces until they are well browned on all sides, about 20 minutes.

Peel the potatoes and cut them into about 1½-inch chunks. Peel and slice the onions.

Transfer the chicken to a plate and brown the potatoes in the same pot. Remove the potatoes with a slotted spoon and place them on a different plate from the chicken. Brown the onion until a deep color but not burned, about 10 minutes. Use a wooden spoon to keep it moving and to scrape away any bits that have stuck to the pan from the chicken or the potatoes. When the onion is browned, remove it with a slotted spoon and place it on yet another plate.

Turn off the heat and carefully pour the grease out of the pot. Return it to the stove, pour in the white wine and deglaze the pot by using a wooden spoon to scrape up the bits stuck to the bottom. Turn the heat on to medium-low and continue to deglaze for 2 or 3 minutes.

Return the chicken to the pot, cover it with half the onion and season with salt and black pepper. Add the potatoes in a single layer and then the remaining onion. Season with salt and black pepper. Pour enough of the boiling water into the pot to barely cover the contents. Slip in the rosemary. Slowly bring the contents to a boil, reduce the heat to low and simmer, with the cover askew, for 45 minutes to 1 hour, or until the chicken is almost falling off the bone.

Serve the chicken and vegetables, covered with the gravy, in pasta bowls.

X.

𝒰 Beccamortu

WHEN THE TRAGEDY OF DEATH struck in Bruculinu, the first person called to the scene was the undertaker, the *beccamortu*. The word mean "the plucker of the dead," but most people didn't know that grim translation. The concept of undertaking itself was grim enough.

The *beccamortu* held a position of great respect in the community. Together with the priest and the doctor, he completed the ministerial trinity of our bodies and souls. He was considered to possess a profound understanding of death, an almost empirical knowledge of its mystery. Due to his firm grasp on this ultimate turn of fate, he was a recognized expert on all aspects of temporal life. His council was sought on matters ranging from political advocacy to house buying.

The undertaker in the old neighborhood whose demeanor most suited his profession was Bruno Caratozzolo. When I knew him, he was past middle age, squarely built, with an open round face and a head full of neatly groomed white hair. Always dressed in a dark suit and a black tie, his manner was quietly direct and calming.

A part of the undertaker's work included grief therapy. At this, Mr. Caratozzolo was masterly. Decades of practice had taught him how to bring even the most emotionally bound to profound tears of mourning. Spotting those in need of his special talent, he would move across the funeral chapel toward them. With great compassion in his eyes, he'd sidle up next to them. Swiftly and silently, he'd place one hand firmly around their waist, and the other securely on one elbow. Holding them up thus, he'd whisper a phrase from his carefully composed stock of condolences. "He was a good man, we all miss him." Or, "She was a great mother, a living saint." Or, perhaps, for the tragedy of the death of a child, "There is a new angel in Heaven today." Upon hearing these words, in the safety of Mr. Caratozzolo's grasp, the aggrieved ones would collapse into wailing sobs. All those present, touched by the moment, would join in, expressing grief, beginning their own healing. A funeral was considered successful by the family if it provided release for the sad but didn't go overboard. At Bruno Caratozzolo & Sons Morticians and Funeral Chapels, proper handling of all matters funereal was ensured.

NOT ALL THE UNDERTAKERS IN THE NEIGHBORHOOD presented an impeccably professional image. Due to their odd hours, some were a bit slovenly. Others, as a way of coping with the work, had developed black senses of humor. A few had adopted eccentric lifestyles.

At the corner of Hart Street and Central Avenue was Tomasso's Funeral Home, in its second generation of operation. The current Tomasso was a man in his late thirties. His choirboy good looks and well-toned form did not conjure the image of his profession. In addition, Mr. Tomasso was well known throughout the neighborhood as a joker.

If business was slow, he would stand in front of his establishment and, with the drollest of deliveries, beckon passersby to stop in and "rest" for a while. In polite conversation, when asked how things were going, he might reply, "Business is great! They're just dyin' ta get in."

Sometimes he'd step into Al's Barber Shop a few doors away. For many, just the sight of the *beccamortu* gave them "the heebie-jeebies." If Mr. Tomasso found a new client of Al's looking disturbed by his appearance in the shop, he'd inquire after the poor man's health, as if to say, "I see the dead all the time, and, brother, do you look bad."

As his unsuspecting patsy grew more and more nervous, Al and the regulars who knew the routine bit their tongues to suppress laughter. Finally, just when the man was convinced that he was at death's door, Mr. Tomasso, in doctoral fashion, would ask him to stand up. He'd reach into the pocket of his black coat, take out a tape and start measuring him for a coffin. Embarrassed but relieved, Mr. Tomasso's victim burst into laughter along with all the other men in the barbershop.

When the uproar ceased, Mr. Tomasso would say something like "But seriously, boys, ya never know when it's gonna be ya time. If ya wanna make some plans, come over an' see me." When the atmosphere in the room had sufficiently chilled, he'd add, "Ya could lie down in a couple, just for size." The slight smile on his face made everyone realize that he'd gotten them all again. Their laughter spilled out into the street as he made his exit.

There was a great deal more, however, to Mr. Tomasso's personality than jokes. Standing at the back of the church during funeral services, he could be found crying, especially if he knew the deceased. Everyone in the neighborhood knew Mr. Tomasso was too thin-skinned for his work, but he went on and we respected him for it.

THE UNDERTAKER LORENZO PULITO was a most unlikely candidate for the profession. Mr. Pulito was a short, dark man with sharp, pointy features. His upper lip was decorated with a pencil-line mustache, enhancing the ratlike image. His black hooded eyes held the mournful gaze of his calling and were, at the same time, a caricature of sexiness.

His usual, overly formal attire of morning coat and striped trousers was impeccably tailored to his diminutive form. His wing-collared shirt, starched to a cardboard finish, was background to onyx cuff links and studs. His black cravat was secured with a pearl stickpin the size of a chickpea. A homburg, dove gray spats and gloves completed the ensemble. In all, he looked more like a tango dancer than an undertaker.

When Mr. Pulito smiled, his lips parted in a straight line, revealing the *pièce de résistance:* a large diamond embedded in his upper left canine. He revealed this misguided marvel of dentistry sparingly, for dramatic effect. Locking one in his gaze, he'd turn his head to one side, showing off the rock to best advantage. Then, quickly closing his mouth, the sparkler would vanish like a shooting star.

The hearse used by the Pulito Mortuary was as distinctive as its chauffeur. Purchased just after the First World War, it had the old-fashioned look of a horseless carriage. Beveled windows ran along its sides, and the coffin could be seen through discreetly parted curtains. Ornate brass sconces at each end of this vitrine punctuated the view.

Mr. Pulito sat behind the wheel in the open cab, his face set in a most serious expression, contrasted by the jaunty angle of his homburg. Beside him on the floorboards sat an antique windup phonograph on which he played recordings of stately funeral music. The driving speed was slow, partly to maintain the tone of the occasion and partly to prevent the needle from skipping.

When not in use, the hearse was parked in the funeral home's garage, where it was kept in showroom condition. In the early 1940s, I am told, this chore was assigned to Mr. Pulito's teenage son. Familiarity with the profession had made the youth somewhat im-

153

mune to the purpose of the vehicle. He thought nothing of inviting friends to assist him with the washing and simonizing.

At first, his chums were not charmed by the chore, the vehicle or the macabre location, but then they discovered the phonograph. After spinning a few big band tunes on it while they worked, they, too, found immunity to the trappings of death. In short order, girlfriends were invited to the garage to practice new dance steps. It was a party.

At the end of the session, to avoid detection by the elder Pulito, the funeral selections were returned to their proper place on the phonograph. One Saturday, however, the boys forgot, and the first funeral on Monday morning was accompanied by "Stompin' at the Savoy."

The worst-kept secret in the neighborhood was that Mr. Pulito had a mistress. It was rumored that Mrs. Pulito and the husband of the woman not only knew of this liaison, but were romantically involved with each other. I doubt that this aspect of the scandal was true; it is precisely the kind of tidy resolution the community would have designed to lend an ironic sense of propriety to the disgrace. In any case, the affair continued for decades.

Mr. Pulito and his paramour thought their behavior was highly discreet, but in reality their actions were about as unnoticeable as a fishmonger's call. One of their more flagrant public displays occurred every time Mr. P. had a funeral to direct.

On the way to the cemetery, it was customary for the deceased to be driven past his former residence for one last good-bye. Mr. Pulito always plotted the processional to pass under his mistress's bedroom window. He'd stop the hearse right there, bringing the entire funeral entourage to a halt. Pointing the phonograph's horn up at her window to herald his arrival, he awaited acknowledgment for this tribute of his undying love.

The darkened room hid the inamorata's face as a delicate hand sensually parted the lace curtains, giving the all-clear sign that Mr. Pulito had been looking for. Fixing his sparkling smile in the direction of the boudoir, he'd give her the eye, as if to say, "I'll be seeing *you* after the burial."

DEATH IN BRUCULINU was encased in a shroud of custom and tradition. Every aspect was ritualized, down to the finest detail. If the candidate was dying at home, children of tender age were sent to a cousin's house, shielding them from the instant when life turns to death. As the priest or the doctor made the final pronouncement, the assembled family began mourning their loss. Some cried in silence, while others wailed, in extreme cases slapping their own faces and pulling their hair. They were calmed by those more in control.

The undertaker's arrival in his shiny black hearse announced the sad news to the block. Word traveled up stairs and from building to building. Neighbors began to gather on the street, forming a kind of honor guard on either side of the front door of the deceased.

As the corpse was removed, men stood in silence with their heads uncovered, and women sniffled, mumbling prayers. When the closest surviving relatives appeared to accompany the body, those holding vigil uttered gasps and condolences.

Before leaving, the undertaker affixed a small bunch of lilies of the valley or stocks to the front door. For the death of an adult, they were tied with purple and black ribbons, and for a child or an infant, with pure white ones. All who passed the doorway lowered their voices and crossed themselves. No children played in front of a house with a death marker on the front door.

Over the next 24 hours, while the body was being prepared, the family readied for the wake. Relatives and friends were notified of the sad news. Those present at the final moment relived the emotional experience with every phone call. In the house, clocks were stopped at the moment of death. TV and radio were forbidden, their distraction deemed inappropriate and disrespectful. Mirrors were covered, partly to avoid the frivolity of vanity, and partly so that people would not see their own expressions of grief. Women donned their blackest dresses. They wore no makeup. Hairdos lost their style from lack of attention and from the long black veils covering them. Men, their judgment impaired by bereavement, didn't shave, avoiding despair's temptation of the razor against their own necks.

O N THE FIRST EVENING OF THE WAKE, the family assembled in the waiting room of the funeral home. Escorted by the undertaker, they moved down the hall to the closed double doors of the funeral chapel. Opening them with a slow, quiet motion, the undertaker beckoned the family to enter.

The lighting was low and theatrical, the air redolent of flowers, the scent embedded in the walls and carpet after so many years. The room was filled with neat rows of folding chairs, set up like a theater. At the front, on a kind of cloth-covered altar, the late loved one was laid out in an open casket. In Bruculinu, except in cases of severe accident and disfigurement, this presentation was the norm. The skilled mortician used his artistry to create the illusion of peaceful sleep on the loved one's face. All ravages of disease were covered with seamless expertise. The very old were made youthful, giving grown children a final reminder of how their parents looked in years past.

This first viewing elicited quiet tears of mourning. Sometimes, in true Sicilian fashion, the moment became highly dramatic. A new widower, seeing his departed wife, would call out, "Sweetheart, wake up! Please, please wake up!" A woman might straighten her late husband's tie or ask someone, "Ya got any cigars? He always had cigars stickin' outta his pocket."

The immediate family of the deceased virtually moved into the funeral home for the three days of the wake. They left only to eat, and then in rotation, or when the funeral parlor closed for the night. As the days passed, their eyes became rimmed with red from constant tears.

E VERYONE WHO CAME TO PAY HIS RESPECTS signed a guest book and gave a cash gift to the family to help defray the funeral expenses. A trusted friend or cousin was placed in charge of these accounts. Careful records were kept so that the generosity could be reciprocated when the unfortunate opportunity presented itself.

The undertaker, always familiar with the family, had a good sense of what they could afford to spend for his services. He skillfully steered the bereaved away from fancy coffins and linings he knew were out of their range, while at the same time keeping up his profit margin. It was a delicate operation. Occasionally when necessary, the undertaker offered his services gratis.

T HE LAST NIGHT OF THE WAKE was the most intense. Relatives and friends arrived from great distances. Wakes, like weddings, were reasons for the whole family to assemble. Adjoining funeral chapels were opened to accommodate the overflow. When the atmosphere became a bit too festive for the occasion, people moved to the public areas of the funeral home or to the ever-present bar across the street.

A priest leading a recitation of the Rosary, or a widow's wail, refocused the visitors on the purpose of their vigil. In addition, every family had at least one member who could be relied upon to perform a truly heartrending act of mourning. The crowd awaited the grand entrance of these mourners with great excitement and anticipation.

When I was a boy, no wake in my family would have been complete without an appearance by Cousin Tony Civello. He was a jolly,

burly fellow in his mid-fifties, with a round red face and large strawberry nose. As a boy, his left eye had been put out by a baseball. It
turned pale yellow, giving him a somewhat monstrous look. His
other eye was of the clearest blue, filled with laughter and the devil.
As children, we were all struck by this distortion. "Did Cousin Tony
look at you?" we asked one another, "Wid his eye?!"

We saw Cousin Tony only at large family gatherings. At weddings, he was the life of the party, always telling a joke, or going up
on the stage to sing with the band. Tony was a bit of a tippler, and although his whiskey voice did not have the clearest tone, his lusty
exuberance more than made up for it. In the unlikely role of master
mourner, he was incomparable. He dressed for the part in a black
sharkskin suit, thick white silk shirt and black necktie. His jacket's
handkerchief pocket was filled with a neatly folded, enormous white
linen, bordered in black satin.

Word of his arrival at the front door spread throughout the
chapel like wildfire. Giving the audience just enough time to settle,
Cousin Tony burst into the room, as if he'd just heard the tragic
news. (In reality, he'd been spending the past two days preparing
his wardrobe.) Stopping short just inside the entrance, he demanded
in a booming voice, "Oh, dear God! Wat happen'd hea?" All eyes
fixed on him as he made his way down the aisle to the front. Approaching the closest relatives, he'd roar, "Katie, wat happen'd hea?
Oh, my God, Bessie, wat happen'd? Charlie, ansa-me, wat happen'd?"

As Tony asked and reasked the existential question, everyone's
eyes filled up with tears. When he sensed emotions about to overflow, Tony would turn and see the dearly departed for the first time.
Opening his face to the audience, so they could see his grief, he
wailed to Heaven. He'd pull the black-bordered handkerchief out
of his pocket with the grandest of gestures and, with polished timing,
collapse to his knees in uncontrollable weeping.

It was a moment of exquisite catharsis. There wasn't a dry eye in the house. Afterward, people gathered around Tony, making sure he was all right, and thanking him for helping them "ta get it out." Some even complimented him on his performance.

T HE NEXT MORNING, black limousines took the immediate family to the funeral home for one last look. With respectful attention, the funeral director closed and latched the coffin. The deceased and the family were now chauffeured to the church. This was the undertaker's big chance to advertise. Someone in the church might take notice of how well attended the grieving were, or how smoothly the operation ran. They would remember this when their own need arose.

For the funeral of one well known in the community, the church would be filled to overflowing. The priest could give a grand eulogy, whether or not he had known the person. The service itself was often punctuated by sobs and sniffling. At its conclusion, the cars were filled with the living and the dead and driven at processional speed to the cemetery.

The graveside provided a setting for gestures of mourning, operatic in scope. As the priest prayed in Latin, blessing the coffin with holy water, it was gently lowered into the ground. There was guaranteed to be at least one close relative so overcome with grief, that she wanted to throw herself in after it. Sometimes it took the strength of several strong men to dissuade her.

On the way back home, for the first time in days, women tried to arrange their hair; men evaluated the stubble on their faces. The living were beginning to rally.

T HERE WERE ALWAYS A COUPLE OF RELATIVES who had a more unresolved relationship with death than the rest. They preferred not to visit the funeral home at all, much less attend the burial service. Their feelings were respected, and they were entrusted with the important tasks of child care and the preparation of the after-burial luncheon.

As for every other major event in Bruculinu, a specific meal was also served for this sad occasion. It opened with a shot of brandy or whiskey, followed by chicken soup and the boiled chicken. No matter what the season, the meal never varied. It was designed not only to remove the chill of a cemetery in winter, but the chill of death itself.

As the family sat around the dining table, eating a dessert of biscotti and strong black coffee, someone might uncover the mirrors or turn on a radio just to hear the baseball scores. Although mourning would continue for weeks, months and in some cases, years, the ordeal was over.

To help in this transition, our wise elders had a barrage of proverbs at the ready. One of the ancient Sicilian adages, often quoted by older family members at these times, says:

Povera idu chi dunnu 'i spaddi a rrina,
Chiddu chi rrestu si rrimina.

Translated literally, it means, "Pity he who gives his back to the sand. Those who remain will turn themselves around." It embodies the greatest of all death's lessons: life goes on.

Brudu 'i Gaddina

$\mathscr{C}$ hicken Soup

C HICKEN FEET ADD A HEARTINESS to the soup that cannot be
achieved by any other means.

For 8 servings

1   4-pound chicken, preferably free-range,
    including the neck, gizzard, liver, heart and feet
5   quarts spring water
6   Roma tomatoes
3   large carrots, cut into thirds
3   celery ribs, with leaves, cut into thirds
2   large onions, quartered
1   small bell pepper, halved, cored and seeded
12 sprigs Italian parsley
24 whole black peppercorns
    Sea salt
    Black pepper
1   pound orzo, pastina or little star pasta
¾   cup grated imported pecorino cheese, preferably Locatelli

Rinse the chicken under cold running water and drain. Remove
and discard all the fat from around the crop and the cavity. Put the
chicken, water, tomatoes, carrots, celery, onions, bell pepper, parsley and peppercorns in a large stockpot.

Place the pot over medium heat with the cover askew. Bring to
a boil, skimming the foam that rises to the top, then reduce the
heat to low. Simmer, with the cover askew, for 3 hours, removing

foam as necessary. Check occasionally to make certain the simmer is maintained. Do not let the broth boil.

Turn off the heat and transfer the chicken to a platter. Strain the soup through a fine-mesh strainer into another large pot or bowl. Transfer the cooked vegetables to a food mill and puree twice, changing after the first time to a smaller-holed disk.

Remove the fat from the broth with a fat separator or large spoon. Mix the puree into the broth and heat it, uncovered, over low heat. Taste for salt and pepper, adding more if necessary.

Fill a large pot with 6 quarts water. Add 2 tablespoons salt and bring to a boil. Add the pasta and cook until al dente. Drain thoroughly.

Serve the soup with a ladleful of pasta in the bottom of the bowl and a small sprinkling of grated cheese on top. The chicken may be served on the side or shredded into the bowl with the pasta.

Viscotta 'i Marsala

$\mathcal{M}$ arsala Biscotti

THESE COOKIES, MADE WITH MARSALA from Sicily, are an excellent accompaniment to dessert wines and sherries.

For 3 dozen biscotti

3 cups bleached all-purpose flour
1 cup cake flour
  Pinch of baking powder
½ pound (2 sticks) unsalted butter
1 cup sugar
2 large eggs, beaten
⅓ cup sweet Marsala wine
1 teaspoon vanilla extract

Sift together the all-purpose flour, cake flour and baking powder twice. Transfer to a large bowl. Using an electric mixer or by hand, cut in the butter until the mixture has the consistency of cornmeal. Stir in the sugar and then the eggs. Stir in the Marsala and vanilla and knead in the bowl just enough to produce a soft, elastic dough. Divide the dough into 2 balls, cover with floured cloths and refrigerate for 1½ hours, or until firm enough to roll.

Preheat the oven to 400°F, with a rack positioned in the upper third.

Remove one of the balls from the refrigerator. Take a small piece of dough about the size of a whole walnut and roll it between your hands into a thick rope about 5 inches long. Place the rope on a baking sheet and form it into an S shape. Continue placing the bis-

163

cotti on the sheet 1 inch apart, until the baking sheet is filled. If necessary, use 2 baking sheets, but bake them one at a time.

Bake for 12 to 15 minutes, or until the biscotti are pale golden. Let cool for 5 minutes on the pan, then transfer the biscotti to a cooling rack. When completely cooled, store in an airtight container.

Nucatuli

$\mathcal{H}$azelnut Cookies

THESE CRUNCHY COOKIES ARE GREAT with morning coffee, or mourning coffee, as the case may be. This recipe is an adaptation of an ancient one from Polizzi Generosa. It contains a small amount of honey. The honey taste does not appear until the last bite. For some reason, it inspires you to eat another cookie.

For 7 dozen cookies

3½ cups (1 pound) shelled raw hazelnuts (filberts)
3¾ cups all-purpose flour
1¼ cups cake flour
    Pinch of baking powder
1 teaspoon ground cinnamon
8 tablespoons (1 stick) unsalted butter
2¼ cups sugar
4 large eggs, beaten
¼ cup honey
1 tablespoon cold milk, plus more if needed

Preheat the oven to 450°F.

Toast the nuts for about 10 minutes. Be sure they don't burn. When they are cool enough to handle, rub them together to remove as much of the brown powdery skin as possible, then let them cool completely. Coarsely chop them into halves and quarters and set aside.

Sift together the all-purpose flour, cake flour, baking powder and cinnamon twice. Transfer to a large bowl. Using an electric mixer or by hand, cut in the butter until the mixture has the consistency of cornmeal. Stir in the sugar and then the eggs. Stir in the nuts. Thin the honey with 1 tablespoon milk and knead it into the mixture to form a soft, elastic dough. If necessary, add additional milk, 1 teaspoonful at a time.

Cut 2 pieces of aluminum foil, each about 16 by 8 inches, and lightly dust the shiny side with flour. Divide the dough in half and place each half on a piece of foil. Roll the dough into logs 12 inches long and 2½ inches in diameter. Wrap the logs in the foil and roll them on the work surface to keep them smooth and round. Freeze the logs for at least 1½ hours, to become quite firm. (The dough may also be frozen for up to 1 week.)

Preheat the oven to 400°F, with a rack positioned in the upper third. Grease 4 baking sheets.

Unwrap the logs. With a sharp knife or one with a serrated edge, use a sawing motion to cut the dough into slices ⅛ inch thick. Place the slices on the baking sheets about 1 inch apart. Bake for about 15 minutes, or until the tops just begin to color. Cool the cookies completely on the baking sheets. The cookies will become crunchy when cooled. Store in an airtight container.

XI.

*I*n the Barber Shop
of Ali Baba

I N BUSHWICK, DURING THE 1950s, males still "took haircuts," they didn't "get styled." In those well-groomed times,
a tonsorial visit was requisite at least every two weeks, at
least every three in the dead of winter. If hair began to meet
one's collar, it was considered slovenly. That person was surely un-
employed or a lowlife or a musician, or all three. People would say,
"Looka dat guy's hair. He oughta go on da corna widda tin cup an'
a violin!" Indigence was no excuse for bad grooming. Haircuts cost
50 cents for boys, 75 cents for adults, 75 cents or a buck, respectively, with tip.

One of the more popular neighborhood barbershops was located
on Central Avenue and Suydam Street. The storefront window was
filled with a lush growth of mother-in-law's tongue, an unlikely
sentry in such a male bastion. A white shade discreetly covered the
glass door. On the sidewalk in front of the shop stood an electric barber's pole, the illuminated red and white spiral spinning into infin-
ity. Modern stylings aside, this centuries-old sign symbolized the
barber as paramedic, schooled in the dressing of sword wounds and
in the art of bloodletting. In mid-twentieth-century Brooklyn, how-

167

ever, the only remnant of this glorious medical past was the surgical cleanliness maintained inside the shop.

One long wall of the shop was covered with gleaming mirrors and shiny white cupboards. Below was a counter of hair tonics, pomades, scissors, clippers and straight razors, all set in neat rows on an immaculate white towel. Prominent among this display was a large glass container with a chrome lid. It was filled with a phosphorescent green-blue liquid in which combs were stored and sterilized. The clear block letters on the front of the jar said BARBASOL.

Facing this wall unit were two white porcelain and red leather barber's chairs. A series of bright chrome levers at the base could make the seats rise, swivel or recline. Farther along this wall was a sink for washing hair and an enormous steaming device for towels. The other walls of the shop were lined with a mismatched assortment of chairs, for waiting. Interspersed was a collection of end tables. These held stacks of reading materials, ranging from Italian newspapers to comic books to girlie magazines.

The barber's name was Al. He was a short man with a trim build. His hair and pencil mustache were impeccably groomed. Al's costume never varied. It had an almost military aspect to it. He wore a starched white smock over a starched white shirt. The perfectly tied knot of a dark silk necktie could be seen over the top button of the smock. His trousers were dark and well pressed, his black shoes polished to a mirror finish.

Although there were two barber's chairs in the shop, Al owned and operated it alone. He and his wife lived in the apartment behind the shop, but in all the years he cut my hair, I never saw the apartment nor the wife.

W HEN I WAS A SMALL BOY and heard the words "Al the Barber" spoken by my grandfather in his heavily Sicilian-accented English and by American-born adults in their Brooklynese, my ears heard "Ali Baba." Long after the truth came to light, I held onto this fantasy of Arabian adventure. It helped buffer the squirmy, itchy experience of a haircut.

I would sit in the great barber's throne, fitted with a booster seat, covered from the neck down in a voluminous pinstriped chair cloth. The mist from the towel steamer mixed with the perfume of rosewater and Lilac Vegetal hair tonics. I imagined myself deep in the maze of some Oriental Casbah, as the great Ali Baba, in disguise, held a straight razor to the back of my neck, cleaning away soft baby hairs. Together that night, we would ride our trusty steeds to the palace of the evil caliph, to steal back the people's gold, which had been confiscated by corrupt tax collectors. With a sweeping display of courage and heroism, we would snatch the beautiful princess from the clutches of the evil one. When we returned to the secret cave, I would bellow, "Open Sesame!" to reveal the hidden portal. Ali Baba's scissors responded with a "chop-chop-squeak."

A T FIRST I WENT TO THE BARBER with my grandfather on Saturday mornings. The shop was filled with older immigrant gentlemen, queuing up for their weekly shaves, haircuts and shampoos. As they waited, they read their newspaper, *Il Progresso Italo-Americano*. They conversed in Sicilian, speaking in quiet tones, as if they were in church. The misty perfumed air of the shop mingled with the acrid smoke of their Italian cigars, creating a kind of incense.

In the last century, many of these men had been boys together in the same Sicilian town; their connections easily spanned 60 or 70 years. As immigrants, they may not have risen to great heights of wealth and position, but they had made good lives for themselves and their families and were proud and contented. They enjoyed the respect given them as elders and treated one another likewise. Therefore, if someone said or did anything boorish or boastful, the others would demur behind their newspapers, to preserve dignity. One could surmise their displeasure or suppressed laughter only through the intensity of the smoke signals rising behind the papers.

I loved listening to their tales of Sicily, which were almost as exotic as my Arabian fantasies. I had a pretty good time being the only boy in a room full of grandfathers. It is amazing how much candy grandpas can carry in their vest pockets.

AFTER I WAS EIGHT, trips to Al the Barber changed. From then on, I went on Friday afternoons, in the company of what seemed like every other boy in my school. The thrill of the Orient and the gentilesse of the old men were gone from the experience. All that remained was the close stuffy air, and we boys, with our sticky, inky fingers. We were bored with the comic books, by now memorized. We were testy and quarrelsome. The former Ali Baba tried pitifully to control this restless mob.

The possibility of redeeming these lost Friday afternoons lay in the speed with which one made it from the school, down the street, into the shop. The good sisters led us in silent lines, two by two, class by class, from the school door to the corner and across Central Avenue. At this point the line dispersed into pandemonium. The doomed among us made a mad dash for the barbershop, 20 feet away. The upper grades were at the front of the parade, and descending class order fixed the odds for getting a good place in Al's waiting line. Sometimes you got lucky. Mostly, I watched the hope of a stickball game or of a scullsy tournament fade, as Al swept away the mounds of hair cuttings into a pile.

I especially felt this despair when there was snow on the ground. Brooklyn usually has only one or two good snowfalls a year, and all of us looked forward with great excitement to playing in the frozen dunes. We'd form the snow into blocks with our hands and build forts and igloos. Shielded by these fortifications, we'd lob snowballs at our opponents and their fort. Kids of all ages, and sometimes even adults, joined in the melee. Missing such an opportunity because of a haircut was too much to bear.

As I scurried home from the barbershop on those bitter evenings, the wind would quickly evaporate the alcohol in the Jeris Hair Tonic soaking my head. The cold would freeze the remaining liquid to my hair, even under the protection of a hat with built-in earmuffs. When I arrived home and lifted that hat, the pompadour, combed with Al's master touch, presented itself intact, like a molded dessert transported to a picnic in a pie basket.

This Howdy Doody hairstyle amused everyone in the house. As it defrosted, their laughter turned to awe, the Jeris still working to hold every hair in place. By morning, the pompadour had collapsed, as had the snow forts down in the street.

A T 10 YEARS OF AGE, my fifth-grade classmates and I discovered the girlie magazines in Al's shop, located at the bottom of one of the stacks of comics. We would linger in the stack, ostensibly searching for a favorite Superman. With studied nonchalance, we'd sneak a peek at the covers, which always pictured a buxom beauty in a state of dishabille. Her costume was no more revealing than ordinary street fashions of a decade later, but to 10-year-old boys in 1958, this was pretty hot stuff.

Al, clipping away, kept a careful eye on these goings-on through the mirror. If one lingered too long, he'd order, "OK! Take a comic an' sid-down! OK?!" Whenever he'd vanish into his apartment, we would storm the stacks. Always catching us on his return, he'd snatch the contraband out of our hands and, waving it in the air, scream, "Nice! Cat-lick schoolboys! Very nice!" Al went on with his tongue-lashing, opening the magazine and referencing particularly torrid shots. "Looka dis! An' dis! Ya like dis filtt?!" (His display showed us much more than we could have sneaked on our own.) "I'm gonna tell da nuns! I'm gonna tell ya muddahs!" At this we'd all look penitent, as angelic as altar boys. Actually, we knew that Al wasn't "gonna tell NO-body about NUT-in." To tell on us would be to tell on himself for having the magazines in the first place.

O NE FEBRUARY HAIRCUT DAY, when I was 12, I had fared particularly badly in the line at Al's. I was last. While Al cut and we made small talk, the door opened, admitting a cold gust of wind and a broad man in a black suit. He bore a serious expression. Upon seeing him, Al immediately put his comb and scissors down on the counter. The man said something to him in a low voice. Al snapped to attention and spoke out clearly in clipped tones. "Louie Sip put a ten spot on 682. Big Chas put 50 on 756."

"Just-a minute," the man interrupted. "Wat about da kid?" he said, referring to me.

"Don' worry 'bout it," said Al. "Da kid's aw-right."

He continued with a few more names and numbers. The man checked them against a list written on a small pad. When Al finished his recitation, the man put the pad and pencil back into his pocket. He gave Al a very serious look and left. Al locked the door after him and quickly finished my haircut in silence. When I left, he opened the door just enough for me to pass, telling me to take care on my walk home. I heard the lock turn behind me. The light in the barber's pole went out.

B ENEATH THE SURFACE of this working-class Brooklyn neighborhood were layers of intrigue and secret identities. Perhaps everyone else knew that Al was a numbers runner, but this was the first I'd learned of it, although I had always suspected that Ali Baba was up to something.

The number is the last three digits of the pari-mutuel tally of the money bet at the track that day. This tally was published in the evening paper for all to see. The number was impossible to fix, and the 600-to-1 payoff was very attractive, although the odds against winning were 1000 to 1. Even so, the possibility of big winnings interested everyone. Most people bet a buck or two, but bets of a quarter or 50 cents were not uncommon. For a special number, like a birth or death date, one might bet a great deal more, even up to 50 bucks. There were those, too, who bet hundreds of dollars, often borrowed from loan sharks. In addition to the compulsive gamblers, many a workingman found himself in deep with "da shylocks" from a failed effort to make it big. These debtors, however, were the exceptions. Usually people didn't hurt themselves. Playing the numbers was an exciting diversion for practically everyone in the neighborhood.

For the people running the numbers business, huge sums of money were at stake. The operation involved three levels of employees. The runner took the bet. He gave that list and the money in a sealed envelope to the pickup man, who carried it to the comptroller. Accounting records, winners' lists and the money were sent off to the "bank." A large numbers bank could have in its employ, from different neighborhoods, 3 comptrollers, 9 pickup men, and 180 runners. Each runner took about $250 in bets a day, meaning that the bank could gross $45,000 a day, 365 days a year. After salaries, bribes, percentages and payouts, the bank surely netted $8,000,000 a year!

The runner received a small percentage of the bets he took, along with large tips from his winners. Sometimes a runner "gone bad" would hold out a large bet to increase his take. As long as that number didn't hit, his scam could remain undetected. If it did come in, he would be in big trouble.

For example, suppose there was a barber who was a numbers runner. Maybe it's winter, the haircut business is a little slow, and the wife wants a new coat with a fur collar. So there's this guy who comes in once a week and lays 50 bucks on his mother's death date. He's been doing this for seven years and the number has never hit. The barber decides one week to hold back the 50 from the pickup man. As fate would have it, the number comes out. Fifty bucks at 600 to 1 means that the barber has to find 30 grand to pay the guy. For him that is 30,0000 haircuts at a buck apiece!

THE FOLLOWING SATURDAY, my grandfather came home from the barbershop with a small square of tissue paper on his chin. Al, for the first time in 17 years, had nicked him. Al's hand, he said, was shaking so hard that he could barely hold the razor.

On the next haircut day, my classmates and I went through the usual drill to get a good place in the line. We were stopped by a locked door. Peering into the window, through the mother-in-law's tongue, we saw an incredible sight. All the mirrors and tonic bottles were smashed to bits. The barber's chairs were turned over. Broken glass and mounds of wadded towels and chair cloths covered the floor, along with a papier-mâché of Barbasol, comic books and girlie magazines. Al's Barber Shop was no more.

We gazed in silence, our mouths and eyes opened wide. We were mesmerized by the scope of the destruction. I wondered if Al himself was somewhere in the tangle, if perhaps he had been fashioned into a kind of barber's pole. Fortunately he was nowhere to be seen. Suddenly I felt a group thought overtake the crowd: maybe we'd never have to get our hair cut again.

But by the very next haircut day, a new barber was found. He had been scouted by the grandfathers and met, marginally, with their approval. The new barbershop was not the same as Al's. It was now 1961, and in a few short years, nothing much of the old neighborhood would be the same.

For months, the men and boys of the neighborhood speculated on what had happened to the now missing Al the Barber. I, of course, knew the truth: he had been trapped by the evil caliph and had narrowly escaped from the merciless palace guard. In a show of exquisite bravery, he had released his beautiful princess from the clutches of the wicked one. Together they had fled on his magnificent white steed to another kingdom far, far away, maybe New Jersey. Al was now in disguise as a Good Humor man but would soon resume his secret destiny, fighting injustice and seeking adventure.

Naturally, I could never tell anyone what I knew. After all, "Da kid's aw-right"—Ali Baba said so.

Pasta chi Ciciri

*P*asta with Chickpeas

S UPPER ON THOSE HAIRCUT FRIDAYS was always meatless, as dictated by the laws of the Church. Fried, baked or poached fish was often served. During the colder months, Papa Andrea would prepare a hearty *minestra*, a soupy pasta dish, like this one. We could feel its warming effects to the tips of our toes.

For 6 servings

2   cups (1 pound) dried chickpeas
1   tablespoon chopped leaves of wild fennel or bulb fennel
    Sea salt
½   cup plus 2 tablespoons extra-virgin olive oil
1   medium onion, finely chopped
1   pound medium shell pasta
6   sprigs Italian parsley, chopped
    Black pepper

Put the chickpeas in a colander and wash them under cold running water. Check for small stones and other debris. Soak them overnight in a 3½-quart nonreactive pot, covered with a generous inch of water. If, after soaking, you need to add more water to keep them well covered, do so. Add the fennel and 2 tablespoons salt to the chickpeas. Cover and cook them over low heat until tender, about 3 hours, depending on the size and age of the chickpeas. Stir occasionally and add more water as necessary. After about 2½ hours, or when the chickpeas are slightly underdone, turn off the heat and leave the pot on the stove with the cover in place.

Fill a large pot with 6 quarts water, add 2 tablespoons oil and 2 tablespoons salt and put it on the stove to boil.

Meanwhile, put the onion and the remaining ½ cup oil in a skillet over medium heat. Sauté until the onion is pale golden, about 10 minutes. Add the onion and oil to the chickpeas. Taste for salt, adding more if necessary.

When the water comes to a boil, add the pasta and cook until al dente. Drain the pasta but not too thoroughly: the dish should be a bit soupy. Transfer the pasta to a heated bowl and toss with the chickpeas and parsley. Add black pepper and serve very hot.

'A Frocia

Sicilian-Style Omelette

O FTEN THERE WOULD BE AN OMELETTE on Friday night. Papa Andrea's omelettes were flavored with grated pecorino cheese and parsley and folded perfectly in thirds. Prepared with a dozen eggs, the omelette was large enough to feed the entire family.

For 6 servings

¼ cup extra-virgin olive oil

12 large eggs

¼ cup milk

2 cups grated imported pecorino cheese, preferably Locatelli

4 sprigs Italian parsley, chopped, plus more for garnish

Black pepper

Pour the oil into a well-seasoned 12-inch skillet over medium-low heat and heat slowly.

Beat the eggs, milk, cheese and parsley together with a whisk until fluffy. Season with black pepper.

When the oil is nearly smoking, pour in the egg mixture. Reduce the heat to low, cover and cook for about 20 minutes, or until the bottom is pale golden and the top is set. Check from time to time by lifting an edge with a spatula. Make sure that the bottom is not turning brown, as this will make the omelette brittle and impossible to fold. If it is browning, turn the heat down even lower. When the omelette reaches the proper stage, remove the cover, turn off the heat and let it settle for a moment. Fold it in thirds by carefully bringing one edge to the center with a spatula and then the other.

With a spatula in each hand, transfer the omelette to a platter. After a moment, flip it over so that the folded side is down. If necessary, the omelette may be kept warm in a 250°F oven for up to 15 minutes. Garnish the platter with parsley and serve.

Nsalata 'i Tunnu

Sicilian Salade Niçoise

ON A HOT AND HUMID SUMMER DAY in Bruculinu, my favorite Friday dinner was Papa Andrea's interpretation of salade niçoise, which he called *nsalata 'i tunnu,* tuna salad. The tang of the vinegar and lemon juice was refreshing and restorative.

For this dish, I have coordinated the preparation of the component salads, but you may serve each one separately.

For 6 servings

FOR THE POTATO SALAD

2½ pounds white or red new potatoes or Yukon Gold
   or Yellow Finn potatoes
   Sea salt
½ medium onion, thinly sliced
⅓-½ cup extra-virgin olive oil
   Black pepper

FOR THE GREEN BEAN SALAD

2½ pounds green beans
1 garlic clove, peeled and left whole
   Sea salt
¼ cup white wine vinegar or champagne vinegar
   (7% acidity)
   Extra-virgin olive oil

FOR THE EGG HALVES
6   large eggs

FOR THE TUNA SALAD
24 ounces canned chunk light tuna, packed in spring water
1   medium onion, finely chopped
    Grated zest and juice of 1½ lemons
⅔   cup extra-virgin olive oil
    Black pepper
2   tablespoons capers, rinsed and drained
    Sea salt

FOR THE TOMATO SALAD
6   ripe Roma tomatoes
    Sea salt
    Dried oregano
    Extra-virgin olive oil

FOR THE GARNISH
12-ounce can anchovies, packed in olive oil
Large green olives
Oil-cured black olives

Prepare the potato salad: Peel the potatoes, cut them into 1½-inch cubes and put them in a pot of lightly salted cold water over medium-high heat. Bring to a boil, and cook until cooked through but still firm, about 15 minutes. Drain the potatoes and transfer to a large bowl. While they are still very hot, add the onion and toss. Pour in the oil and toss again. Taste for salt, adding more if necessary, and add several grindings of black pepper. As the potato salad cools, it will absorb the olive oil. Do not cover or refrigerate.

Prepare the green bean salad: Clean the green beans and snap off the ends. Place a steamer on the stove with the garlic in the water. When it comes to a boil, put the beans in the steamer basket. Steam the beans until tender, 8 to 12 minutes, depending on their thickness. Transfer to a platter. While they are still hot, season with salt and toss. Add the vinegar and toss again. Drizzle with oil, toss again and let cool at room temperature. Do not refrigerate.

Prepare the eggs: Pierce the large end of each egg with a pin to prevent cracking. Put the eggs in a small pot, cover with cold water and cook for about 10 minutes after the water comes to a boil. Drain the eggs and run them under cold water to stop the cooking and loosen the shells, but do not peel the eggs until assembling the salad.

Prepare the tuna salad: Put the tuna in doubled cheesecloth. Twist and squeeze to remove all the water. Put the tuna in a bowl and lightly mix in the onion, lemon zest and juice with a fork. Lightly mix in the oil and black pepper and then fold in the capers, taking care not to crush them. Taste for salt and add if necessary. The tuna salad may be refrigerated in a tightly sealed container.

Prepare the tomato salad: Just before you are ready to assemble the salad, cut the tomatoes lengthwise into quarters or sixths.

Assemble the salad: Choose a platter large enough to hold everything. Place the potato salad at one end. Place the tomatoes in a layer next to the potato salad. Season them with salt and generously sprinkle with dried oregano. Drizzle with oil.

Arrange the green bean salad in a pile beside the tomatoes, across the plate. Spoon the tuna onto the platter next to the beans. Peel the eggs and cut them in half lengthwise. Drape each half with an anchovy and a bit of the anchovy oil. Place the eggs and the olives around the rim of the platter and serve.

XII.

The Feast

I N BRUCULINU, in addition to the traditional American holidays of Thanksgiving, Christmas and the Fourth of July, we had feast days of our own, imported by the Sicilian immigrants of my grandparents' generation—holidays whose observance marked an unbroken chain stretching back across the pounding Atlantic to the peaceful seaside and mountain towns of Sicily, connected, in turn, to millennia-old traditions.

Foremost among these holidays was the Feast Day of St. Joseph, March 19. In the old neighborhood, we called the two-week celebration surrounding it simply "The Feast."

To the Sicilian people, Joseph's profound commitment to his familial responsibility has made him the exemplar of one of the traditional Sicilian ideals of manhood, *omu di panza*, a "man of stomach," one who has the guts to do the right thing. Church art often depicts St. Joseph carrying a staff that is topped with early spring flowers. He has become a Christianized "Father Spring," replacing an earlier god as the focus of a vernal equinox festival. By March 19, spring's renewal is very much in evidence throughout Sicily.

By March 19 in Brooklyn, however, the arrival of spring is not so evident. From the beginning of the month, discussions of erratic March weather patterns raged throughout the neighborhood.

Everyone knew the old adage: in like a lion, out like a lamb; but the question on everyone's mind was how would the weather be for The Feast. In typical Sicilian fashion, five people could raise seven opinions.

The more devout smiled, knowingly, at these discussions. They knew them to be a waste of time, for the great saint would, certainly, supply good weather, and whatever the reason, spring always managed to appear just in time for The Feast. Everyone agreed that even the rain was a good luck omen. Without knowing why, the sons and daughters of the immigrants, Brooklynites from birth, supported their elders' agrarian interpretation of spring weather.

IN PREPARATION FOR THE FEAST, the streets in the quarter mile around St. Joseph's Church were closed to traffic. They were studded with tall wooden support beams, held in place by a tangle of guy wires. To the heights of these supports were rigged massive metal frames, holding arrangements of lights, arching the street. These structures were repeated, in exact duplication, every 10 yards.

From the windows of the school atop the flat-roofed, baroque-style church, we watched the progress of the installation, enraptured. Our Dominican nun teachers could not divert our attention. The good sisters' endless annual lectures on the sinful, pagan evils of The Feast never diminished our excitement. "Da Feast is comin'!" was the buzz in every classroom.

THE STREETS THEMSELVES were plated with tented booths. The food sellers were local, but the game-of-chance booths belonged to outsiders who worked the church feasts and street festivals along the eastern seaboard. Entire families would set up housekeeping in these tents. We children were warned to avoid these carny folk, lest we be robbed, or worse, stolen away.

184   On the nights of The Feast, however, the supporting structures,

the seaminess and the sin all disappeared in the glow of a million lights.

On the morning of the feast day itself, a great wooden statue of St. Joseph was carried through the streets in procession. Larger than life, it had been commissioned from a master Sicilian statue maker. The saint's features were meticulously carved and painted. His eyes held one in their gaze from many angles and for a great distance. His clothing was real cloth, topped with a long green mantle.

The statue rested on a large base, decorated with lilies, tulips, other early spring flowers and loaves of bread, symbolizing the images of St. Joseph as god of spring and as patron breadwinner. Attached to the sides of the base, in the style of a sedan chair, were two sturdy, long poles. The statue and its base were so massive that it took 16 strong men to carry it, balancing these poles on their shoulders. Their hands folded in front of them, they moved in perfect cadence, as their bodies swayed under the weight.

Preceding the statue was an army of acolytes holding candles or swinging thuribles. Enshrined in their midst was a priest carrying a long pole topped with a golden cross. Following the statue was a band, playing *sicilianae* in stately rhythm. And behind the musicians was a prowl of old women in black, carrying round loaves of bread before them.

As the procession moved slowly and solemnly throughout the neighborhood, every few yards it would stop to allow throngs of people to approach the statue. With the help of the bearers, they would pin money to the saint's mantle. By the time the statue returned to the church, it was covered in 5-, 10-, 20-, even 50- and 100-dollar bills, quite a show of wealth for this working-class community. The statue and its "cape of money" were left on display at a side altar of the church for the duration of The Feast. Groups of parishioners and visitors gathered around it, gazing in wonder, or trying to count the loot.

In those days, churches were not locked. Needless to say, there was no thief in the entire borough foolish enough to steal from St. Joseph in a Sicilian church. Sacrilege aside, there was always the presence of a bulky serious fellow in a dark suit, surreptitiously guarding it, just in case.

ANOTHER ANCIENT SICILIAN TRADITION for this time is the St. Joseph's Table. In exchange for answering a prayer or out of devotion to the saint, an individual holds a yearly feast for a certain number of pitiable orphans, in the name of St. Joseph. The devotees are assisted in keeping their solemn vow by family and neighbors, turning the event into an elaborate celebration for the entire community. In Bruculinu, the most stunning of these tables was sponsored by Maria Roccaforte.

Maria was born in 1891 in Santa Margherita di Belice, a mountain town in southwestern Sicily. She had immigrated to America as a girl, and by 1922 was married and the mother of four. She worked as a seamstress in a Brooklyn dress factory, doing piecework. Maria's sharp, dark eyes and her determined no-nonsense will contrasted with her small, delicately boned stature. She was devout and pious, but by no means an aesthete or ethereal.

When she was 31, Maria had a dream. As she told it, St. Joseph appeared to her. Startled, she asked, "What do you want?" St. Joseph said, "I want you, Maria, to feed six orphans at a feast in my honor." She said, "But St. Joseph, I'm a poor woman." He said, "Don't worry, Maria, it will cost you only one dollar."

"But how?" she demanded, thinking that perhaps the apparition wasn't St. Joseph at all, but some trick of the devil. The good saint wrote in the air, listing all of the items she would need and their cost. Being quick at addition, from tallying the chits on her piecework, Maria informed the saint that the list added up to only 98 cents. Nearly at the end of his patience, he said to her, "Buy more napkins." With that, she woke up, certain she had been visited by a heavenly presence.

Maria Roccaforte dutifully followed the wishes of St. Joseph. The feast for the orphans that year did, indeed, cost her exactly one dollar. Year after year, her St. Joseph's Table grew, becoming an event attended by the whole neighborhood. Everyone who visited left a small donation. And so, for the next 65 years, until her death at 96, Maria Roccaforte's St. Joseph's Table never cost her more than a dollar, including napkins.

For the celebration, Mrs. Roccaforte's Stockholm Street apartment was transformed into part shrine, part cornucopia. The furniture was removed and replaced by tiered tables, swathed in white cloths. The tiers reached nearly to the ceiling and were covered with hundreds of large votive candles, each candle with a white label affixed to its glass, so that visitors could write down their reasons for lighting them. Other tiers were covered in flowers and potted palms.

The highest tier in the main room displayed an altarpiece with a cross, flanked by a statue of the Virgin in prayer and St. Joseph holding the infant Jesus. It was decorated with lilies and candles and crowned with Christmas lights. Beneath was a table set for seven: the six orphans and St. Joseph. Not the actual saint, of course, but a proxy named Mr. Guarofalo. He was, minus the beard, a dead ringer for the statuary representation.

In other rooms, the tiered tables were covered with food. The dishes were all meatless—appropriate for a Sicilian holy day. Mountains of stuffed artichokes and bell peppers and cords of fried asparagus and zucchini were but a few of the vegetables represented. There were schools of fried fish, and a harvest of pasta tossed with garlic and olive oil, or with fava beans or green peas or with chickpeas. The pasta was prepared in batches to keep it hot because no self-respecting Sicilian would ever eat cold pasta, not even for St. Joseph.

One room was filled with bread, made for the occasion and do-
nated by the Giangrasso Bakery, the best in the neighborhood. The
more intricately sculpted loaves were made with yellow durum
wheat, the same grain used for couscous and pasta, having been
brought to Sicily from North Africa in the ninth century. This crusty
bread, covered in sesame seeds, is called *pani 'i casa*, bread of the
home. For this feast day, in its decorative form, it is renamed *pani 'i
San Giuseppi*, St. Joseph's bread. Pastries abounded, because St.
Joseph is also the patron saint of pastry cooks. Oranges, pineapples
and bananas filled in any empty spaces that could be found.

Every one of the hundreds who passed through Mrs. Roccaforte's door during those three days was fed and given a roll, an orange and some cookies to take home. If his name was Joseph, a loaf
of bread was added. This food was treated as religious artifact, and
people crossed themselves before eating it. Even the sick and dying
were carried up the stairs to this apartment, set for miracles. If nothing else, they left with a greater sense of inner peace.

M RS. ROCCAFORTE CHOSE WISELY the children who were to
be the pitiable orphans. Called the *virgineddi*, the little virgins or innocents, they could be neither too little nor too pitiable.
Tiny children could not eat enough to fulfill her vow: St. Joseph
must be pleased. Moreover, if the orphans did not perform well the
crowd surrounding the table would lose interest and stay home the
next year. Mrs. Roccaforte would lose face and barely be able to
show herself around the neighborhood.

One year, my cousin Felicia and I were chosen to be two of the
"pitiables." Both of our fathers had passed away when we were small
children, so we were technically eligible. As 12-year-olds, however, we
did not appreciate being thrust into the center of this spectacle, but
we had no way to tell our families we would not accept the honor.

At noon on March 19, we assembled in Mrs. Roccaforte's hallway. When everyone had arrived, she went inside and closed the door. Mr. Guarofalo, in the role of St. Joseph, knocked on the door. "Who is it?" asked Mrs. Roccaforte, in Sicilian. "I need a place to stay, and something to eat," he replied.

"We have no room, go away" was her stern answer. He knocked again, receiving the same reply. The third time, in response to her question, he said, "It's St. Joseph with Mary and Jesus." With that, the door was thrown open, and we were ushered inside, amid the cheering crowd. Felicia and I, along with the other four *virgineddi* and "St. Joseph," were seated at the table of honor. We were all given a small drink of sweet vermouth as a welcoming toast. Mr. Guarofalo made sure that the bottle stayed near him for regular refills.

The grand luncheon began with pasta. Felicia and I ate heartily. When we had finished, the same selection was passed among the crowd of onlookers. Our bowls were filled with a different variety, and we proceeded with vigor, as expected. By the fourth bowl of pasta, we began to slow down. This was, however, only the beginning. Vegetables, fish and later, sweets and fruits, were piled onto our plates in prodigious quantities. My cousin and I, flashing a look between us, understood that we had no choice. We must eat! The crowd cheered us on, joining in the feeding frenzy. Four hours later, barely able to stand, we were mercifully released from the table. Mr. Guarofalo, too, could barely stand, but for a different reason.

Waddling our way through the backslapping crowd, we thanked Mrs. Roccaforte. "St. Joseph will bless you, my children," she said, lovingly touching our faces. Then she dropped her hands to her side, adding, "But only you didn't eat."

As we padded our way home, Felicia and I talked about the afternoon. We realized that in spite of the sometimes comedic form, we had been part of a deeply spiritual experience, and we still talk about it today, more than 35 years later. Still, it is difficult to fathom that this all took place in the United States in 1960. On the other

189

hand, we knew that Beaver Cleaver would not be attending a St. Joseph's Table that night in his TV town.

I N OUR HOUSE, the holiday was always celebrated with a special dinner, prepared by my grandfather. The main course was the most traditional of all Sicilian dishes for the Feast Day of St. Joseph, *pasta chi sardi*, pasta with fresh sardines. The consumption of this food on this day was obligatory, nearly devotional. The dish consists of a long tube pasta, such as bucatini or perciatelli, mixed with fresh sardines, wild fennel, pine nuts and currants. Each city or village, neighborhood or family, in Sicily has its own interpretation of this dish. Sometimes tomato or saffron is added. In other places, the dish is served baked, with toasted bread crumbs sprinkled on top. In still others, all the sauce ingredients are pounded together into a paste and then mixed with the pasta.

As anyone who has ever eaten a badly prepared version of this dish can attest, it can taste a bit like a piece of the dock, but Papa Andrea's recipe is the most delicate and elegant of any version I have ever tasted. He began by making a Sicilian-style classic French *fumet* that he called a *fumettu*. This stock base is perfumed with anchovy and finished with extra-virgin olive oil. He tossed his cooked pasta with fennel leaves, pine nuts and currants, then placed it in an oven pan, layered with fresh sardine fillets, sauced and baked.

An invitation from Papa Andrea for the Feast of St. Joseph was highly prized. It gave family and friends the opportunity to wish their paterfamilias well. It was also assured that they would be eating the best *pasta chi sardi* in Bruculinu—maybe in the world!

Papa Andrea accommodated anyone who wanted to be invited. The large kitchen in our apartment under the rattling Myrtle Avenue el fairly groaned under the assemblage of tables and chairs, as 30 or more guests gathered. Aunt Mae, in charge of place settings, abandoned her usual fastidiousness, deciding that as long as everyone had a pasta bowl, a fork and a napkin, she could relax her standards for this one occasion.

Pan after pan of *pasta chi sardi* was brought to the table. Everyone ate with gusto. Covered dishes were prepared for those unable to attend and later transported through the streets with the reverence of a priest carrying the Eucharist to the sick.

The meal finished with *sfinci 'i San Giuseppi*. These are balls of choux paste, deep-fried until hollow and puffed to golden perfection. When cooled, they are split and filled to overflowing with sweetened ricotta, chocolate chips and candied fruits. In centuries past, nuns in cloistered convents made and distributed these pastries throughout the towns and cities of Sicily. In our house, in mid-twentieth-century Brooklyn, they were made by the masterly hands of Papa Andrea.

AFTER DINNER, we ambled over to The Feast. As we turned onto Suydam Street, The Feast presented itself in all its glory. Our ears filled with a symphony of voices, pierced by the sound of spinning wheels of fortune and the screams or groans of the players. Mothers called after lost children, amid the pop of shooting galleries. Great gales of laughter rose from strolling groups of families and friends. There was the excited giggling of innocent young girls, experiencing perhaps for the first time the attentions of awkward young suitors. It was, after all, spring.

The Sicilian band from the morning's procession changed its style for the evening festivities. The tunes were faster now, more sensual, with playful North African rhythms.

Nuns peeked through the curtains of the convent's windows, in spite of their admonitions. We would wave to them with great enthusiasm. Ignoring us, they would move away quickly or pretend to be absorbed in adjusting a fold, feigning ignorance of the goings-on all around them.

The tantalizing aroma of the food was pervasive. There were booths selling the freshest raw clams and the most tender octopus, cooked in a piquant tomato sauce. Many other booths sold *zeppole*, a kind of Italian doughnut. Taken directly from the fryer, they were placed in small brown paper bags and dusted heavily with powdered sugar. The bags soon became sodden with grease. Eaten very hot, the pastries were delicious. The fact that they later sat in your stomach like little cannonballs deterred no one from eating them, for St. Joseph.

Along with *zeppole*, these booths sold other fried delights. Creamy potato croquettes, rich *arancine* and exotic chickpea-fritter sandwiches, *pani e panelli*, appeared in various stages of preparation from booth to booth. A pandemonium of yelling customers, their outstretched hands waving dollar bills, tried to place their orders with the stone-faced fry cooks. The ordeal made the food taste even better.

Some booths specialized in nuts, seeds and dried salted beans, and had grand displays of red and white pistachios, hazelnuts, almonds of every description, dried salted chickpeas and fava beans, pumpkin seeds and Indian nuts. These arrays were arranged by color and texture, nut by nut, into fantastic geometric patterns recalling the thousand-year-old influence of Islam on Sicilian culture and art. Other booths sold loose taffy, almond nougat, halvah and huge puffs of cotton candy. The neighborhood pastry shops were also represented, each offering their version of the specialty of the day, *sfinci 'i San Giuseppi*.

No feast could be complete without the sausage sandwich. Sicilian pork sausages, flavored with fennel seeds and black pepper, were grilled over charcoal, placed in a cradle of crusty bread and topped with sautéed bell peppers and onions. Their preparation created enough smoke to fill the streets, beckoning one, as if in a trance, to their pleasure. Perhaps I have enshrined the childhood memory, but no sausage sandwich, anywhere in the world, has ever tasted as good to me as those I devoured at The Feast.

In the shadows of some booths, men of the neighborhood would sneak shots of strong, homemade liqueur, toasting St. Joseph and celebrating their manhood. A parish priest might join them, showing his humanity. In an odd way, his presence sanctified the good fellowship.

Everyone took home a souvenir. The prizes won at the games ranged from stuffed animals to elaborate electric kitchen gadgets. Statues of St. Joseph and other religious articles were sold everywhere. People tried to bring food home, but it always lost its special flavor along the way.

For a boy of seven, the best memento was a tin sword, medieval in style, with glass jeweled hilts and brightly colored cardboard scabbards. We would tie our coats around our shoulders, turning them into capes. Thus arrayed, we'd roam The Feast, like a division of tiny Norman paladins come to beat back the infidel. And the nut sellers would yell to us in English or Sicilian, "Get outta here wid dat sword!" protecting the artistry of their displays from pillage.

Today, the tin swords are broken or forgotten, the prizes old and obsolete. Someone, somewhere, still cherishes a nostalgic statue of St. Joseph, but the lights of our feast have long been put out. The most lasting souvenir will always be the remembrance itself, magnified through childhood memories, highlighted through the passage of years.

Pani e Panelli

hickpea Fritter Sandwiches

THIS DINNER MENU FOR THE FEAST OF ST. JOSEPH begins with *Pani e Panelli,* Chickpea Fritter Sandwiches. *Panelli* are unique to the province of Palermo. They are made with chickpea flour, which is dissolved in boiling water to form a thick paste. Tradition-ally this hot paste is thinly smeared over wooden forms or the back of plates. When cooled, it is cut and fried. A simpler method, how-ever, is to pour the hot paste into a loaf pan, chill it and then cut it into thin slices.

Some Italian specialty shops stock chickpea flour, although surer sources are health food stores or Middle Eastern markets.

For 8 servings

Olive oil, for greasing the pan and frying
4   cups (1 pound) chickpea flour
Sea salt
Black pepper
30   thin slices St. Joseph's Bread (page 198)
or Italian bread

Grease a 9-by-5-inch loaf pan generously with olive oil.

Bring 5½ cups water to a boil in a heavy medium pot. Stir in the chickpea flour very slowly to avoid lumps. Add 2 teaspoons salt and several grindings of black pepper, stirring constantly. Cook over low heat for 3 to 5 minutes, or until the paste is thick enough to stand easily when pushed away from the sides of the pot. Immediately pour the paste into the loaf pan. Smooth the top and let it cool to room temperature. Refrigerate, uncovered, for at least 1½ hours to set.

Turn the paste out of the pan. Using a sharp knife, cut it into about 40 ³⁄₁₆-inch-thick slices. (Any unused paste may be stored, well covered, in the refrigerator for several days.) Pour ¾ inch oil into a large skillet over medium heat. When it is very hot, fry the *panelli* in batches, turning once with flat tongs or a flat spatula, until the slices are a rich golden color on both sides but not too crisp. Drain on brown paper or paper towels. Season with salt and serve in a single or double layer between thin slices of bread. *Panelli* taste best when eaten hot but not steaming.

Pasta chi Sardi

*S*t. Joseph's Day Pasta

FRESH SARDINES MAY BE DIFFICULT TO FIND, especially away from the Eastern seaboard. As an alternative to Papa Andrea's baked pasta with fresh sardines, this version of the classic dish uses canned sardines mashed into a paste. It still embodies all the exciting flavors of this uniquely Sicilian dish.

Toasted bread crumbs are served alongside to sprinkle over the top instead of grated cheese. This garnish is used in all Sicilian pasta dishes that have a fish or olive oil base.

For 6 servings

¾   cup plus 3 tablespoons extra-virgin olive oil
     Sea salt
1   cup unflavored fine dry bread crumbs
1   medium onion, finely chopped
⅓   cup pine nuts
1   pound canned skinless and boneless sardines,
      packed in olive oil
4   anchovy fillets, packed in olive oil
1½ pounds perciatelli or bucatini pasta
     Crushed red pepper
     Black pepper
¼   cup chopped golden raisins
2   pinches of saffron, soaked in ⅔ cup water
1   cup chopped leaves of wild fennel or bulb fennel

Fill a large pot with 6 quarts water in which to cook the pasta. Add 2 tablespoons of the oil and 2 tablespoons salt and put it on the stove to boil.

Meanwhile, toast the bread crumbs, by putting them in a small heavy skillet with 1 tablespoon of the oil over low heat. Toast until they are a rich brown. They will cook slowly at first, but once they start to brown, things go quickly. Do not let them burn. Remove from the heat immediately.

Heat the ¾ cup oil in a 9-inch skillet over medium-low heat. Add the onion and pine nuts. Sauté until the onion is a light golden color, about 10 minutes. Remove from the heat and set aside.

Drain the sardines and the anchovies and put them in a bowl. Mash them together.

When the water comes to a boil, add the pasta. After about 5 minutes, when it is halfway cooked, reheat the pine-nut mixture and add the sardine mixture to it. Add a pinch of crushed red pepper, several grindings of black pepper and the raisins. Taste for salt, adding more if desired. Stir the mixture into a paste. Cook for 3 minutes over low heat and stir in the saffron water. Remove from the heat and keep warm.

When the pasta is al dente, drain it and return it to the pot. Toss with the sardine sauce over very low heat for about 2 minutes. Transfer to a large warmed serving bowl. Add the fennel and toss again.

Serve with additional red or black pepper to taste and a sprinkling of toasted bread crumbs.

Pani 'i San Giuseppi

St. Joseph's Bread

S T. JOSEPH'S BREAD is made from durum wheat flour, as is all the bread in rural Sicily. This hard yellow wheat was introduced to Sicily from North Africa a thousand years ago. It is the same grain from which couscous and pasta are made, but for breadmaking it is ground as fine as ordinary flour. Products marketed as "pasta flour" or semolina are too coarse and not suitable for bread. Often called simply durum wheat flour, the proper grind can be found at some Italian groceries and health food stores. Depending on the area in which you live, however, it may be available only through mail-order sources.

To enhance the crust, it is advisable to bake this bread on a baking stone or pizza stone. When baking the bread, place the stone in a cold oven and allow it a good 30 minutes of preheating before use. Do not attempt to remove it until cool, as a rapid change in temperature may cause it to crack.

Serve this bread with Orange and Onion Salad (page 201).

For 1 large ring-shaped loaf, about 3 pounds

- 1½ teaspoons sugar
- 1 tablespoon active dry yeast
- 2½-3 cups warm water (105°F-115°F)
  About 6 cups durum wheat flour
- 1½ teaspoons sea salt
- 3 tablespoons extra-virgin olive oil
- 1 large egg white, slightly beaten

Unhulled sesame seeds for sprinkling on the bread
Coarse-ground semolina or yellow cornmeal,
for dusting the paddle

Mix the sugar and yeast together in a tall warmed glass. Add ½ cup of the water and mix with a wooden spoon. Let stand for 7 to 10 minutes, until the yeast is foamy.

Meanwhile, mix 6 cups flour and the salt together in a large warmed bowl. When the yeast is ready, mix it in. Mix in the oil and 2 cups water. Continue mixing until it forms a ball. If the dough is too sticky, add a bit more flour; if it is too dry, add more water. Turn out onto a floured surface and knead until the dough is smooth, about 10 minutes.

Lightly sprinkle flour on the inside of a warmed bowl large enough to hold the dough when it has doubled. Put the dough in it, cut a ½-inch-deep cross on top with a sharp knife and dust the top with durum flour. Cover with a dish towel and set it in a warm place for 2 to 3 hours, until the dough has doubled in bulk.

Gently punch down the dough. Dust a work surface with fine flour. Roll and stretch the dough into a cylinder 2 feet long. Join the ends together to form an oval-shaped ring.

Dust a paddle or a piece of stiff cardboard with coarse semolina and slip the loaf onto it. Lightly dust the top of the loaf with fine flour and cover it with a dish towel. Let it rise in a warm place for 40 to 50 minutes, until almost doubled in height.

At least 30 minutes before you bake the bread, place the baking stone in the center rack of a cold oven and preheat the oven to 450°F.

When the loaf has completed its second rise, decorate the outer edge. Using a dough scraper, make crisscross hatch marks or cut out triangles along the outer circumference. Embellish and flatten the edge with the tines of a fork or a zigzag pastry crimper. Brush the loaf with egg white and cover it with sesame seeds. Using the point of a sharp knife, cut a 1-inch-deep circular line into the center of the top of the loaf.

Make sure there is enough semolina on the paddle to allow the loaf to move easily. Gently slide it into the oven.

Bake for 45 minutes to 1 hour, or until the crust is a deep rich golden and the loaf sounds hollow when thumped with a knuckle.

Transfer to a rack and let cool before slicing.

Nsalata 'i Aranci e Cipuddi

Orange and Onion Salad

IN BRUCULINU, AS IN SICILY, oranges were used in salad in many ways. This one is with red onion in an olive oil and Marsala dressing. Use St. Joseph's Bread (page 198) to sop up the "little soup," *'a suppedda*, created by the dressing.

Very sour oranges are best for this salad. At different times of year, certain varieties of oranges are more sour than others. A good greengrocer can be helpful in determining which these are.

For 6 servings

6 large oranges
1 large red onion
Sea salt
⅓ cup extra-virgin olive oil
2 tablespoons dry Marsala wine
Black pepper

Cut the ends off each orange. Working over the serving bowl to catch the juice, peel each orange, removing all of the pith. Cut the oranges into sixths, remove the pits and cut away the core. Place the pieces in the bowl.

Peel and halve the onion. Cut it into thin slices and add to the orange pieces. Lightly salt and toss.

Whisk together the oil and Marsala. Dress the salad and toss again. Add a few grindings of black pepper and toss for the third time. Serve slightly chilled, accompanied by St. Joseph's bread.

Sfinci 'i San Giuseppi

*F*illed Puffs

THE QUALITY OF THE TASTE OF THIS DESSERT depends on the quality of the ricotta used to make the filling. It should be white and creamy. Most commercially produced ricotta in this country is too grainy. If you cannot find good-quality ricotta from an Italian market or a specialty cheese shop in your area, a suitable substitute is very simple to make. Since this cheese is made from whole milk rather than whey, it is not truly ricotta, but it does work well in this recipe. Begin its preparation the night before it is to be used.

For about 1½ pounds cheese

3½ quarts (14 cups) whole milk
7 tablespoons white distilled vinegar
(5% acidity—common supermarket vinegar)
⅛ teaspoon sea salt

Scald the milk slowly over medium-low heat, to 185°F, stirring to make sure that the milk does not scorch or burn on the bottom of the pot. Remove the pot from the heat and add the vinegar. Stir well. The milk will have curdled and the cheese will have begun to form. Cover the pot with cheesecloth and let it stand, unrefrigerated, overnight.

The next morning, drain the cheese. This is traditionally done in a straw basket; a colander may be substituted. Line it with 2 layers of cheesecloth, cut generously enough to rise above the sides. Place the colander in the sink. Using a large slotted spoon or a strainer, lift the cheese out of the liquid. When each spoonful stops draining, put it into the lined colander. Put a plate on top of the cheese and press it under a light weight, such as a can of tomatoes, for about 30 minutes. Turn the cheese out into a bowl and mix in the salt. Cover and refrigerate for about 3 hours, or until cold.

For 12 pastries

FOR THE PUFFS

8 cups (2 quarts) corn oil for deep-frying
1 cup unbleached all-purpose flour
8 tablespoons (1 stick) unsalted butter
1 cup water
4 large eggs

FOR THE RICOTTA CREAM FILLING

1½ pounds good-quality ricotta
1¾ cups plus 2 tablespoons (½ pound) confectioners' sugar, sifted
2 tablespoons orange liqueur, such as Curaçao, Grand Marnier or Cointreau
2¼ teaspoons vanilla extract
6 tablespoons semisweet chocolate chips
3 tablespoons chopped mixed candied fruit

Confectioners' sugar for dusting
Candied orange peel, cut into long strips for decoration

Prepare the puffs: Pour the oil into a 6-quart pot over medium heat and slowly heat it to 350°F. Test with a thermometer or by dropping in a square of bread. It should brown quickly, but not burn.

While the oil is heating, sift the flour into a large bowl. Put the butter and 1 cup water in a heavy 2-quart saucepan over medium-low heat. When the butter has melted and the liquid comes to a boil, stir in the flour all at once. Continue stirring and cooking for 2 to 3 minutes, until the mixture is smooth and leaves the sides of the pan. Remove from the heat and turn the paste into a bowl. Let cool for a few minutes.

Using an electric mixer or a wire whisk if mixing by hand, add the eggs, one at a time. Beat each one in thoroughly before adding the next. Beat vigorously until the mixture is shiny and elastic.

When the oil is ready, take a mounded tablespoonful of the batter, and using a second tablespoon, form it into a ball. Use one of the spoons to scrape it off the other to drop it into the oil. It will fall to the bottom. As it cooks, it will rise to the top. Fry until the puffs are a rich golden brown and hollow inside, 10 to 15 minutes. Be sure the puffs are evenly colored on all sides. They will turn on their own, but sometimes they need a little encouragement from the edge of a slotted spoon. Do not fry more than 5 at a time, as they will not have enough room to puff up. Remove the puffs from the oil with a slotted spoon and drain on brown paper or paper towels.

The puffs may be made up to 1 day before serving. Store them overnight loosely covered with waxed paper in a dry place.

Prepare the ricotta cream: Pass the ricotta through the largest-holed screen of a food mill to break up the curds. Mix in the confectioners' sugar with a wooden spoon. Do not use an electric mixer, as it will destroy the curds. Mix in the liqueur and vanilla, and then fold in the chocolate chips and candied fruits. Cover and refrigerate.

Fill the puffs: Just before serving, make a slit in the top of each puff. Using a pastry bag or a teaspoon, fill to overflowing with the ricotta cream. Dust the puffs with confectioners' sugar and decorate with candied peel.

XIII.

$\mathcal{E}$asta

EASTER IS THE MOST IMPORTANT HOLY DAY of Christendom, celebrating the Resurrection of Christ and his triumph over death, thereby raising the possibility for all humanity to share in the eternal life of the soul.

In Bruculinu, not many could express this basic concept of Christianity so concisely. Our religious style was more emotional. "Easta," as we called it in our Brooklynese, was celebrated with religious procession, fervent commitment, family banquets and new clothes.

The Church sets the date for Easter on the first Sunday, after the first full moon, after the vernal equinox. All the other movable holy days are calculated from it. It is, in a sense, the first day of the Church's calendar, designed to coincide with spring's renewal. In Bruculinu, there were neither fields to sow nor lambs to slaughter. Our more urban rite of spring began with the Feast of St. Joseph on March 19 and reached its apex with Easter Sunday.

IN JANUARY, after the excitement of the Christmas season had passed and the novelty of winter weather had worn off, Bruculinu snuggled in for the long, dreary winter ahead. The sun didn't shine for days at a time, obscured by overcast skies. Dark, ominous clouds

hung over us, filled with potential sleet and snow. Streets were covered in sheets of ice, and, in order to avoid slipping, people adopted
a peculiar gait, reminiscent of high-stepping horses in slow motion.

For children, this bleak season was endless, brightened only by
an occasional blizzard. At school, lights were left on all day, so we
could see the board. The warm, close air in the classrooms made
everyone sleepy. Often we drifted off, carried by the counterpoint
of the howling wind outside and the hissing steam radiators inside.

During the bleakest part of February, our school, St. Joseph's on
Suydam Street, closed for a week to conserve fuel. This winter recess was called Coal Week. We children heard "cold week," as so
many of us were laid up with winter illness. Shiny black Lincolns
and Cadillacs stopped in front of buildings all over the neighborhood, bringing doctors on house calls, their black bags filled with
cold stethoscopes and painful needles of penicillin.

The first indication that winter might end was the arrival of Ash
Wednesday. It marked the first day of Lent, the religious season 40
days before Easter. Lent, as defined by the Church, is a time of
penance, designed to prepare and focus the faithful on the great religious mysteries of Easter to come. Coaxed by the nuns, we made
Lenten promises of self-mortification and sacrifice, as if the weather
wasn't mortifying enough. We dutifully "offered up" sweets or TV
shows, promising to do without them, except on Sundays, for the
endless six weeks.

Ash Wednesday itself was quite a spectacle. All day long, the
church was crowded with lines of parishioners, waiting "ta get ea-
shes." Upon reaching the altar rail, they knelt in solemnity. The
priest, in full regalia, would lean over them and paint a tiny cross in
ashes with his thumb on their forehead, mumbling in Latin, "From
dust thou art and to dust thou shalt return."

The cross always looked more like a smudge than anything else,
but the nuns instructed us that it should not be washed off, under

pain of mortal sin. Neither could the ashes be brushed away, but rather they had to disappear in their own time. So as not to disturb the holy ashes, thereby avoiding the flames of eternal perdition, some overzealous children walked home without their winter hats. The cold, damp February wind blew in their ears and up their noses, often provoking another visit from the doctor and his black bag of needles.

ABOUT THE TIME EVERYONE HAD REGAINED HEALTH and was growing weary of Lenten promises, the clothing stores on Knickerbocker Avenue decorated their windows with the latest spring styles. Often, people turned up their noses at the more outlandish creations, but the Easter windows were decorated early enough so that by the time we went shopping, we had grown used to the current fads.

Some of the boys' parents, looking for a bargain, went shopping at a discount clothing store, Robert Hall. To fashion-conscious 11-year-olds, this option was considered terribly outré. "Where d'ja get dat suit," someone might inquire, "Robert Hall? Looks like ya muddah robbed it an' ya faddah hauled it!"

Most of us found ourselves being taken on shopping expeditions to the Knickerbocker Boys and Young Men's Shop. It was one of those apparel stores from the late fifties decorated like a bar in a fancy men's club. It was a deep, wide space with racks of suits three levels high along the walls. The place was dimly lit by elaborate wrought-iron chandeliers with amber-colored glass globes. The ceiling was painted tobacco brown, and the shag carpeting was an autumn tweed. The furnishings consisted of knockoff claw-footed tables on which were piled pants, shirts or neckties. Scattered about the store were several deeply tufted, fake red leather sofas for waiting. During the Easter onslaught, waiting could take hours.

When it was finally your turn, the serious salesman would hold a suit coat for you to try on, just for size. His first selection was always a real clunker—loud, brassy and extreme, obviously the result of a misguided deal the store had made with the wholesaler. Judging by the well-honed technique the salesman used to sell that particular garment, his commission on its sale must have been substantial. He used his position as arbiter of good taste to support the dictum "Dis is wat der all wearin'."

Out of respect for our parents' wishes, he never spoke directly to us, but all the while used us as allies to help make the sale. In 1958, for example, boys' suit coats lost their lapels. Most parents thought this modification outrageous. Afraid of looking "doofie" in the critical eyes of our peers, we tried to cajole or argue our parents into capitulation. They generally countered with such clichés as "If all your friends go an' jump off da Brooklyn Bridge, are yous gonna go an' follow 'em?"

Sometimes these discussions grew quite loud, with boys and parents taking their squabbles out onto the street. Most of the time, however, the salesman successfully effected a compromise and made the sale. The parents, distracted by the salesman's clever maneuvers, acquiesced. But in the end, our elders' original judgment had been correct. The clothing always outlived its faddish styling, and those who looked "boss A" on Easter looked "doofie" by the end of June.

IT WAS ON EASTER that girls were first allowed to wear hose or heels, or to put on makeup. For their twelfth Easter, all the girls made their debut as adolescents. So that their appearances would not shock anyone on their Easter visits, their parents made warning phone calls to the grandparents weeks in advance. These calls fostered endless discussion among the grandmothers in both languages. "Ain't she too young for dat?" they disapproved. "Kids ta-day, dey wanna grow up so fast," they lamented. Not wanting to interfere, they kept these discussions to themselves. In unhappy resignation, they asked, "Watta ya gonna do?"

But on the day, the feared floozies never materialized. The girls' high heels were Queen Anne–style, dainty and demure. Their hose showed off the promise of shapely legs and well-turned ankles. Their ever-so-subtle makeup accented blossoming beauty. The grandmothers wept at seeing their baby granddaughters "all grown up just like dat." The girls' springtime marked the passage of their own years.

PALM SUNDAY, one week before Easter, was the preview. The church filled once more with what the nuns cynically called "A & P Catholics," those who came to church only for ashes and palms. Everyone was very well dressed, but careful not to tip his hand regarding the elegance in store for the following week.

Throughout the morning, grandfathers across the neighborhood were kept busy folding palms into crosses, employing a kind of Sicilian origami. The palm crosses came in all sizes. Small ones were pinned to lapels and dresses; larger ones were hooked to saints' statues or crucifixes in the home. We took the largest palm crosses to the cemetery, leaning them against the headstones of dearly departed relatives. At the cemetery, we could measure the progress of a more bucolic spring in the budding trees and early flowers. We returned home with glowing reports of renewed verdancy.

In the neighborhood during Holy Week, which begins with Palm Sunday, people conducted the business of Easter clothing and food shopping in pious tones. On Holy Thursday, the mood brightened a bit, as we celebrated the Eucharist, but the next day, Good Friday, was the darkest day of the Christian year.

The Passion of Christ, as the time between his betrayal in the garden and his death on the cross is called, was commemorated with the kind of drama only Sicilians could achieve. In church, the altar was stripped of its cloths, candles and decoration. The door of the tabernacle was left open, revealing it to be empty inside.

It was an austere sight, and young and old alike were impressed by its severity. Between noon and three, the hours representing Jesus' time on the cross, a funeral dirge wound its way around the neighborhood. In the lead was a black coffin carried on the shoulders of eight pallbearers. A priest in purple vestments followed, flanked by two altar boys. One held a crucifix on a long pole, and the other a pair of sticks, beating out a slow, sober rhythm.

The old women in black came next, some walking barefoot, others on their knees, as a kind of penance or devotion. Their wailing could be heard from a great distance, mourning the loss of Jesus as if it had just happened. Bodies quaking with emotion, fists beating their chests, they screamed phrases over and over, such as "*Jesu miu e mortu*" (My Jesus is dead) or "*Hannu mazzatu Jesu-cristu*" (They have killed Jesus Christ). Some women became so overcome that they passed out right there in the street and had to be carried away by relatives or friends. Sometimes, small children who had seen their grandmothers in such a state became frightened and woke up with nightmares for weeks afterward.

In other parts of America, there were Easter parades and egg hunts and visits from the Easter bunny. But this procession of ours was never pictured in the rotogravure of any newspaper.

O N EASTER MORNING, the whole neighborhood rose early. To hail the risen Christ, we all dressed carefully and slowly in our new clothes, finding the hidden pins in shirts, removing tags from the waistbands of trousers and cutting open jacket pockets. Women and girls spent long minutes in front of the mirror applying their makeup and styling their hair, placing their hats just so. Finally, family by family, we slowly walked to church, parading our new wardrobes before the whole neighborhood.

At Mass, we checked one another out. Particular attention was paid to the wealthier trendsetters of the parish, but for the most part we each liked our own outfits best. Some people's ensembles displayed outrageously bad taste, loud colors or strange styles. There were women whose hats were so elaborate we imagined they might burst into a Carmen Miranda number right in the middle of the Agnus Dei.

If Easter was early or cold, we wore topcoats, then removed them inside the church to show off the goods. At the same time, we were careful not to wrinkle our sleeves from the weight of the coat across our arms. Early Easter was a blessing for the poorer parishioners. They could leave on their coats, avoiding the critical or, even worse, pitying looks of their neighbors.

After church, the streets filled with people promenading their way to visit family. There was such a tangle of generations living in the old neighborhood that it wasn't possible for everyone to be together for holiday dinners. Dates were carefully apportioned so as not to slight one side of the family or the other. Visitors carried Easter lily plants or cut flowers to the parents or grandparents they wouldn't be seeing later. These visits offered further opportunity to show off our new clothes, defining our newly risen selves.

A T ABOUT ONE-THIRTY, my aunts and uncles and cousins arrived for Easter dinner. There was great show of admiration as each family strode into the parlor. "Stand back," Aunt Jo might say to the girls. "Lemme get a good look at-cha." Uncle Duffy would jokingly say to us boys, "Hey, fellas, ya clean up pretty good." The mood sobered as someone brought up the memory of a close relative, now passed away. "Oh, if only they could be here, they'd be so proud." The quiet tears were always turned to laughter by Uncle Charlie, who would say in mock mourning, "Mama, the tears, will they stain my new suit?"

Hats, both men's and women's, were carefully placed on a bed for safekeeping, as all 18 of us took our places around an assemblage of tables that filled our large kitchen. Aunt Mae had starched the linens especially for the occasion. A bouquet of flowers decorated the table's center but was moved aside to make room for the real flower of our celebration: Papa Andrea's food.

The dinner began with an artichoke heart salad. The halved hearts were arranged on an oval platter, layered in the spade shape reminiscent of an artichoke leaf, with anchovies draped across the top. The small, pale green stalks and leaves from the heart of a bunch of celery grew up from its center. The artichokes were cooked with lemon and dressed with a drizzle of the finest olive oil. The flavor was subtly sweet and sour. Accompanied by an assortment of olives, it was the perfect way to open a grand banquet.

The first course was *tumala d'Andrea*, my grandfather's adaptation of a rice bombe conceived by a tenth-century emir of Sicily, Ibn-al-Tumnah. In my grandfather's version, rice, mixed with grated cheese and eggs, is placed against the walls of a mold to form a shell. The interior is filled with pasta and tomato meat sauce and dotted with peas. It is then baked and unmolded before serving. The result is surprisingly light, with delicate, refined layers of flavor.

For Easter, two five-quart *tumalas* were needed to satisfy all the guests, invited or unexpected. One Easter, my grandfather made one, and my mother made the other. A friendly competition arose between father and daughter as to whose would look and taste best. The old man gave his daughter knowing looks that implied her doom at every turn of the preparation. She pressed on.

When it came time for the baking, the *tumalas* were placed in the oven in identical bowls, his on the right and hers on the left. At one point during the baking, Papa Andrea stepped out of the kitchen, and my mother switched the positions.

At last, the baking complete, it was time to unmold. My mother went first with Papa Andrea's. It was a beautiful golden color and he complimented his daughter on her good work. Now it was the master's turn. With the practiced dexterity of years of experience, he deftly turned "his" *tumala* onto the platter. It, too, was of exactly the same perfect shape and color. With certain laughter in his eyes, Papa Andrea said to his daughter in Sicilian, "You see, my child, this is how the *tumala* should look."

"Oh yes?" she responded in the same tone. "You know, Papa, I switched them in the oven, the one in front of you is mine."

Without missing a beat, the old *monzù* answered, "I know, my dear. I switched them back."

The second course was leg of lamb. This traditional Easter fare was eaten throughout Bruculinu, reflecting the Sicilian practice of thinning the flocks at this time of year. In our house, it was crusted with pecorino cheese and bread crumbs.

As one of the accompaniments, Papa Andrea prepared sheets of his special stuffed zucchini. The zucchini were filled with a mixture of bread crumbs and ricotta salata cheese, seasoned with cognac. They had a pillowy texture, with a subtle taste, that turned from sweet to sharp and salty, embodying the basic elements of Sicilian cuisine.

A green salad came next, its vinegary dressing always refreshing at the end of the meal. By this time, someone had always managed to spill something on his new clothes. My mother, an expert on spot removal, evaluated the cause of the stain and the fabric involved. Most of the time, she successfully removed the spot with careful applications of talc or salt or soda water. When her efforts were unsuccessful, she always told the story of Ziu Turiddu and the Opera, for comic relief.

Ziu Turiddu was one of my grandmother's brothers. He was a bachelor until well in his forties, spending most of his free time engaged in sports, and participating in the activities of the *clubbu*. But his greatest passion, by far, was the opera. Every Sunday during the season, he went to the Metropolitan Opera House as part of the famous "standing-room-only" audience. These opera buffs were the hall's toughest audience. Their boos or bravos instructed the less expert on the quality of a performance or new work.

Before going into the City, Ziu Turiddu sat down with the family for Sunday dinner, dressed in his Sunday best. Each week without fail, he managed to spot the tip of his collar or cuff with tomato sauce, provoking him to bring all the saints down from Heaven in a torrent of colorful Sicilian blasphemies.

My grandmother, trying to remedy the situation, would produce an arsenal of household spot removers. Unfortunately, usually nothing worked. Turiddu's brother, Uncle John, might produce a piece of tailor's chalk from his pocket, but the white was different from that of the fabric, and although it covered the red of the tomato sauce, it dulled the finish. The children, my mother and her brothers and sisters, found all this very funny but didn't dare laugh.

The clock was ticking, and Ziu Turiddu had to get going. As if by conspiracy, the whole family lied through their teeth, telling him, "Even if ya know it's der, ya can't see it at all, really." When retelling the story for the benefit of the "anointed" at our Easter table, my mother added, "But, really, it looked like polka dots." Everyone laughed, and the person with the blemished shirt or necktie didn't feel so bad, restoring good Paschal spirit.

J UST BEFORE DUSK, my cousins and I readjusted our clothing and went out for another tour of the neighborhood. This time, we were sent on a mission to Palermo and Canepa, the best pastry shop in the quarter, to pick up the traditional Sicilian Easter dessert, *cassata alla Siciliana.*

The shop was filled with people in their Easter finery. For the occasion, the usual assortments were removed from the showcases and replaced by the Easter selections. One case overflowed with marzipan Paschal lambs with hand-sculpted fleeces, in all sizes, reclining on green straw. Their faces wore a direct, somewhat sensual expression. In another case were sheet pans of small, sweet ricotta-filled turnovers called *cassateddi*.

One entire section of refrigerated cases was reserved for *cassata alla Siciliana*. The word *cassata* means treasure chest, and this exquisite confection is just that. Only one bite is needed to understand why *cassata alla Siciliana*—elegant, sublime and exceedingly decadent—is the queen of Sicilian desserts. At first glance, it appears to be made of green porcelain topped with a beautifully arranged cornucopia of ceramic fruits. The inside of this sybaritic delight reveals a filling of sweetened ricotta, dotted with chocolate bits and chopped candied fruits and perfumed with vanilla and lemon liqueur. This filling is held in place by a light and airy layer of sponge cake, tangy with the delicate essence of lemon zest, moistened with orange liqueur flavored syrup. The outer wall is made of green almond paste covered with a glaze of opaque lemony icing.

Our mouths watered as we looked at the case. When it was our turn, the small teenage girl who was our server went into the back to get the *cassata* my mother had ordered. At the pastry shop, as well as at the butcher's and fishmonger's, we were instructed by our elders never to accept goods from the showcase. These might not be as fresh as those from the back, their flavors compromised by the constant change of temperature from opening the case. To have to ask for this consideration from a regular vendor was considered an insult.

The young girl returned with a pink box tied with string. The box was so tall in comparison to her diminutive height, that the whole shop of waiting customers gasped as she craned her neck to see where she was going. Having happily avoided a disastrous misstep, she handed me the box, and we were off for home.

We placed the *cassata* in a cleared space on the table, where it was cut, plated, and served. We ate this wonderfully damp dessert in hushed silence, as if in church, the sparks of flavor tickling our palates.

The silence afforded me a chance to evaluate the wrinkles in my new clothes. I knew that for next Sunday they would be laundered and pressed, but they wouldn't feel the same again. "Easta" was over. These new clothes, as a measure of the year's growth and maturity, would eventually grow old. But the cycle of renewal and rebirth would continue, marked by each successive Easter for the rest of my life.

Nsalata 'i Trunzi 'i Cacuocciuli

Hearts of Artichoke Salad

MY GRANDFATHER ARRANGED HIS ARTICHOKE SALAD with the
heart of a head of celery sticking up in the center, and with
the top layer of artichoke hearts draped with anchovies. When I'd ask
him why, he'd smile at me and say, "Because that's the way you do
it." I knew there was more to the story.

Years later, in Los Angeles, I planted a vegetable garden. The first
time I saw an artichoke plant, I recognized the resemblance to the
heart. And spreading the leaves of an organically grown artichoke
to prepare it for stuffing, I found a large worm inside. At last I understood Papa Andrea's little joke: the anchovies represented the
worms.

During the heights of the spring and fall artichoke seasons,
medium-sized artichokes can often be found at a good price. This
preparation offers the possibility of cooking the day before use,
freeing time for the cook on the day of a large dinner party.

Serve with an assortment of olives and crusty bread. For smaller
parties, the recipe may be halved.

For 12 servings

16   medium artichokes, about 5 inches long and
       3½ inches in diameter, with long stems
8   lemons
1½   tablespoons sea salt
1   cup extra-virgin olive oil
1   celery heart, small inner part only
     12-ounce can anchovies, packed in olive oil

Pour cold water into a large bowl. Before cutting the artichoke, juice 4 of the lemons and add the juice and rinds to the water. Pass a knife through another lemon prior to each cut. This will help prevent the artichoke from turning black.

Working with 1 artichoke at a time, cut off ¾ inch from the top. Remove the outer leaves to the place where the leaves are thin and pale green. Cut the artichoke into quarters. If the stem is curved, be sure that it, too, is cut evenly into quarters. With a sharp paring knife, trim away the dark green base of the leaves around the heart. Peel the stem and cut away the end. Carefully remove the spiny choke and the purple leaves with a paring knife or a spoon and discard them. Place the quarters in the lemon water.

Meanwhile, fill a large pot with 4 quarts water and put it on to boil.

When all of the artichokes have been cleaned, juice the remaining 4 lemons. When the water comes to a boil, add the juice and rinds of the lemons, the salt and the oil. Drain the artichokes and add. Turn down the heat and simmer, covered, for 8 to 10 minutes, or until the artichokes are three-quarters cooked, that is, still a bit crunchy. Remove the pot from the heat and carefully transfer the artichokes and lemon rinds to a roasting pan about 16 by 12 inches and at least 2½ inches deep.

Pour in the pot liquor and cover the pan with aluminum foil, shiny side down, or a dish towel. To prevent the artichokes from turning brown, be sure that the foil touches the liquid. Let cool thoroughly, then put the pan in the refrigerator for at least 3 hours or overnight.

About 1 hour before serving, assemble the salad. Place a layer of artichokes, cut side down, on a serving platter. Arrange them in a spade shape, like an artichoke leaf. Overlap the stems. Place the next layer on top of the first, and so on. Stand the celery heart straight up in the center, like a plant growing out of it. If necessary, the celery heart may be anchored to the platter with a marble-sized piece of bread moistened with water. Drape anchovies over the top and serve.

Tumala d'Andrea

*R*ice Bombe

T UMALA WAS MY GRANDFATHER'S SIGNATURE DISH. As a boy, I watched from the other end of the kitchen table as he prepared it. As a teenager, I helped. As an adult, I have prepared *tumala* many times, and over the years its magnificence has awed my guests. I even found the old porcelain bowl my grandfather used to mold it, forgotten in a high cupboard of my aunt's kitchen.

Recently I came across a home movie from 1957. In it, Papa Andrea is cutting and serving *tumala* to a tableful of relatives. The 85-year-old *monzù* moves the knife with the agility and grace of a much younger chef. I had always thought that *tumala* was simply cut into slices and served, but Papa Andrea cut the slices again halfway up and put them on the plates rice side down. This method helps keep the slices intact and creates a more appealing presentation. Papa Andrea has been dead for more than 30 years now, but he is still teaching me about food and the wonders of his artistry.

Guests always ask for seconds, but if you have any left over, reheat it wrapped in foil in a hot oven.

Mold and bake the *tumala* in a 5-liter (approximately 21 cups) stainless steel mixing bowl, measuring about 11 inches in diameter at the top, and standing 5 inches high.

For 12 servings

Sea salt

5½ cups (2¼ pounds or 1 kilo) Arborio rice

5 large eggs

4½ cups grated imported pecorino cheese, preferably Locatelli

2   28-ounce cans peeled Italian plum tomatoes
4   ounces fresh crimini mushrooms (or 4 ounces white mush-
    rooms plus 3 dried porcini mushrooms)
1   medium onion, finely chopped
5   tablespoons extra-virgin olive oil
¾   pound ground veal
¼   pound ground pork
2   tablespoons tomato paste dissolved in ⅓ cup water
    Black pepper
3   sprigs basil, chopped
1   tablespoon sugar
4   scrapes freshly grated nutmeg
1   pound ziti tagliati or penne lisce
1   cup fresh or frozen peas
    Butter and bread crumbs, for the bowl

The night before or at least 6 hours before the *tumala* is to be prepared, cook the rice. Fill a large pot with water. Add 1 tablespoon salt, bring to a boil and add the rice. Stir from time to time to prevent sticking. When the rice is cooked al dente, remove the pot from the stove and add cold water to stop the cooking process. Drain thoroughly and put the rice in a large mixing bowl. Allow the rice to cool for 5 minutes.

Beat 4 of the eggs. Using a wooden spoon, thoroughly mix the eggs and 2 cups of the cheese into the rice. Put the mixture in a large shallow serving bowl and smooth the top. Cover with a dish towel and put it in a cool place (not the refrigerator) to rest overnight or for at least 6 hours.

On the day the *tumala* is to be served, prepare the tomato sauce and cook the pasta. To prepare the sauce, place a food mill fitted with the smallest-holed (1⁄16 inch) disk over a bowl. Mill the tomatoes in order to remove the seeds, which can make the sauce bitter. Scrape the pulp from the bottom of the mill into the bowl. Set aside.

If using the dried mushrooms, put them in a small bowl, cover with boiling water and let stand for 5 minutes. Lift the mushrooms out of the liquid with a fork, leaving behind the debris, and coarsely chop. Wipe the fresh mushrooms clean, using as little cold water as possible to remove dirt. Trim the stems, discarding any that are dried out. Coarsely chop the caps and remaining stems.

Put the onion and 3 tablespoons of the oil in a heavy medium saucepan over medium heat. Sauté until the onion is translucent, about 5 minutes. Add the mushrooms, increase the heat to high and season with salt. When the mushroom liquid has mostly evaporated, add the veal and the pork. Sauté, stirring with a wooden spoon to break up any clumps, until browned. Reduce the heat to medium and stir in the dissolved tomato paste. Let the mixture thicken for about 1 minute and add the tomatoes. Stir well. Season with more salt and black pepper and add the basil, sugar and nutmeg. Reduce the heat to low and simmer the sauce, uncovered, stirring from time to time, for 40 minutes. Do not let it boil. When it is ready, keep it hot while you prepare the rest of the *tumala*.

About 25 minutes before the sauce is ready, fill a large pot with 6 quarts water. Add the remaining 2 tablespoons oil and 2 tablespoons salt and bring to a boil. Add the pasta and cook until slightly underdone. Drain well and toss with just enough sauce to coat it. Using a slotted spoon, remove about three quarters of the solids from the sauce and mix into the pasta. Mix in ½ cup of the remaining cheese and the peas. (Too much sauce liquid will cause the *tumala* to crack when it is unmolded.) Set aside to cool to room temperature. Remove the sauce from the heat and set aside.

Preheat the oven to 400°F, with a rack positioned in the center.

Begin to assemble the *tumala*. Grease the stainless steel bowl generously with butter. Coat the inside of the bowl thoroughly with bread crumbs all the way to the top edge. Sprinkle an additional tablespoon of bread crumbs on the bottom of the bowl.

Line the bowl with the rice mixture, making a ½-inch-thick wall. Gently press the rice against the bowl with your hand, moistened with water to keep it from sticking. Be sure there are no thin spots. Build the wall of rice up to the top edge of the bowl.

When the pasta is at room temperature, spoon it into the rice-lined bowl to within 1 inch from the top. Make sure there are no empty spaces. Cover the top with the remaining rice. Fold the top edge of the rice wall over the top layer of rice, so that the *tumala* is recessed ½ inch into the bowl. The top layer must be flat and sealed well all around, since it will have to support the weight of the *tumala* when it is unmolded. Beat the remaining egg and brush it over the top to ensure a good seal.

Bake the *tumala* for 1 hour, or until the top is light golden. Immediately upon removing the *tumala* from the oven, carefully run a knife around the top edge of the bowl to release it. Let the *tumala* rest in the bowl for 10 minutes. Meanwhile, reheat the tomato sauce.

Place a serving platter on top of the bowl and turn it over. You may want to get help. This step may require two people. Gently lift off the bowl. If it is stuck, don't panic. Try tapping on the bowl or twisting it gently. Persevere! It will release. Let the *tumala* rest for 5 minutes, then bring it to the table.

Use a large, sharp chef's knife to cut a tapered slice about 4 inches wide at the bottom. Do not remove it. Holding the knife blade parallel to the serving platter, cut the slice about one third of the way up. Carefully lift out the top portion and place it, rice side down, in a pasta bowl. Place the bottom portion in another pasta bowl. (It is already rice side down.) Continue in this manner, until you have about 16 slices. Spoon a small amount of tomato sauce on each slice and sprinkle with grated cheese and a grinding of black pepper before serving.

Arrustu 'i Agneddu Impannatu

Roasted Leg of Lamb

with Pecorino and

Bread Crumbs

COATING A LEG OF LAMB with ewe's milk cheese—pecorino—is a pairing direct from the mountains of Sicily. The sharpness of the cheese greatly enhances the sweet flavor of spring lamb.

For 12 servings

½   cup unflavored fine dry bread crumbs
½   cup grated imported pecorino cheese, preferably Locatelli
3   sprigs rosemary, leaves only
    Black pepper
    Sea salt
1   8-pound bone-in leg of lamb
1   cup dry white wine

Preheat the oven to 375°F, with a rack positioned in the top third.

Put the bread crumbs, cheese and rosemary in a small bowl. Mix in the pepper. Lightly salt the lamb on all sides. Place the lamb in a large roasting pan on a roasting rack or on 2 doughnuts of aluminum foil. Spread the bread-crumb mixture on top of the lamb, pressing it against the meat.

Roast the lamb for 2 hours 40 minutes, about 20 minutes per pound, or until a meat thermometer reaches 130°F for medium-rare or 135°F to 145°F for medium. After the first 2 hours, slowly pour the white wine over the roast, being careful not to disturb the crust.

Transfer the lamb to a warmed serving platter and let it rest in a warm place for 15 minutes. Thinly slice the meat and serve with the pan juices.

Cucuzzeddi Chini

$\mathscr{S}$tuffed Zucchini

O NE OF SEVERAL SIDE DISHES on our Easter table as well as on many other Sundays throughout the warmer months of the year was stuffed zucchini. Its delicate texture complements roasted or grilled meat dishes. It may also be served as an appetizer.

The cheese used in the stuffing, ricotta salata, a pressed ewe's milk ricotta, is easily found in Italian markets and specialty food shops. The cheese is made in several textures. For this recipe, the moister kind is best. This recipe may be reduced proportionately.

For 12 servings

12 zucchini, 5 inches long, 1½ inches in diameter and as
    straight as possible
1   teaspoon finely chopped garlic
¼   cup extra-virgin olive oil, plus more
    for brushing the zucchini
¼   cup cognac
    Sea salt
    Black pepper
¾   cup unflavored fine dry bread crumbs
1   cup coarsely grated ricotta salata
3   large eggs, beaten

Wash the zucchini, pat them dry and cut them in half lengthwise. If they are curved, cut them with the curved side up. Hollow out the zucchini halves with a melon baller or spoon, leaving a ⅛-inch shell. Chop the flesh medium-fine and mix it with the garlic. Heat

226

the ¼ cup oil in a skillet over medium-high heat and sauté the chopped zucchini and garlic until cooked but still firm, about 5 minutes. Turn off the heat to avoid a flare-up, and add the cognac. Carefully turn the heat back on and cook until the alcohol evaporates, 1 to 2 minutes. Lightly season with salt and pepper. Remove from the heat and stir in the bread crumbs. Turn the mixture into a large bowl to cool.

Preheat the oven to 375°F.

When the mixture is at room temperature, stir in the cheese and eggs. Brush the zucchini shells inside and out with olive oil and fill them with the stuffing. Smooth it flat; it will mound as the eggs expand during cooking.

Bake for 50 to 60 minutes, or until the zucchini shells are quite soft and the stuffing is firm and golden on top. Let cool for 5 minutes before serving.

If the dish is to be served as an appetizer, serve it warm, not hot, for easier handling.

Cassateddi

Sweet Ricotta Turnovers

CASSATEDDI MEANS "DEAR LITTLE TREASURE CHESTS." Traditionally, they are made for Easter in several different styles. This version has a rich *pasta frolla* folded over ricotta flavored with sugar, cinnamon, cocoa, candied fruits and pistachios.

Well covered in a cool place, *cassateddi* will keep for a week.

For 3 dozen turnovers

FOR THE FILLING

1   pound good-quality ricotta or ⅔ of the recipe
    for cheese used in Filled Puffs (page 202)
1¼ cups confectioners' sugar
2   large eggs, beaten
1   teaspoon European-process unsweetened cocoa powder
½   teaspoon ground cinnamon
2   tablespoons chopped candied fruits
⅓   cup unsalted shelled pistachios, halved or coarsely chopped

FOR THE PASTRY

3   cups bleached all-purpose flour, plus more if necessary
1   cup cake flour
    Pinch of salt
12 tablespoons (1½ sticks) unsalted butter
1   cup granulated sugar
6   large egg yolks
1   tablespoon cognac
⅔   cup milk, plus more if necessary

2 large egg whites, lightly beaten
Nonpareils in the colors of the season

Prepare the filling: Pass the ricotta through the largest-holed disk of a food mill to break up the curds. Mix in the confectioners' sugar with a wooden spoon. Do not use an electric mixer, which will destroy the curds. Thoroughly mix in the eggs, then the cocoa and cinnamon. Fold in the candied fruits and pistachios. Cover and refrigerate until needed.

Prepare the pastry: Sift together the 3 cups all-purpose flour, the cake flour and salt into a large bowl. Using an electric mixer or by hand, cut in the butter until the mixture has the consistency of cornmeal. Thoroughly mix in the sugar. Work in the egg yolks one at a time with a wooden spoon or spatula. Mix in the cognac. Slowly add the milk, kneading in the bowl just until a smooth dough is formed. If the dough is too sticky, add small amounts of flour; if too dry, add a few teaspoonfuls of milk. Form the dough into a ball, cover with a lightly floured cloth and let it rest at room temperature for 15 minutes.

Divide the dough into quarters. Working with one quarter at a time and leaving the rest refrigerated, roll out the dough on a lightly floured surface to 3/16 inch thick. Cut it with a cookie cutter into 4-inch circles.

Preheat the oven to 375°F, with a rack positioned in the upper third of the oven.

For each turnover, place a level tablespoon of the filling in the center of one half of the circle, about ¼ inch in from the edge. (Bear in mind that the filling will expand when cooked and that overstuffing will cause the crust to crack.) Brush the edges of the dough with the beaten egg white. Fold the top half of the dough over the filling to enclose it and press or crimp the seam together to form a tight seal. Place the turnover on an ungreased baking sheet. (You will need to use 3 baking sheets, but bake them one at a time.) When the sheet is full, brush the top of each turnover with egg white and sprinkle with nonpareils.

Bake for about 20 minutes, or until the turnovers are barely golden on top. Cool on a rack and serve at room temperature.

Cassata alla Siciliana

*C*assata

THE ORIGINS OF *CASSATA* ARE UNCLEAR. One theory, widely believed in Sicily, was related to me by a Sicilian pastry chef. It seems that one day in the sixteenth century, a famous chef to one of the grand families of Sicily found that a large quantity of ricotta in the kitchen was about to spoil. Sweetening it to mask any sour taste, he covered it in an airtight casing of sugar syrup over almond paste. Thus *Cassata alla Siciliana* was born.

On closer reflection, this story is surely apocryphal. Until the mid-nineteenth century, the price of sugar remained high and only the wealthy could indulge in its pleasure. Anyone who could afford the amount of sugar needed to prepare such a dessert would not have been concerned over the spoilage of ricotta, as common in Sicily as sheep.

A more likely theory is that *cassata* is North African in origin, its rudimentary form dating back to the tenth century. The word itself may be from the Arab word *qa'sat,* a type of large baking pan. Over the centuries, it developed into this luscious baroque beauty of international renown.

In America today, *cassata alla Siciliana* is difficult to find. Most pastry shops or restaurants that do offer it sell a somewhat pedestrian version. It is possible, however, to make it at home. Although the recipe directions are lengthy, they are by no means difficult to execute. Components of *cassata* are used in many other Sicilian and Italian desserts as well.

The traditional *cassata* mold, made of metal, glass or ceramic, is about 9 inches in diameter at the bottom and has sides sloping slightly outward, so that the top diameter is about 10 inches; it is about 3 inches deep.

If you do not own a traditional *cassata* mold, use a similarly shaped flat-bottomed vessel that has sides at least 3 inches high and a diameter no greater than 10 inches. The *cassata* will fill 3½ quarts, so the vessel should hold at least that amount. In a pinch you may use a straight-sided 10-inch springform pan. Although it is not quite large enough to hold the full yield of this recipe, the *cassata* will still be impressive.

PREPARING THE *CASSATA*

In cooking, as in comedy, timing is everything. Preparation of the *cassata* needs to begin five days before it is to be served, so that the almond paste and the sponge cake have time to set up. The finished *cassata* itself needs three days to "ripen," *pi fari maturari,* as the Sicilians say.

Five days before the *cassata* is to be served, prepare the almond paste and the sponge cake. In the evening of this day, prepare the ricotta, if the correct type cannot be purchased. Also prepare the soaking syrup. Four days before the *cassata* is to be served, prepare the ricotta cream and assemble the *cassata,* prepare the glaze and un-mold and decorate the *cassata.*

For one 10-inch *cassata,*
about 24 servings

CHAPTER XIII.

Five days before the cassata is to be served, prepare the almond paste.

Pasta Riali

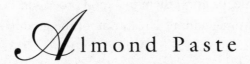

lmond Paste

ALMOND PASTE WAS, at one point during the sixteenth century, Sicily's largest export. It was prized in royal courts as far away as Scandinavia. In recent years, it has become the fashion to prepare uncooked almond paste. All of the ingredients are placed in a food processor and machined into a paste. I find the result to be vastly inferior in flavor, structure and texture to the traditional cooked method. Whole, blanched almonds may be used, but do not use slivered almonds for this recipe. They tend to be dry and powdery and have lost much of their flavor. It is best to begin with shelled raw whole almonds and blanch them yourself.

For about 1¾ pounds paste

12 ounces (2¼ cups) shelled whole almonds, raw or blanched
2¼ cups (1 pound) granulated sugar
Confectioners' sugar, for dusting
1 cup water
2 tablespoons light corn syrup
1 teaspoon almond extract
4-5 drops green food coloring

If using almonds with skins, you will need to blanch them. Fill a medium saucepan with water and bring to a boil. Drop in the almonds and blanch them for 2 minutes, or until the skins loosen. Drain well. When they are just cool enough to handle, "shoot" them out of their skins into a large bowl of cold water to keep them from turning brown. Drain and pat dry.

Pound the blanched almonds to a very fine consistency in a mortar and pestle, or grind them in a food processor. Process about ½ cup nuts at a time, adding 1 teaspoon of the granulated sugar to each batch. Pulse in short bursts until the almonds are very finely ground, about 30 seconds. Do not overprocess the almonds, or they will turn to nut butter.

Have ready a surface at least 16 inches square on which to knead the almond paste after it has cooked. The best material to use is marble, since it is always 10 degrees cooler than the temperature of the air. A stainless-steel work surface can be substituted, as can a shallow glazed ceramic bowl at least 12 inches in diameter. Dust the surface with confectioners' sugar. Fill the sink with a few inches of cold water. This will serve as a water bath in which to quickly cool the pot of almond paste when it is done.

Place the water, corn syrup and remaining granulated sugar, in that order, into a 6-cup heavy-bottomed saucepan. Stir gently to combine the ingredients and moisten the sugar. Place the pot over low heat and stir gently until the sugar is melted and the solution is translucent. Do not create turbulence in the pot.

Stop stirring, turn up the heat to medium-high and boil until the syrup reaches the firm-ball stage, which is 248°F. This temperature must be exact and is best determined with a mercury candy thermometer.

Although corn syrup inhibits the formation of sugar crystals during cooking, as the sugar boils, crystals may still form around the edge of the pot. Their presence will ruin the smoothness of the almond paste. They are easily melted by putting the lid on the pot for a few seconds. The steam will liquefy the crystals. Wash them down the sides of the pot with a pastry brush dipped in water.

Be watchful as the syrup approaches the firm-ball stage. The moment that it reaches 248°F, turn off the heat and quickly stir in the almonds with a wooden spoon. Stir constantly, making sure that the mixture does not stick and that the almonds do not take on any color. When the mixture can be pushed away from the sides of the pot with the spoon, it is done. Immediately place the bottom of the pot in the water bath for a few seconds to stop the cooking process. Slowly begin to pour the mixture onto the sugar-dusted work surface. If it begins to overflow the edges, wait until it stops and then continue pouring.

Let the mixture cool for 3 to 4 minutes before touching. It is very hot. When the mixture has cooled to 110°F—slightly warm to the touch—sprinkle with the almond extract and begin to knead. At first, use a wet metal dough scraper to fold the edges to the center. As the ball begins to form, wet your hands and continue to knead the paste until it is smooth and elastic and takes on the consistency of pasta dough. Work 4 to 5 drops of green food coloring into the paste, until it is a uniform light green.

Form the paste into a log 3 inches in diameter. Let cool to room temperature, dust with confectioners' sugar and wrap in aluminum foil. Refrigerate overnight to set.

On the same day, prepare the sponge cake.

Pan 'i Sponza

Sponge Cake

S PONGE CAKE was originally named in Sicilian *pan 'i sponza.* *Sponza* is the Sicilian word for sponge. The Italian "continentals," missing the point entirely, thought they were hearing *Spagna,* Italian for Spain. Because Sicily was under Spanish rule for 400 years, there was some sense to this misnomer. Sicilian sponge cake, *pan 'i sponza,* is still known throughout Italy as *pan di Spagna.*

For a 10-by-2-inch cake

Butter for greasing the pan
1¼   cups cake flour, plus more for dusting the pan
1½   cups sugar
6   large eggs, separated
2   tablespoons water
1¼   teaspoons finely chopped lemon zest
⅛   teaspoon powdered eggshell (see page 44)
     or ¼ teaspoon cream of tartar

Preheat the oven to 350°F, with a rack positioned in the center. Grease and flour a 10-inch round cake or springform pan. Sift together the 1¼ cups flour and 2 tablespoons of the sugar.

Using an electric mixer or by hand with a wire whisk, beat the egg yolks, 1¼ cups of the sugar and water together until the mixture turns pale yellow and forms ribbons, about 7 minutes. Fold in the lemon zest. Beat in the flour mixture a little at a time, adding more only when the previous addition has been absorbed.

In a clean grease-free bowl, copper if possible, begin to beat the egg whites with a clean mixer or a clean whisk. If any oils from the egg yolks touch the egg whites, they will not stiffen. When the whites begin to change color, add the powdered eggshell or the cream of tartar, and continue beating until the whites form peaks that are stiff but not dry. Continue to beat, sprinkling in the remaining 2 tablespoons sugar, a little at a time.

Beat a few tablespoons of the whites into the yolk mixture to lighten it. Quickly but gently fold the rest of the whites into the yolk mixture with a rubber spatula.

Turn the batter into the pan and bake for 30 to 40 minutes, or until the cake is light golden and a toothpick inserted near the center comes out clean. Refrain from opening the oven door as much as possible, since a sudden gush of cold air or even a heavy thud in the kitchen can cause the cake to collapse. If you must, peek in and close the door gently.

When the cake is baked, turn off the oven and let the cake cool in the oven with the door ajar. When it is completely cooled, turn it out onto a rack. Store it, loosely covered, until needed or up to 4 days. Be sure to save all of the crumbs or bits of crust for later use during assembly.

That evening, if it is necessary to do so, prepare the ricotta, doubling the recipe on page 202.

On the evening of the fifth day, prepare the soaking syrup.

Sciroppu

Soaking Syrup

A N AMOUNT OF HEAVY SOAKING SYRUP, flavored with orange liqueur, is needed to coat the sponge cake.

For about ½ cup syrup

5 tablespoons water
½ cup plus 1 tablespoon granulated sugar
2 tablespoons orange or lemon liqueur such as Cointreau, Grand Marnier, Triple Sec or Limoncello

Pour the water into a small saucepan. Stir in the sugar. Bring to a boil over medium heat. Remove from the heat and pour the syrup into a small bowl to cool.

When it reaches room temperature, reserve a couple of table-spoons for thinning the sugar glaze later. Flavor the remainder with liqueur. Cover and store overnight in a cool place.

Four days before the cassata is to be served, begin assembling it.

LINING THE MOLD

Cut 2 pieces of kitchen parchment paper long enough to line the mold and extend to 2 inches above it. Crisscross the lining to cover the entire interior surface of the mold. To keep it from slipping, "spot-weld" the parchment in several places with dabs of jam or honey. Fold the lining above the mold back out of the way.

ALMOND PASTE LAYER

Dust a marble slab or work surface with confectioners' sugar. Place one third of the cold almond paste on the slab and flatten it. Put the remainder back in the refrigerator. Roll out the paste with a heavy rolling pin to a strip ¼ inch thick, 3 inches wide and about 11 inches long. Roll the rolling pin in one direction only; a back-and-forth motion may cause the paste to stick to it. If necessary, wet the rolling pin to further discourage sticking. With a sharp knife, trim the paste strip to exactly 3 inches wide. Using a wet metal spatula to lift it off the slab, place it along the wall of the mold against the parchment. Be sure that the paste does not slip onto the bottom surface of the mold. Repeat the process, slightly overlapping the strips, until the wall of the mold is lined with a uniform layer of almond paste. If any thickening occurs at the seams, smooth them by running a wet finger along the joint. Be sure that it does not thicken at the joint. Place the mold in the freezer, uncovered, to set the almond paste. Form the unused paste into a small log, cover and refrigerate for possible repairs.

SPONGE CAKE LAYER

If the top of the sponge cake has cracked and separated, remove it and reserve for future use.

Cut the sponge cake horizontally into 2 equal halves. This is best accomplished with an adjustable cake cutter. An alternative method is to use a length of kitchen twine. Place toothpicks around the outside edges of the cake to mark the center. Using these as a guide, hold the twine taut and draw it through the cake. These methods, as opposed to using a knife, will make a straight cut and keep the cake from crumbing excessively.

Using a long, sharp, serrated knife, cut one of the halves into ½-inch-wide strips, and cut the strips into 3-inch lengths. Save all scraps. Cut the outer crust off the other half, saving the cut-off portions.

Remove the mold from the freezer and fit the whole cake half on the bottom of the mold, bordered by the almond paste. Trim if necessary. Save the crumbs and cut-off portions.

Gently press the cut 3-inch strips of cake vertically and flat against the almond paste, fitting them together tightly. Trim them even with the top edge of the paste. The sponge will be a buffer between the almond paste and the ricotta cream. Contact between the two will make the almond paste gooey, so be sure that the strips fit closely together.

Using a pastry brush, sprinkle the cake sides and bottom with the flavored soaking syrup. The cake should be moist but not sodden. Put the mold back in the freezer for about 15 minutes to set.

While the cake is setting, prepare the ricotta cream.

Crema 'i Ricotta

Ricotta Cream

SWEETENED RICOTTA FILLING is the heart and soul of this dessert. Although the ingredients and preparation are the same as for many other Sicilian desserts, the flavor and texture will be different in the *cassata* because it has been sealed in the syrup, almond paste and sponge-cake casing.

For the ricotta cream, double the recipe on page 203.

FINAL ASSEMBLY

Cut out a circle of sturdy cardboard equal in diameter to the top of the *cassata*. Set it aside until needed.

Remove the mold from the freezer and fill it with the ricotta cream. Make certain there are no empty spaces. Using a rubber spatula, flatten the top even with the almond paste and sponge cake.

Crumb all of the bits of cake and spread them evenly on top of the ricotta cream. Sprinkle with the remaining flavored soaking syrup. Cover with parchment paper and the cardboard circle and press gently to maintain flatness. Cover with plastic wrap and then aluminum foil. Refrigerate for at least 4 hours to set. Put the *cassata* in the freezer for 15 minutes before unmolding and glazing.

While the cassata sets, prepare the sugar glaze.

Zuccaratura

*S*ugar Glaze

FOR *CASSATA*, the sugar glaze is traditionally made with fondant. This basis of all confection is sugar syrup boiled to the soft-ball stage and worked into a smooth, creamy consistency. For the purpose of glazing, it is loosened with lemon juice or soaking syrup.

For about ⅔ cup glaze

½ cup water
1 tablespoon light corn syrup
1 cup plus 2 tablespoons (½ pound) granulated sugar
2 tablespoons lemon juice
Reserved unflavored soaking syrup

Have ready a large work surface at least 16 inches square on which to knead the fondant, preferably marble, though a stainless steel or a shallow ceramic bowl at least 12 inches in diameter will do. Moisten the surface with ice water. Fill the sink with a few inches of cold water to serve as a water bath in which to quickly cool the pot of syrup when it is done.

Place the water, corn syrup and sugar in that order in a small heavy-bottomed saucepan. Stir gently to combine the ingredients. Place the pot over low heat and stir gently until the sugar is melted and the solution is translucent. Do not create turbulence in the pot. Stop stirring, increase the heat to medium-high and boil until the syrup reaches soft-ball stage, 240°F on a candy thermometer. If crystals form, put the lid on the saucepan to let the steam liquefy the crystals. Wash them down from the sides of the pan with a pastry brush dipped in water.

The moment the syrup reaches 240°F, cool the bottom of the pot in the water bath for a few seconds. Pour the syrup onto the work surface or platter. Do not scrape the pan. Let it cool until it is 110°F, slightly warm to the touch.

To work the fondant, use a wet metal dough scraper to fold the edges to the center. As it starts to become opaque, knead it with your hands, moistened with water. When the fondant is smooth, creamy and totally opaque, transfer to a bowl and mix in 2 tablespoons of the lemon juice with a wooden spoon. It should be the consistency of yogurt. If it is too stiff, add soaking syrup, ¼ teaspoon at a time.

Cover with plastic wrap. Be sure that the wrap makes contact with the surface to prevent a skin from forming.

Store in a warm place until needed. If the glaze begins to harden, place the bowl in a bowl of warm water to soften.

When the assembled cassata has been in the refrigerator for at least 4 hours and in the freezer for 15 minutes, unmold it.

UNMOLDING THE *CASSATA*

Remove the wrapping and cardboard. Peel off the top parchment paper. Replace the cardboard and, with a fluid motion, turn over the mold. Remove the mold and gently peel away any paper that may have stuck to the *cassata*.

If the almond paste does not meet the bottom, adjust it by cutting pieces from the leftovers, fitting them and smoothing with a wet metal spatula. If the repair process has caused the *cassata* to warm, put it back in the freezer for a few minutes before glazing.

243

G L A Z I N G   T H E   *C A S S A T A*

Brush a thin translucent layer of glaze on the sides of the *cassata*. Do the same on the top. After a few minutes, brush on another layer of glaze. Be sure the sides are well coated but that the almond paste does not become deformed from the weight. Reserve a small amount of glaze for possible repairs during decoration. Spread the rest over the top in an even layer. Put the *cassata* in the freezer for 10 minutes to chill and slightly set the glaze.

D E C O R A T I N G   T H E   *C A S S A T A*

C a n d i e d   F r u i t

For one 10-inch *cassata*

4   candied orange slices, cut into eighths
3   candied pineapple slices, halved
3   candied cherries, halved
2   candied half pears
2   whole candied cherries

Plan your decoration pattern on a paper circle first to avoid damaging the glaze. You are limited only by your imagination. Place as many pieces of orange slices as will fit around the top edge. Arrange them as closely together as possible, with the rind facing out. Arrange the pineapple slices in a symmetrical pattern inside the orange slices, with the cut side facing out. Place half a candied cherry in the hole of each slice.

Arrange the pear halves in the center of the *cassata* with the small ends touching, to resemble a butterfly. Place a whole cherry above and below the point where the pear halves meet.

STORING THE *CASSATA*

Put the decorated *cassata*, uncovered, in the refrigerator for 6 hours or overnight, or until the glaze is no longer sticky but is smooth to the touch.

Cut a length of waxed paper long enough to encircle the *cassata*. Fold it in half and place it around the *cassata* like a collar. Tape it together in several places. Cover the *cassata* with aluminum foil and refrigerate for at least 3 days before serving, to "ripen."

SERVING THE *CASSATA*

Cut the *cassata* with a large, sharp knife, or one with a serrated edge, warmed in hot water. If necessary, wipe the knife with a damp cloth after every few slices.

XIV.

*L*emon Ice
to the Heart, L.A.M.F.

UGUST IN BROOKLYN IS UNBEARABLE. Temperatures well into the nineties mix with an equally high humidity to create a thick muggy mess. There is no breeze. The dim hope of relief flickers in the promise of rain showers, although these often serve only to raise the already impossible humidity.

It is too hot to sleep or to stay awake, to go out or to stay home; too hot to talk, to eat, to laugh or to cry; too damned hot even to make love. As people plod on as best they can, tempers shorten. Dante's motto of despair may as well have been written on the final Gothic column of the Brooklyn Bridge.

The temperature in our railroad flat under the Myrtle Avenue el rose higher than that in the street. The dense hot air waved at the windows through immaculate white lace curtains. The massive iron structure of the elevated train line warmed in the summer heat. It gave off a sweet, fetid smell, like a giant cast-iron skillet heated for the first time after years of disuse. When a train rolled by overhead, tiny flakes of rust showered down. Illuminated by shafts of sunlight coming through the tracks, they looked like gold dust.

No children played on Myrtle Avenue, under the el. We played around the corner on Cedar Street in the full summer sun; but during heat waves, our games of stickball, scullsy or crack-top were canceled. We sought relief in the shade of someone's stoop. There we'd play cards or exchange stories of recent family vacations "up da country" or "down da shore." Those of us who had not been there dreamed of such luxury.

Sometimes an older brother or father would produce a monkey wrench to open the johnny pump. One strong boy would crouch behind the hydrant, deflecting the water's flow into a cascade with a metal trash can lid. Along with the rest, I pranced, fully clothed, in the ice-cold water. The force of it took my breath away.

The joys of this urban waterfall always ended too soon. "Chickie, da cops!" someone would yell. We'd leap away from the johnny pump, feigning innocence, but our wet clothes spoke for themselves. The cops gave us the obligatory lecture on civic responsibility and wasting water and closed the valve. But it was obvious that what they really wanted to do was jump in too—badge, gun, handcuffs and all.

The wet street quickly dried. The humidity turned our soaked dungarees and polo shirts and our slushy sneakers into sticky, clammy discomfort. Inevitably, we all had to go up and change into hot dry clothes.

THE ONLY LIVING THING that seemed to thrive in this inferno was our landlord's fig tree. It grew in a postage-stamp-sized garden at the Cedar Street side of our building, surrounded by a tall picket fence. Each October, our landlord, Mr. Raimondi, carefully wrapped his fig tree in layers of newspaper, tar paper and burlap, to keep off the winter frost. Each spring, he gently unwrapped it, and by August it was resplendent in full fruit.

It was the only natural thing of significance in this urban land- 247 scape, the only link Mr. Raimondi and the other immigrants on the block had to the gardens and orchards of Sicily, left behind over 50 years earlier. Perhaps Mr. Raimondi's fig tree was the only reason for summer on our block at all. When we ate its sumptuous sweet black figs, all the heat and humidity did seem to have a purpose.

S UPPERTIME BROUGHT NO RELIEF. My mother and aunts returned from their city jobs, their crisp cotton dresses and white gloves wilted from the 45-minute crowded subway ride home. As each walked through the door, the words "Boy! It's hot!" and their English and Sicilian variants filled the house in chorus and fugue. They'd change their business clothes for more comfortable attire and join my grandparents and me at the kitchen table.

For these August heat wave suppers, Papa Andrea prepared an assortment of salads. Green beans vinaigrette and potato salad in olive oil with capers and onion were beautifully arranged on an oval platter. Hard-boiled egg halves, draped with anchovy, adorned the rim. Deep red sliced tomatoes covered in dried oregano with a drizzle of olive oil and a mixed green salad were always on the table in this season.

There might be tuna dressed with olive oil and lemon juice, or an assortment of Italian cold cuts circled by green and black olives. For dessert, there were summer melons, or sweet juicy plums or perfectly ripened fleshy peaches.

This food and its vinegary, pungent, sweet flavors were restorative, the crisp coolness offering satisfying refreshment. The only dissonant element was the bread, its crust made soggy by the ever-present humidity.

D USK FOUND US STILL AT THE TABLE, searching for some new relief. When my mother felt even the slightest movement of air, she would stop the conversation, saying, "Shh! a breeze," as if keeping quiet could trick the heavens into sending a gale. Aunt Jo suggested turning off the light in order to make it cooler. "Lemon ice" was all Aunt Mae needed to say. Everyone agreed that the coldest of all desserts was our best hope.

Sicilians have had a love affair with icy confections since ancient times. During the Roman occupation, fruit juice was mixed with snow from the mountains. Later, the dessert we call sherbet was introduced by the Saracens. *Sarbat* was made by freezing jasmine-flower water or cinnamon oil and sugar. As time passed, Sicilians became world renowned at the art of the frozen dessert. The mass emigration in the early part of this century carried this passion to America.

During the summer months, every pastry shop in the old neighborhood made lemon ice. The best was from Circo's, at the corner of Knickerbocker Avenue and Hart Street. Mr. Circo knew just the right amount of lemon juice to mix with just the right density of sugar syrup, creating a lemon ice with just the right tartness and sweetness.

Limunata is Sicilian for lemon ice. In the Brooklynese of the old neighborhood, the translation was pronounced as one word. "Lemonice" was not only the favorite flavor, but it became the generic term for all ices. A sign in Circo's window read:

LEMON ICE FLAVORS
Lemon
Strawberry
Cherry

Back in the apartment, the quantity of each lemon ice flavor to be purchased was decided. I was given the money and sent on the two-and-a-half-block walk to Circo's.

In the early 1950s, the streets of Bushwick had always been safe for anyone at any hour. In that sweltering summer of 1957, however, things began to change for a nine-year-old boy out alone. Street gangs had begun to hang out around the neighborhood. Most of these were pretty harmless S.A.C.s, but some of the larger gangs did have sizable economic interests from the selling of truckloads of stolen cigarettes and illegal fireworks. The members of the Ellery Bops were known for their fair play and courage in defending their turf as well as for sticking up for noncombatants against more barbaric gangs like the Halsey Bops.

Smaller gangs were affiliated with the larger ones. Gang members ranged in age from about 13 to 20. In addition, the larger gangs all had younger auxiliaries, for which recruitment began at nine. The Ellery Tots and the Halsey Tots, for instance, took up the turf wars where their older brothers and cousins left off.

The Tots, in imitation of the Bops, would accost us kids as we walked by, giving the command "Sound your clique." The proper response was to sing out the name of your gang proudly, military fashion: "Ellery Tots to the Heart" (the phrase indicating great commitment), or "Halsey Tots L.A.M.F." L.A.M.F. stood for "like a muddafucka," which is to say, fierce, violent, out of control.

Nongangsters also had a response, "I'm cool, man." To some gangs, and especially to the younger members, not having a clique meant that you were fair game with no chance of reprisal. The child gangsters played this call-and-answer game constantly, talking the talk, but when it came down to it, walking the walk showed them to be the baby punks they were. Still, my observations from some 40 years distance don't quite convey the very real threat we felt at the time.

The adults had no idea of these goings-on. If they had, they obviously would not have sent me out into a night filled with such danger. I was never involved with a gang, but we shared the same streets, and the cardinal rule for surviving those streets was clear:

keep your mouth shut. When asked, we told the adults that L.A.M.F., tagged all over the neighborhood, meant, "Let's All Make Friends."

I SET OUT FOR CIRCO'S and planned my route. I cut through the gas station onto the first half block of Hart Street. It was cool, dominated by the old two-lane bowling alley. The regulars who bowled there were good guys, though a bit dim-witted. They believed that automatic pinspotters were a fad, soon to die out.

The next block, between Central and Wilson, was gang turf. I took a one-block detour to Suydam, walking past the church and the school. I turned back onto Hart from Wilson for the last block to Knickerbocker Avenue. This block had older Sicilians sitting in front of their houses in folding chairs, trying to catch a breeze. They smiled at me, and we exchanged *buona seras* as I passed.

The sidewalk in front of Circo's was crowded with sweaty, exasperated people, waiting to buy lemon ice through the window. Mr. Circo did not rush. He meticulously packed each order in pleated paper cups for one or two scoops, or round white cardboard containers for pints and quarts. He worked slowly and carefully, never slopping any ice on the outside of the cup. I joined the exasperated. Finally, my order was packed, placed in a white paper bag and ready to go.

There is an art to carrying home lemon ice in a heat wave. One cannot cradle it close to the body, as it will melt. You must carry it by the fold of the paper bag, out in front of you. Two fingers of your other hand may be placed underneath, for support.

I walked very fast, but could never run, which might have caused the bag to break. All in all, not a very tough looking gait with which to meet the dangers ahead. And because time was of the essence, my walk home did not permit any detours.

The old folks on Hart now greeted me as if I were a long-lost 251 grandson. At the time, I thought they imagined that I was bringing the lemon ice to them.

Crossing Wilson Avenue, I steeled myself for the interrogation and what might follow. What if the Tots beat me up? Or, worse, what if they stole the lemon ice?

I saw them. They saw me seeing them. In a moment they had peeled themselves off their stoop and had surrounded me. There I stood, motionless, with the white paper bag out in front of me. The ices began to drip.

"Sound your clique." The drops hitting the pavement magnified the pounding of my heart. All that came out of my mouth was "Lemonice." "Ya goofin' on us or wat?" they came back and began to square off. Suddenly, an older, teenage voice boomed out from the top of the stoop. "Hey! Let 'im alone. Can't yas see he's bringin' lemonice home ta his muddah?"

I got the lemon ice home in time. We ate it out of tall water glasses, scooping it with spoons and long, hard biscotti. We laughed as one by one we all ate it too quickly, giving us that strange, sharp, momentary headache. The lemon ice did indeed provide us with enough relief from the heat to get to sleep.

THE GANG BOYS ON HART STREET never bothered me again. Whenever I walked down their street, "lemonice" was all I needed to say to gain safe passage. I used it all the time, whether I was going to Circo's or not. Lemon ice to the heart. Lemon ice L.A.M.F.

L i m u n a t a

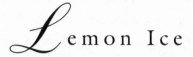emon Ice

THE LEMON ICE WE ATE IN BRUCULINU was different in texture from the Sicilian kind. In Sicily, it was more like a grated-ice drink than a solid, frozen dessert. In an effort to turn Mr. Circo's product into the real thing, we ate it out of tall glasses, hoping that the heat of our hands would turn it into the granular delight of my grandparents' memory.

This lemon ice recipe, as well as the other ice recipes in this chapter, may be made in a smooth, solid style by freezing it in an ice cream machine. But to enjoy true Sicilian-style ices, follow my adaptation of the ancient freezing method. Eat the ice with a spoon or scoop it with Orange Biscotti (page 259).

For 6 servings

1¼ cups spring water
1 cup sugar
4-5 lemons, depending on their size and sweetness

Heat the water and the sugar together in a small saucepan, stirring, until the sugar dissolves and the liquid turns clear. Remove from the heat and cool to room temperature.

Juice the lemons and pour the juice into a medium bowl. Add the sugar water slowly to the lemon juice until the desired sweetness is reached. Chill thoroughly, uncovered, in the refrigerator. Pour the chilled mixture into an 11-by-7-inch metal baking pan and put it in the freezer for 30 minutes.

Scrape down the sides and bottom of the pan with a metal spatula. Chop the already frozen lumps into slivers. Return the pan to the freezer. Repeat this process every 30 minutes, until the ice becomes slushy with slivers of ice in it. Depending on the temperature of the freezer, the process can take up to 2½ hours.

The lemon ice can be held in this state for a few hours by transferring it from the freezer to the refrigerator.

Granita 'i Fraguli

*S*trawberry Ice

FRESH STRAWBERRY is truly the flavor of summer. The addition of a very small amount of sweet vermouth to this ice heightens the sweet-tart flavor. If you are fortunate enough to have wild strawberries available to you, use them, adding an extra third of a pound of whole berries.

For 6 servings

¾ cup spring water
1 cup sugar
¾ pound strawberries
1 tablespoon sweet vermouth

Heat the water and the sugar together in a small saucepan, stirring, until the sugar dissolves and the liquid turns clear. Remove from the heat.

Wash and hull the strawberries. Puree them in a food mill fitted with the medium-holed disk into a medium bowl. Scrape the pulp from the bottom of the food mill into the bowl. Add the sugar water slowly to the strawberry puree until the desired sweetness is reached. Stir in the vermouth and chill thoroughly, uncovered, in the refrigerator. Pour the chilled mixture into an 11-by-7-inch metal baking pan. Follow the method for freezing described in the recipe for Lemon Ice (page 253).

Granita 'i Girasi

C herry Ice

A NOTHER FRESH SUMMER FRUIT USED to create a popular ice flavor in Bruculinu was cherry. While eating it, we children compared the depth of color on our bright red tongues.

For 6 servings

¾   cup spring water
1   cup sugar
1¼   pounds sweet cherries

Heat the water and the sugar together in a small saucepan, stirring, until the sugar dissolves and the liquid turns clear. Remove from the heat and cool to room temperature.

Wash and pit the cherries. Puree them in a food mill fitted with the medium-holed disk over a medium bowl. This process also serves to remove a great amount of the skin. Scrape the pulp from the bottom of the food mill into the bowl. Add the sugar water slowly to the cherry puree until the desired sweetness is reached. Chill thoroughly, uncovered, in the refrigerator. Pour the chilled mixture into an 11-by-7-inch metal baking pan. Follow the method for freezing described in the recipe for Lemon Ice (page 253).

Gelatu 'i Cannedda

$\mathcal{C}$innamon Gelato

ONE OF THE OLDER SICILIAN GELATO FLAVORS is cinnamon. Some argue that it is the first—the flavor that began the love affair between Sicilians and their frozen confection.

The centuries-old style of gelato used in this recipe differs greatly from the modern form found today in America. Although it contains no milk, cream or egg yolks, egg whites provide it with velvety smoothness. Because this dessert contains raw egg whites, use only the freshest eggs from small producers. Cinnamon oil, rather than ground cinnamon, is used as the flavoring. This product is available at pharmacies and in some health food stores, as is the inexpensive glass dropper used to measure it. Following tradition, cinnamon gelato is colored red, visually accentuating its spicy flavor.

For 8 servings

     4 cups spring water
    1½ cups sugar
    20 drops red food coloring
     8 drops cinnamon oil
     1 large egg white

Heat 2 cups of the water and the sugar together in a medium saucepan, stirring, until the sugar dissolves and the liquid turns clear. Remove from the heat and mix in the food coloring and the remaining 2 cups water. Let cool.

Using a glass dropper, put the cinnamon oil in a medium stainless steel or glass bowl. Measure the oil with great care (9 drops are too much). Mix the sugar water into the oil.

In another bowl, whisk the egg white until frothy. Slowly whisk in the liquid. Process the gelato in an ice cream machine, following the manufacturer's instructions. Line a rectangular mold or small loaf pan with plastic wrap. When the gelato is done, spoon it into the mold or pan. Cover well and freeze for at least 3 hours, or until set. About 10 minutes before serving, remove the gelato from the freezer to unmold it. Cut it into slices and transfer the slices to plates.

Viscotta 'i Aranci

Orange Biscotti

THESE SIMPLY PREPARED BISCOTTI are an excellent accompaniment to fruit ices. They are also good with coffee at breakfast or for dunking in milk.

For about 2½ dozen biscotti

2   cups bleached all-purpose flour, plus more
      for dusting the pan
2   teaspoons baking powder
      Pinch of salt
8   tablespoons (1 stick) unsalted butter, plus more
      for greasing the pan
1   cup sugar
4   large eggs
⅓   cup orange liqueur, such as Curaçao,
      Grand Marnier or Cointreau
      Zest of 2 oranges, finely chopped

Preheat the oven to 350°F, with a rack positioned in the upper third. Grease and flour a 13-by-9-inch baking pan.

Sift together the 2 cups flour, baking powder and salt into a small bowl. In a separate large bowl, cream together the butter and sugar with an electric mixer. Beat in the eggs, one at a time. Beat in the orange liqueur and the zest. Stir in the dry ingredients. Immediately turn the batter into the pan. The batter will be heavy; smooth it with a rubber spatula to spread it evenly.

259

Bake for about 20 minutes, or until the cake is golden brown and a toothpick inserted near the center comes out clean. Remove from the oven. Do not turn off the oven.

Leaving the cake in the pan, cut it on the diagonal into ¾-inch-wide strips. Cut the longer strips in half. Let cool for a few minutes. Using a metal spatula or a knife, coax the strips out of the pan and place them on a wire rack. Return to the oven and bake until toasted golden brown on both sides, about 14 minutes.

Cool the biscotti on the rack. When they are cool, stack them crisscrossed on a small serving plate, three or four across. Store them uncovered.

XV.

*G*oin' Up Da Country

EGINNING IN THE MID-1950s, many families from the
old neighborhood bought summer houses in the rural
regions of Long Island, New Jersey, Connecticut or
upstate New York. Children and their grandparents
spent the entire summer away, joined by parents on weekends and
for their usual two weeks' vacation. We called this jubilant event of
summer migration "goin' up da country."

Finding the money for a country place was not easy, but somehow people managed. Most of our parents had spent their childhood
summers on the streets of Bruculinu, and they wanted something
better for us: a chance to be out in the clean, fresh country air.

The landscape of northeastern America was, of course, quite
different from that of the Sicilian mountains. But the country pace,
rustic settings and the lushness of summer reminded our grandparents of the old country. They were more at home here than in the
great city and smiled all season.

ONE SPRING EVENING IN 1953, Uncle John came over for a visit.
He happily announced that he and Aunt Mary had just pur-
chased land in Putnam County, New York, near the lake. Putnam
Lake was one of several man-made lakes established in the 1930s in

261

the part of New York State which borders Fairfield County, Connecticut. Uncle John went on to say that the property included a small bungalow and the foundation for a house. He dreamed of someday building a great sprawling summer house for the whole family.

The first time I remember "goin' up da country" was in 1954, the summer before my first year of grade school. My mother, Aunt Mae and Aunt Jo arranged their vacations for the last week of July and the first week of August. Along with my grandparents and me, our entire household made the journey together, driven by Uncle Bob in his black Nash.

In those days there were no highway connections directly from Brooklyn to Putnam Lake. Much of the route followed long stretches of empty, gravel-covered roads. Uncle Bob drove slowly because my grandmother was prone to car sickness. And he didn't want to damage the car's well-waxed finish or pit his windshield with flying gravel.

The country roads were not posted as to direction or destination. We navigated by landmarks rather than signage, as in a treasure hunt. It was easy here for city-folk Brooklynites to get lost, and we did. As we snailed our way in the overcrowded car, the short 70-mile trip turned into an ordeal of well over three hours.

At long last, Aunt Mae sighted Uncle John stooped over his vegetable garden. We had arrived. Aunt Mary and the rest appeared to greet us. They hadn't seen us for several weeks, but behaved as if our reunion followed a lifetime's separation.

Uncle John had described the country place well, but seeing it for ourselves gave us new perspective. The small log cabin was more like a shack than a bungalow. It was set in a clearing at a perilous tilt. A few yards away was the cinder block foundation. The front end was a story high, but the rear was mostly below grade, up from the ground only a few inches.

Near the rear of the structure was a hand pump, the only source of water. At a short distance stood an outhouse, complete with a crescent-moon cutout in the front door. Nothing in my short years had prepared me for this. I was as lost in this bucolic setting as a farmboy would have been on the streets of my world. My feet seemed as overwhelmed as I and refused to budge.

Three of my cousins, Felicia, Frank and Jo Ann, emerged from the shack. They kissed the newly arrived adults hello. They all wore bathing suits, their bodies nut brown from a month in the sun. Each carried a large, black inner tube slung across their shoulders. They were on their way to the lake, and Frank ordered me to change into my suit and join them. "Dis-a why we come-a," said Uncle John, "*pi picciriddi*—fa da kids-a."

I returned awkwardly, my body ghostly white. Frank presented me with an inner tube of my own. It was as if I'd been given the orders of some strange knighthood. I, too, placed the tube across my shoulders, and the four of us started down the road to the lake. I tried to negotiate the unfamiliar setting. I was amazed at my cousins' nonchalance at the incessant buzzing and swarming of insects and the tiny gnats that flew up our noses.

Frank, a relentless joker, painted a fantastic picture of the great peril to be found in the woods. "Dat der is da poison sumac," he said. "Don't neva touch it. My gran-pa, ya uncle John, tol' me dat's how he lost all his hair." Felicia and Jo Ann nodded in solemn agreement. He pointed out other terrors, both real and invented. "Der," he said, "dat's poison ivy, an' dat-der's da cure, milkweed, growin' right next ta it." He nodded at all manner of bushes with red berries that were sure to hold instant death if swallowed. Maintaining a safe distance, he showed me real beehives and wasp nests. When we passed an old, crumbling house, Frank ordered us to walk by quickly. "Dat's da haunted house," he whispered, but his inadvertent smile let me in on the joke.

263

At the lake, there was a clearing, euphemistically called Johnson Beach. It was one of 12 clearings that had been covered with sand when the lake was established in the 1930s, but now the beach was a kind of alluvial mixture of sand, mud and pebbles. Even so, for a pack of city kids, the lake was the most beautiful natural thing we'd ever seen.

Before we went in the water, Frank solemnly laid out the safety rules. Under no circumstances could any of us go into the lake without the presence of an adult relative or close family friend. This was not a problem, as the "beach" was littered with people to whom at least one of us had some entangled familial relationship.

The adults made a line with their bodies in the water. No child in an inner tube or life jacket was permitted beyond this point. "Out der" was the deep water and danger. All were determined that there would never be a tragic accident on their watch. As we splashed about, this army of lifeguards kept a careful eye for tired children or those whose lips had turned blue, decreeing who could stay in the water and who had to get out. This whole section of Putnam Lake might have been called "Bruculinu North."

A large wooden raft was anchored several hundred feet out in the lake. This was the domain of the older boys and girls. Children from about the age of nine, who had acquired enough swimming expertise to reach it, were permitted access. To be able to go to the raft expressed a childhood rite of passage. It was an important event, the initiates admired by all.

The first child of our family to achieve this goal was Felicia's brother, John. He was four years older than we, deadly handsome and very cool. If Frank was the lieutenant, John was the captain. He spent most of the time with his buddies at the raft, and we watched them in awe. Years later this raft would become an important meeting place of our adolescence, but for now none of us even suspected that future.

DINNER, ESPECIALLY ON WEEKENDS when the party exceeded 20, was a remarkable event. A collection of folding metal tables snaked their way under a spreading crab apple tree next to the shack. It was laid with oilcloths and set with an odd collection of plates and flatware, castoffs of the whole family.

Meals were wholesome and hearty, our appetites heightened by the fresh air and activity. Great platters of pasta were generously portioned and served. Marinated chicken, cooked over an open fire, might follow as a second course. There was always a big bowl of mixed green salad and the most delicious green bean and potato salad I have ever eaten. It was redolent of vinegar, perfumed with raw onion and olive oil. For dessert, there was applesauce, which Aunt Mary had made from the crab apples in the tree above our heads.

As evening fell, most of the family walked down to the lake to watch the sunset. In Bruculinu we rarely saw the horizon, let alone this incredible light show of pink and purple. As the fireball fell quickly into the lake, we stood transfixed until the last rays left the sky.

The walk home in the pitch-black night was guided by flashlights and aided by lightning bugs. Sometimes a flashlight's beam would move in a frenzy, illuminating trees or disappearing in the night sky, signifying that someone in our party was dancing to avoid the bite of a mosquito, in this country the size of a hummingbird.

We returned to find the shack transformed into a kind of dormitory. The floor of all three rooms had been covered with an assortment of daybeds and mattresses. By now, the older adults had repaired up the road to Frank and Jo Ann's other grandparents' house, but often there were more than a dozen children and adults bedding down in the shack.

I tried to sleep, but the night sounds were unfamiliar. Instead of the rumble of passing el trains, there was the rhythm of crickets and the hooting of owls. My body remembered the rippling lake, and

I felt its gentle rocking. Soon, imagining the whole tilted shack afloat like a cartoon houseboat, I drifted into sleep.

BY 1956, the house was built: not the country palace envisioned by Uncle John, but a more *ad hoc* structure, cobbled together by his son Donald and his son-in-law, Steve Toto. In a two-week frenzy, they turned the foundation itself into a house. The result was a long, narrow building that burrowed into the ground. From the front, it looked like a movie set. From the side, it resembled a bomb shelter.

The men laid a tar-paper roof on the foundation and partitioned the interior into rooms. There was a bedroom for Uncle John and Aunt Mary, and each of the families of their three children. There was also a small bathroom and the blessed arrival of indoor plumbing.

A large central room served as kitchen, dining room and living room. Its walls were covered with giant turquoise and white harlequin print wallpaper. Much of the space was filled with a table and benches with 20 places. It was so large that it had to be built in the room and was unable to fit through the door.

When it rained, children and adults crowded into the room to talk or play cards. The din was immeasurable. It became so loud, thick and stuffy that the Harlequin's pantaloons seemed to dance right off the wallpaper. Even so, it was still a great relief from the dog days of inner-city Brooklyn.

When the rain stopped, we disembarked from the low, narrow house, as if from Noah's Ark. The wonderful smell and renewed lushness filled our senses. Our ears, still ringing from the noise inside the house, soon healed in the after-rain stillness. The sun's rays once more found their way to earth, as rainbows arched the sky and birds resumed their song. Soon it was summer again, calling us to the lake and its new waters.

CHAPTER XV.

B Y THE LATE SIXTIES, the family had outgrown the funny little
house at Putnam Lake. By this time, we all had moved from
Bruculinu into suburbs near and far. We had grown into young
adults with lives of our own. The lake community itself, now joined
to the city by superhighways, was no longer rural but itself a distant
suburb of the great metropolitan sprawl.

In 1970, my cousin Felicia married. The newlyweds bought
Uncle John's property, and within several years built a house there
that far surpasses his original dream. The first time I saw it, I recognized nothing of the old country place or the landscape. While taking me on a tour of the new house, Felicia led me through a small
door under the stairs that led down to the basement. There, to my
astonishment, as if in some archaeological catacomb, was the old
country house. It was preserved intact, down to the now-faded
wallpaper.

I remembered myself at different ages in every corner. I could almost hear the sounds of voices now silent, and the feel of summers
now gone. We climbed the stairs again to the present, and the door
closed behind us. Smiling at the memory of then, we ran down to the
lake for a swim, as if it were for the first time.

Pipi suttu Cinniri

$\mathscr{P}$eppers Roasted in Ashes

WHENEVER PEPPERS roasted on top of the gas stove or in the broiler appeared at our table, the immigrant Sicilians reminisced about the flavor of peppers roasted in ashes in rural Sicily. In inner-city Brooklyn, there was, of course, no place to make a wood fire, so that flavor could only remain a memory for them and a mystery for us. In the country, however, we made peppers cooked in ashes to our hearts' content.

For an antipasto, this simple dish is served with olives and freshly baked Italian bread.

For each serving

2 whole Italian peppers without deep dents,
   about 5 inches long, with stems attached
   Sea salt
   Pinch of dried oregano
   Extra-virgin olive oil

Build a fire of small pieces of firewood or dried twigs in a grill or fireplace. (Charcoal briquettes are not suitable because of their strong flavor.) When the fire has burned down to glowing embers, bury the peppers in the hot ashes. Roast until the skin is charred.

Remove the peppers from the ashes. When they are cool enough to handle, peel away the burned skin. Leave the peppers whole, with the stems attached. Arrange the peppers on a serving platter, season with salt and oregano and drizzle with olive oil. Serve at room temperature. The peppers are best eaten with the fingers, whole and in one bite, holding a slice of bread underneath to catch the juices.

Italieddi e Fasoleddi

Pasta with Italian Green Beans

THE SUNNY TASTE OF THIS RUSTIC SICILIAN DISH is sure to bring fresh country air into the most urban kitchen. The green beans used here are broad and flat. One variety, Romano, is often marketed as Italian green beans. A common feature of these beans is that they do not have strings. Sicilians cook their beans until quite tender and sweet.

Ditali, or ditalini, pasta is one of the more used shapes in Sicilian peasant dishes. It is a very small tube, about ⅜₆ inch long. Since it is originally from the Italian peninsula, Sicilians call this pasta *Italieddi*, little Italians.

For 6 servings

1   6-inch stem wild fennel or bulb fennel
6   broccoli leaves
8   radish greens
8   beet leaves
5   tablespoons extra-virgin olive oil
    Sea salt
1   35-ounce can peeled Italian plum tomatoes
1   medium onion, finely chopped
1   tablespoon tomato paste dissolved in ⅓ cup water
    Black pepper
2   teaspoons sugar
4   sprigs Italian parsley

1½   pounds flat green beans
 1   pound ditali, or ditalini, pasta
⅓   cup chopped fresh basil
5-6 ounces ricotta salata in a chunk
     Crushed red pepper

Clean the fennel, broccoli leaves, and radish and beet greens and tie them up in cheesecloth. Fill a large pot with water, add the packet of greens, 2 tablespoons of the oil and 2 tablespoons salt and put it on the stove to boil.

Place a food mill fitted with the smallest-holed disk (¹⁄₁₆ inch) over a bowl. Mill the tomatoes in order to remove the seeds, which can make the sauce bitter. Scrape the pulp from the bottom of the mill into the bowl.

Put the onion and the remaining 3 tablespoons oil in a heavy medium pot over medium heat and sauté the onion until it turns translucent, about 5 minutes. Stir in the dissolved tomato paste. Let it thicken for about 1 minute and add the tomatoes. Season with salt and pepper and the sugar and parsley. Reduce the heat to low and simmer the sauce, uncovered, stirring from time to time, for 40 minutes. Do not let it boil.

Meanwhile, cut the green beans on a slight diagonal into 1-inch-long pieces. When the pasta water comes to a boil, drop in the beans, cover and boil for 7 minutes. Add the pasta and cook it, uncovered, until al dente. Discard the cheesecloth packet. Drain the pasta and beans until slightly soupy. Transfer to a warmed serving bowl and toss with the tomato sauce and basil.

Serve with ricotta salata coarsely grated at the table and crushed red pepper to taste.

Gaddina all'Apertu

Sicilian-Style Barbecued Chicken

THE BASE OF THE MARINADE for this chicken is orange juice. The acid in the juice acts as a tenderizing agent, while its flavor adds tangy counterpoint to the bitter and sweet herbs and spices. The cognac adds a slight sweetness, and its alcohol helps to bring all of these flavors together. The olive oil also helps. The result is an explosion of flavor, each bite revealing something new.

For 6 servings

12 pieces of chicken, any combination of breasts, thighs and drumsticks
    Sea salt
    Black pepper
6   scallions
2   cups freshly squeezed orange juice
¼   cup cognac
¼   cup extra-virgin olive oil
3   garlic cloves, pushed through a garlic press
¼   cup chopped Italian parsley
4   sprigs marjoram, chopped
3   sprigs rosemary, leaves chopped
⅛   teaspoon freshly grated nutmeg

Wash the chicken pieces and pat dry. Place on a platter in a single layer and season with salt and pepper on both sides. Clean the scallions and thinly slice the white parts. Tie the remaining green parts into a brush to be used later to baste the chicken. Layer the chicken pieces with the sliced scallions in a large bowl. Whisk together the remaining ingredients in a medium bowl and pour the mixture over the chicken. Cover with plastic wrap, refrigerate and marinate for 6 hours or overnight.

To cook the chicken in a 26-inch covered kettle grill, light 60 charcoal briquettes and let them burn down. When they begin to turn white, arrange them in 2 narrow strips, placing a pan in the center to catch the drippings. Put the grill rack in place.

Place the chicken pieces directly over the coals. Brown each piece on both sides, then move it to the center of the grill over the drip pan. When all the pieces are in place, baste, dipping the scallion brush into the marinade, and cover. Grill for 55 to 60 minutes, pouring the remaining marinade over the chicken after the first 35 minutes. (If you are using a different type of grill, follow the manufacturer's instructions. Excessive charring will destroy the delicate flavor of the chicken.)

When the chicken is cooked, transfer it to a warmed platter and serve. By this time, the pan drippings will be mostly grease and unusable as a sauce, but the chicken will have enough flavor without it.

Nsalata 'i Fasoleddi Virdi e Patati

*G*reen Bean and Potato Salad

WE USUALLY SERVED THIS SALAD WARM, but you may also chill it slightly and enrich it with the addition of tomato wedges and sliced hard-boiled eggs. Taste and adjust the seasonings.

For 6 servings

3 pounds small red new potatoes, about the size
  of small limes
  Sea salt
2 pounds flat Italian or round Blue Lake green beans
1 large red onion
½ cup red wine vinegar
⅓ cup extra-virgin olive oil
  Black pepper

Scrub the potatoes and put them in a pot with lightly salted cold water to cover over medium-high heat. Bring to a boil, and cook until the potatoes offer little resistance when pierced with a fork, 20 to 30 minutes.

Meanwhile, clean and snap off the ends of the green beans. Place a steamer on the stove. When the water comes to a boil, put the beans in the steamer basket. Steam the beans until tender, 8 to 10 minutes, depending on their thickness.

Halve the onion, thinly slice it, separate the pieces and put them in a large serving bowl. Mix in the vinegar. When the green beans are cooked, drain and put them in the bowl. Season with salt and toss.

When the potatoes are cooked, run cold water into the pot to stop the cooking process and drain them thoroughly. When cool enough to handle, slip them out of their jackets.

Put the potatoes in the serving bowl, season with salt and toss. Add the olive oil and toss again. Finish with a few grindings of black pepper. Serve warm.

XVI.

${\mathcal{M}}$arilu Preziosa

THE FIRST TIME I REMEMBER SEEING HER was in 1957.
She was sent from the other fourth grade class to mon-
itor ours. I learned her name, carried on a current of
whispers: Marilu Preziosa.

She stood poised in front of the class, trying to be serious despite
the antics of giggling girlfriends. She was dressed in a red sweater,
plaid skirt, little white anklets and saddle shoes. The early spring sunlight filled the room, transforming shafts of chalk dust into star-
dust, playing off her shining dark eyes and jet-black pigtails. I am still
swooned by the memory of the first time those dark eyes turned in
my direction, still blushed and dry-mouthed and prickly skinned
from my first innocent nine-year-old crush.

Six years flew by, bringing the early sixties and adolescence. The
whole world was experiencing great social change, but not, for the
moment, our corner of Brooklyn. Things remained pretty much
the same for my crowd as they had been for teenagers through the
forties and fifties. We attended boys' or girls' Catholic prep schools,
danced Friday nights at the church's community center and went
to Mass on Sunday. We were "da good kids."

For Friday-night dances, the community center was pathetically
decorated with a few old balloons and wilted crepe-paper stream-

ers. The room was lit as for brain surgery so that no hanky-panky would escape the watchful eyes of Father Rizzi and our dour-faced adult chaperones. A dress code, strictly enforced, required girls to wear skirts, and boys, jackets and ties. Even so, our raging adolescent hormones had no trouble finding this setting exciting and romantic.

I encountered Marilu again at these socials. Actually, it was she who brought me there. She had grown into a uniquely beautiful young woman. Tall, with long legs and a graceful figure, Marilu had curly black hair, no longer in pigtails, which framed her fair face. Those dark eyes had grown mysterious with a certain sadness behind them, but when she smiled, they took on a silly pixilated expression.

The first dance of our sophomore year was a bit awkward. That most of us had known one another since the first grade didn't much ease the situation. The girls, at one side of the hall, waited hopefully to be asked to dance while the boys milled around the other, as nervous as hell. I carefully positioned any boy I was talking to so I could get the best glimpse of Marilu. No matter how nonchalant I was, Marilu was always staring back, smiling and sighing, giving me looks of encouragement.

Finally, with all the courage I could muster, I walked across the vast, brightly lit dance floor in her direction. I felt as if everyone's eyes were upon me. Stopping in front of her, gulping in air, I stammered, "Um . . . um . . . would you . . . um . . . "

"Yes," she said softly, "I'd love to dance with you."

We didn't exactly glide across the dance floor, but I did manage to avoid stepping on her feet. Perhaps "Coney Island Baby," by the Excellents, was a bit too slow for the shyness of our first time out, but we managed with small talk and smiles.

By November, almost everyone had paired off. Our dance movements to fast songs like "Twist and Shout," by the Isley Brothers, 277 were not lost to the eyebrows of Father Rizzi and the chaperones. Songs like the slow, dreamy perennial by the Harptones, "A Sunday Kind of Love," brought this propriety patrol to action.

Marilu and I danced very closely, silently arranging the future in each other's eyes. Sometimes a forbidden thought passed between us, hands tightening in hands, and around backs and shoulders. We gently rocked, barely moving to the music, until a sharp tap on the shoulder from Father Rizzi and a resounding "Make room for the Holy Ghost!" brought us back to earth. Soon we were soaring away again, as in love as two 15-year-olds have ever been.

The Wednesday evening before Thanksgiving, a dance was to be held at my high school, well known as the social event of the season. For many of us, it would be the first time on a proper date, outside the neighborhood. My friends and I carefully planned and replanned every aspect of the evening, from seating arrangements to after-dance strawberry cheesecake at Junior's Deli. Endless debates on which type of corsage to give were finally settled by our mothers.

Marilu said I needed to ask her father's permission to take her, an extremely old-fashioned request, even for our neighborhood. I dreaded the ordeal, but resigned myself. Sunday morning, she said, would be an opportune time: "He's usually in a good mood then."

Eddie Preziosa was a short, dark fireplug of a guy, always in need of a shave. He never smiled. He and his mother, a stern-looking old woman in black, complete with warts, owned and operated a flower shop. They were like characters out of a fairy tale, the old witch and her ogre son with the beautiful flower garden, imprisoning the lovely young princess. I have always assumed that the bulk of their business must have come from funerals, the flowers far too tainted with misery for happier occasions.

By contrast, Marilu's mother, Emily, was an attractive "American" woman. Eddie had married her during the war, while stationed

in the faraway country of Indiana. Everyone around the neighborhood referred to her as "Eddie's war bride." Whatever sparks might
have flown between Eddie and Emily "over there," here in Bruculinu, living two floors above the shop, with the matriarch below,
they didn't stand a chance. Emily bore her mistake with dignity.

After Mass, I walked to the shop and climbed the two flights of
stairs to their apartment. My knees were feeling a bit wobbly. "How
bad could he be?" I asked myself. "It's just a dance. I'm not asking
the florist's permission to deflower his daughter."

Mrs. Preziosa answered my knock. Although distracted and
somewhat bedraggled, she tried to be welcoming. I could tell by
her demeanor that Mr. Preziosa was not in a good mood. Knowing
why I had come, she pointed me in Mr. Preziosa's direction, as if
sending me to my doom.

I found him in the long narrow living room sitting in a flower-
print armchair, buried in the Sunday paper. He wore black trousers
and an athletic undershirt that showed off his hirsute arms and torso
to unbecoming advantage. His breath snarled heavily through his
nose, like a bull ready to charge. Marilu was also in the room, terrified that her father might sense there was something between us.

Mr. Preziosa gave no greeting, only an abrupt "Wadda *you*
want?" Before I finished asking, he snarled his one-word, negative
reply, returning to his paper. His rudeness was so stunning that
it glued me to the spot. I felt the heat rise in my cheeks, the blood
pound in my stomach and a knot form in the back of my throat.
It took all the strength I had to walk away. I was halfway down
the stairs when my disappointment and anger exploded. As I burst
onto the street, the cold autumn air hit my face, calming me
down.

The next Friday, Marilu didn't come to the church dance. Her
good friend Louise gave me the scoop. It seems that Mr. Preziosa
had been thorny all week. Marilu was getting the third degree morn-

ing and night. "Wat's really goin' on between you and dat guy?" was the grand inquisitor's question.

"I don't want ya ta even talk ta dat creep no more" was his final judgment. The message Louise brought me from Marilu was to meet her at Mass on Sunday morning.

We looked like spies in a dark corner of the side chapel. While our heads stayed locked on the service, our hands discreetly met under a mountain of overcoats and mufflers, the thrill almost too much to bear. After Mass, we managed a quick conversation, shielded from view by a circle of friends. Leaving, Marilu pressed a note into my hand:

> *Dear Vin,*
>
> *I'm sitting here thinking of the wonders of God and how things work out without our pitiful human finagling. Who would have thought that the tall boy with the thick glasses would end up with the skinny girl in pigtails and saddle shoes? Now I couldn't get you out of my heart if I tried.*
>
> *Whenever you need me, just close your eyes and think of me and I am there. It works because I do it often myself, and there you are, looming up beside me like a giant tree, and I am safe. Then I get all warm and happy inside, darling, and I start to sing or do something equally crazy.*
>
> *Now I have to study my Religion notes for Monday's test. Good luck in your midterms.*
>
> *Love,*
> *Lu*

We were "da good kids."

CHAPTER XVI.

MR. PREZIOSA LET MARILU OUT OF HIS SIGHT only to go to
school. He used a subway schedule to calculate her exact arrival time. He was obsessed for reasons that I am sure were beyond
his conscious understanding.

After a couple of months, responding to the supplications of his
wife, he relented somewhat. "Aw rite," he pronounced. "She can
go bowlin' on Sattadays, but dat's it."

The new bowling alley, Ridgewood Lanes, boasted 24 alleys
and automatic pinspotters. On weeknights, it was dominated by
teams of beefy men and plump women in bowling shirts. On Saturday afternoons, it was overrun by a gathering of teens. I suppose
some went to bowl, but everyone I knew came to be social.

Between frames, as I sat on an orange Naugahide banquette,
my arm around Marilu's shoulder, the sound of cracking pins turned
into a desert island surf, the fluorescents into moonlight. We savored
every second of these precious, stolen moments spent together, sharing our lives, making plans for the future, deepening the forbidden
connection between us.

By the spring of 1964, the world's social innovations were beginning to find their way to our neighborhood. They benignly attached themselves to the craze surrounding those four lads from
Liverpool. Hair and clothing styles formed opposing camps in the
neighborhood, but the fact that my generation was emerging dif-
ferently from preceding generations could no longer be denied.
The Beatles were the idols of this newly made youth culture, Beatles'
songs its liturgy. Our lives were changed.

Through that summer, Marilu and I barely saw each other. She
was vacationing with her family in Indiana, I at my Uncle John's in
Putnam Lake. Many letters flew across the country, mailed and received by our confidant, Louise. They grew more and more serious, more and more dreamy, more and more defiant.

The new school year brought an endless wave of sweet-16 par-   281 ties. Little brightly printed invitations arrived in the mail requesting my presence at gatherings as far away as the finished basements of Ozone Park, Queens. Some invitations came from girls I didn't even know, but their postscripts cleared up the mystery: "Marilu will be there."

I'd arrive at the appointed hour, a gaily wrapped bottle of Ambush cologne in hand. The young hostess, thanking me for the birthday gift, would place it on a side table, next to all the other gaily wrapped bottles of Ambush.

Marilu usually arrived early, "to help set up," so there'd be no chance of my running into Eddie, who still chauffeured her everywhere. I would sometimes find her in quiet tears, the injustice of all this sneaking about too much to bear. But the Beatles' songs, and the dancing and the sheer bliss of our youth, soon changed her mood.

Depending on the diligence of parental supervision, there might be a lot of kissing at these parties. Once, while Marilu and I were locked in a dancing embrace, a buddy of mine, stumbling toward us in the darkness, announced, "Cool it! He's early." I found a basement storage closet and hid just as Eddie the Ogre came down the stairs to fetch his daughter.

Through the slightly opened closet door, I could see his simian form, silhouetted by the light streaming down from the house above. I imagined smoke curling out of his nostrils. I could sense that he knew something was up, for in a room full of slow-dancing teenagers, there was Marilu standing in a corner, alone, eating peanuts.

In the dankness of the dark closet, I realized he was winning. By forcing us to sneak and hide, he was turning our pure first love into something else, something prurient and devious, something like him.

MARILU AND I agreed it would be best if we stopped seeing each other for a while. I forced myself to go on dates with different girls, sometimes almost believing that my feelings toward them were deeper than they actually were.

Even if we had wanted to, Marilu and I couldn't meet. Her father accompanied her even to Mass. But we still passed letters through Louise. They were filled with longing and hope.

A watery, adolescent melancholy descended upon me. I wrote tragic, romantic poetry in code and carried a slim volume of lyric verses by Ernest Dowson everywhere. *I have been faithful to thee, Cynara, in my fashion.*

In the summer of 1965, the New York World's Fair became a popular hangout for teenagers. It was an easy place for boys and girls to meet, plus it had the boon of parental approval. Its motto, "Peace Through Understanding," seemed to mirror the altruism of our youth.

One Saturday, I was waiting for my friends at the fountain around the Unisphere, the fair's symbol. I watched the passing throngs of visitors. My friends approached in a smiling group. From the center Marilu emerged. My heart leapt! "Surprise!" she whispered, almost as a question. "Yes," I answered, reaching my arms out to her. "I'd love to dance with you."

What a glorious day we had, there in the faraway land of Flushing Meadows. For those few hours, we were really off the block and out of the neighborhood, free to be two American teenagers in love.

TIME, DISTORTED BY THE MADNESS of the late sixties, gradually moved us apart. For the first few years, I heard news of Marilu from mutual friends, but as the old neighborhood disintegrated and we all scattered, the network was broken.

Although I haven't seen Marilu in over 30 years, there is still a worn manila envelope in the place where I keep those things precious to me. In it are Marilu's fading letters, unused tickets to a high school dance, and the still blushing memory of first love.

Recipes

AFTER THOSE STOLEN MOMENTS WITH MARILU on Sunday mornings, the afternoons were devoted to the weekly family dinner. At two o'clock, all 18 of us filled the large kitchen on Myrtle Avenue. My cousins Caroline and Ken and I, six months apart in age, shared our dramas of adolescence between courses. Sometimes we'd seek the counsel of Carol or the biting wit of Paul, Ken's older siblings. The comfort of Papa Andrea's food always turned the drama into farce, and we laughed, surrounded by the warmth of our family.

Alivi Chini

*S*tuffed Olives

AS THE SICILIANS SAY, the purpose of an antipasto is *u sprog-ghiu pitittu*, to undress the appetite. These olives stuffed with a piquant parsley pesto do just that. Serve them with crusty bread.

For 8 to 12 servings

2 large eggs
12 ounces (about 80) canned extra-large pitted
    California black olives
8 canned anchovy fillets, packed in olive oil
6 cornichons or 4 teaspoons chopped sour pickle
1 tablespoon capers, rinsed and drained
½ teaspoon grated lemon zest
2 teaspoons extra-virgin olive oil, plus more for drizzling
    Black pepper
1 cup finely chopped Italian parsley

Pierce the large end of each egg with a pin to prevent cracking. Put the eggs in a small pot, cover with cold water and cook for 9 minutes after the water comes to a boil. Place the eggs under cold running water to loosen the shells, peel and cut in half. Remove the yolks and put them in a small bowl. Set aside. Discard the whites.

Soak the olives in two changes of cold water to remove excess salt. Using a small food processor or a mortar and pestle, process the anchovies, cornichons, capers and lemon zest to a paste. Add the oil and a few grindings of black pepper. Add the parsley and process for a moment longer. Mash the egg yolks with a fork and mix them in.

The quickest way to stuff an olive is with a cookie press (with the ratchet disengaged) or an icing syringe. Fit it with an appropriately sized tip and fill it with the stuffing. Place the plunger against a work surface with the tip straight up. Holding the olive's hole over the tip with one hand, gently push down the press with the other to fill the olive. An alternative method is to use a small pastry bag with a plain metal tip.

Place the olive in a serving bowl and continue until all the olives are stuffed. Toss with a drizzle of olive oil and a sprinkling of coarse-ground black pepper.

Serve at room temperature. The olives may be stored, well covered, in the refrigerator for up to 5 days. Bring back to room temperature before serving.

Maccarruni 'o Furnu

$\mathscr{B}$aked Macaroni

ALTHOUGH WE ATE PASTA in a variety of ways several times during the week, on Sundays it was always baked with a special meat sauce with a hint of cinnamon.

For 8 servings

FOR THE TOMATO SAUCE

2 28-ounce cans peeled Italian plum tomatoes
1 small onion, finely chopped
3 tablespoons extra-virgin olive oil
4 ounces crimini or Italian brown mushrooms,
   chopped medium-fine
   Sea salt
8 ounces ground veal
2 ounces ground pork
2 tablespoons tomato paste dissolved in ⅔ cup water
1 tablespoon sugar
   Black pepper
   Pinch of ground cinnamon
2 sprigs basil, chopped, or ¼ teaspoon dried basil

FOR THE MACARONI

2 tablespoons extra-virgin olive oil

2 tablespoons sea salt

3 pounds good-quality ricotta

1½ cups grated imported pecorino cheese, preferably Locatelli

10 sprigs Italian parsley, chopped
   Black pepper

1½ pounds ziti tagliati or other medium tube pasta
   without ridges

Prepare the tomato sauce: Place a food mill fitted with the smallest-holed (⅟₁₆ inch) disk over a bowl. Puree the tomatoes in order to remove the seeds, which can make the sauce bitter. Scrape the pulp from the bottom of the mill into the bowl.

Put the onion and olive oil in a heavy medium pot over medium heat and sauté the onion until it turns translucent, about 5 minutes. Add the mushrooms, increase the heat to high and season with salt. When the liquid has mostly evaporated, add the veal and pork. Sauté, stirring with a wooden spoon to break up any clumps, until browned. Reduce the heat to medium and stir in the dissolved tomato paste to thicken for about 1 minute, then add the tomatoes. Stir well. Add the sugar, black pepper, cinnamon and basil. Reduce the heat to low and simmer the sauce, uncovered, stirring occasionally, for 40 minutes. Do not allow the sauce to boil.

Prepare the macaroni: Fill a large pot with 6 quarts water and the oil and salt and put it on the stove to boil.

Meanwhile, prepare the ricotta. Place a food mill fitted with a large-holed disk over a medium bowl. Mill the ricotta to break it up. Using a rubber spatula, mix in ¾ cup of the grated cheese, the parsley and black pepper. Do not use an electric mixer.

When the sauce is ready, add the pasta to the boiling water and cook until it is slightly underdone. Run cold water into the pot to stop the cooking process. Drain the pasta well and put it in a bowl. Toss it with 2 cups of the sauce, then with the ricotta mixture.

Preheat the oven to 400°F.

Choose a 2-inch-deep baking dish just large enough to hold the pasta. Very lightly coat the bottom with tomato sauce. Fill the pan with the pasta. Drizzle the top with a small amount of sauce and sprinkle with ¼ cup of the grated cheese.

Bake for 20 minutes, or until hot and slightly crisp on top. Serve with additional sauce and the remaining ½ cup grated cheese.

Arrustu 'i Vitedda

Veal Shoulder Roast

EXCEPT FOR THE HOTTEST PART OF SUMMER, we always had roast as the second course of Sunday dinner. Whether this roast was pork, lamb or veal depended on the season.

For this veal roast, the shoulder must be boned, trimmed of interior fat and tied or netted. To be certain that the veal has been prepared properly, it's best to purchase the meat from a butcher rather than prepackaged in a supermarket.

For 8 servings

3   pounds russet, Yukon Gold or Yellow Finn potatoes
    Sea salt
1   3½-pound boneless veal shoulder roast,
    about 4 inches in diameter
6   tablespoons extra-virgin olive oil
2   medium onions, finely chopped
    Black pepper
1½   cups dry white wine

Peel the potatoes and cut them in wide slices about ½ inch thick. Soak them in lightly salted water for 1 hour.

After the potatoes have soaked for 30 minutes, preheat the oven to 500°F, with a rack positioned in the upper third.

Form a 12-inch length of aluminum foil, 18 inches wide, into a cylinder. Join the ends to make a doughnut and place it in the center of a 14-by-9-inch roasting pan. Set the roast on this doughnut. Rub the roast very lightly on all sides with salt and olive oil. Press the onions on top and season with black pepper. Put it in the oven and sear for 15 minutes.

Drain the potatoes, coat them with the remaining olive oil and season with salt. When the meat is seared, place the potatoes around the roast. Reduce the heat to 350°F. After about 1½ hours, when the onions are nicely browned, baste the roast with the wine, being careful not to disturb the onions. Gently scrape loose any potatoes that may have stuck to the pan. Cook for 2 hours to 2 hours 15 minutes, until the roast reaches an internal temperature of 140°F. At this point, the meat will offer little resistance when pierced with a skewer.

Remove the roasting pan from the oven and increase the oven temperature to 400°F. Let the roast rest in a warm place for 15 minutes before slicing. Lift the potatoes out of the pan juices, put them in a different pan, and return them to the oven to finish cooking. Degrease the pan juices and keep hot in a small covered saucepan over low heat.

Cut away the strings or netting on the roast and thinly slice. Serve with the potatoes and pan juices.

Castagnoli

$\mathcal{C}$hocolate Nut Truffles

DESSERT ON THOSE SUNDAYS was Sicilian pastry offered by one of the guests, who either brought it along or sent my cousins and me for it after dinner. Never would any guest—no matter how close the relationship—arrive for dinner empty-handed or, as the Sicilians say, *panza prisenza,* presenting the belly.

During the cooler months, my grandfather often made a platter of simply prepared truffles from an old Polizzani recipe. Called *castagnoli,* large chestnuts, their refined flavor suggests a complicated preparation, but, as you'll see, the recipe is very easy to follow.

For about 40 truffles

1   cup plus 2 teaspoons spring water
¼   cup regular-grind espresso or decaf espresso
8   ounces shelled raw whole almonds
8   ounces shelled raw whole hazelnuts (filberts)
1¾ cups sugar, plus more for dusting
¾   cup European-style unsweetened cocoa powder
4   teaspoons ground cinnamon
    Pinch of finely ground black pepper
2   tablespoons grappa or vodka
1   teaspoon vanilla extract
¼   teaspoon almond extract

Make strong coffee by bringing 1 cup spring water to a boil and stirring in the ground coffee. Return to a boil for a few seconds. Remove it from the heat and add the 2 teaspoons spring water, which will cause the grinds to fall to the bottom of the pot. Strain the coffee through a fine-mesh strainer. Let it cool to room temperature.

Preheat the oven to 450°F.

Toast the almonds and hazelnuts together for 10 minutes. Take care that the nuts do not burn. When cool enough to handle, rub the nuts together to remove as much of the brown powdery skin from the hazelnuts as possible. Let the nuts cool completely.

Finely chop the nuts in a food processor with 2 teaspoons sugar to keep them from clumping. Put them in a large bowl. Mix in the remainder of the sugar, the cocoa and the cinnamon. Pour the liquor, vanilla and almond extract into a measuring cup. Pour in enough coffee to make ½ cup. Make a well in the nut mixture and pour in the coffee mixture. Mix together to form a stiff, fairly dry paste. Make certain that the liquid has been well distributed and that there are no lumps. Add more coffee in very small amounts if needed.

Line a work surface with waxed paper. Working with wet hands, roll the mixture into balls about the size of a chestnut and place them on the waxed paper.

Roll the truffles, several at a time, in the dusting sugar, coating them well. Place each truffle in a pleated paper candy cup and serve.

Stored in an airtight tin, the *castagnoli* will stay fresh for about 2 weeks.

Scacciata cu Cipuddi

*S*icilian Pizza
with Onions

IN THE EVENINGS after those Sunday dinners, at about seven o'clock, we began to get hungry again. By this time, the guests had multiplied, as the families of my grandmother's brother, Giovanninu (Uncle John), and other cousins and friends arrived.

Using the dough she had made earlier in the day, my mother began preparing sheets of Sicilian-style pizza. She made the popular mozzarella-and-tomato-sauce variety. Others she very simply topped with anchovies and their oil. My favorite is this one made with smothered onions.

For one 17-by-11-inch pizza

FOR THE CRUST

1   package (2¼ teaspoons) active dry yeast
1   teaspoon sugar
1⅓-2   cups warm water (105°F-115°F)
    About 3 cups durum wheat flour
1   cup bread flour
1   heaping teaspoon sea salt
2   tablespoons extra-virgin olive oil,
    plus more for greasing the pan

FOR THE SMOTHERED ONIONS

3   pounds medium onions
¼   cup extra-virgin olive oil
    Sea salt
    Black pepper

FOR THE PIZZA SAUCE

1   28-ounce can peeled Italian plum tomatoes
3   large garlic cloves, peeled and left whole
¼   cup extra-virgin olive oil
2   teaspoons sugar
    Sea salt
    Black pepper
½   teaspoon dried basil

FOR THE TOPPING

1¼ cups grated imported pecorino cheese, preferably Locatelli
16 black oil-cured olives, pitted
2-3 ripe Roma tomatoes, very thinly sliced

Prepare the crust: Mix the yeast and sugar together in a tall warmed glass. Add ⅓ cup of the water and mix with a wooden spoon. Let stand for 7 to 10 minutes until the yeast is foamy.

Mix the 3 cups durum wheat flour, bread flour and salt together in a large warmed bowl or in the work bowl of a food processor. When the yeast is ready, mix it in with a wooden spoon if mixing by hand, with the dough hook of an electric mixer or by pulsing with the food processor.

Mix in the 2 tablespoons oil and 1 cup of the water. Continue mixing until the dough forms a ball. If it is too sticky, add a bit more durum flour; if too dry, add more water.

If mixing by hand, turn the dough out onto a well-floured work surface and knead for 10 minutes, or until the dough is soft and springy. If using an electric mixer, knead for about 5 minutes after the ball is formed, or until soft and springy. If using a food processor, turn the dough out onto a well-floured work surface as soon as a ball is formed and knead briefly by hand.

Lightly sprinkle flour inside a warmed bowl and place the dough ball in it. Cut a ½-inch-deep cross on top of the dough and dust it with flour. Cover the bowl with a dish towel and set it in a warm place to rise for 3 hours, or until doubled.

Prepare the smothered onions: Peel the onions and cut them into quarter slices, ½ inch thick.

Separate the onion pieces and put them together with the oil in a large heavy skillet. Sauté over medium-low heat for 30 to 40 minutes, stirring from time to time to prevent the onions from burning or becoming crisp. They should remain soft.

Increase the heat to high and let any liquid evaporate. Keep turning the onions to prevent them from burning. Continue to sauté until the onions are a light golden color, about 5 minutes. Remove the skillet from the heat. Season with salt and black pepper to slightly offset the sweetness of the onions. Spread the topping in a single shallow layer on a platter to cool to room temperature.

Prepare the pizza sauce: Pour the tomatoes into a bowl. Squeeze them with your hand to break them into small pieces.

Put the garlic and oil in a large heavy saucepan. Sauté the garlic over low heat until lightly cooked on all sides, and discard garlic.

Turn off the heat to prevent splattering, and add the tomatoes, sugar, salt, black pepper and basil to the saucepan. Cook, uncovered, stirring with a wooden spoon, until a creamy consistency is reached. Turn up the heat to medium and let the sauce gently boil for 15 to 20 minutes, until it is reduced to a thick pulp. Stir from time to time to keep the sauce from burning. Cool it to room temperature before assembling the pizza.

Assemble and top the pizza: About 15 minutes before the dough has finished rising, preheat the oven to 450°F and lightly grease a 17-by-11-inch jelly-roll pan or an 18-by-12-inch sheet pan with oil.

When the dough is ready, gently punch it down and turn it onto a lightly floured work surface. Roll it in an even thickness into a rectangle, about the size of the pan. Lift the dough into the oiled pan and stretch it to fit exactly.

Carefully pour the tomato sauce onto the dough. Use the back of a wooden spoon to spread it evenly, right up to the edge. Sprinkle the grated cheese over the sauce and then spread the onions in an even layer on top of the cheese. Decorate with the olives and tomato slices.

Place the pizza in the oven. Immediately reduce the heat to 425°F. Bake for 20 to 25 minutes, until the top has a nicely baked edge and the crust is golden on the bottom. (Check it by carefully lifting a corner with a spatula.)

Let the pizza cool for several minutes before cutting and serving.

XVII.

All Away Out

S
TARTING IN THE 1960s, as the older generation was fading away, families began to leave the old neighborhood.
Motivated by the desire to make a better life, they moved
in droves to the suburbs, as well as to other parts of
Brooklyn and Queens. The exodus began slowly, but soon it seemed
as though we heard news of families leaving every day. A common
conversation went like this:

"I ain't seen Louie Agusti in a long time. You?" someone might
inquire.

"Oh, dey moved," came the response. "Dey moved all away
out."

For us, Bruculinu was the center of the universe. On our planet,
there was no up or down, no near or far, only close in, or way out.
When someone left, it was as if he had left our very atmosphere for
a strange new world.

Visiting these relatives and friends in their new places was for us
a journey of discovery. I remember one summer day traveling to
see relatives who had moved to the distant reaches of Queens. My
mother and I dressed in our Sunday best. After an endlessly hot
and sticky subway trip of complicated connections, we took a 10-
minute taxi ride to their house, avoiding an additional session with

buses. As we drove down the quiet streets of two-story row houses, the coolness of the shade trees refreshed us. We marveled at the lushness of the old horse chestnuts. "Dis ain't notin'," said the cab driver. "Whea yous is goin', da trees is so tick, ya can't even see da sky." My mother and I fell back into our seats in openmouthed wonder.

Upon arrival, we were taken on the grand tour. Many aspects of the new home were pointed out to us with great pride. The freshly painted white walls were smooth, the plaster without cracks or unsightly repairs. All of the kitchen's cabinets closed perfectly, without gaps caused by decades of paint buildup. The appliances and fixtures were new and unchipped. Everyone had her own room with a door. There were even *two* bathrooms!

Closets were displayed with great pride, for now everything had a place. We walked down the narrow, steep stairs to the basement. It was dominated by a sparkling white Deepfreeze, the dream food-storage unit of every family. One day this space would be finished with knotty pine paneling and wall-to-wall carpeting, just like the family rooms and dens in TV America.

The woman of the house said, "Why don't yous kids go in da backyard an' play." She said the word "backyard" with special emphasis, as if in a foreign tongue.

The backyard was long and narrow, bordered by a chain-link fence separating it from similar backyards. The lawn was carefully maintained, but we all missed the concrete and tar of our streets back in Bruculinu. Here there was no place to play scullsy or Chinese handball, no place to spin a top or ride a milk-crate scooter. The junk man and the knife sharpener and their bells and songs did not play here. There were no coal deliveries, leaving behind lumps for children to try and press into diamonds, like Superman. Here, on this beautifully manicured lawn, in a cage of chain-link fence, there was no street life, no world to study, no lessons to learn.

O THER MEMBERS OF THE FAMILY moved "all away, all away out," as far as Farmingdale, or Hicksville, or Hempstead, Long Island. Whole sections of the neighborhood settled in brand-new tract house communities. Although a butcher, bread baker, doctor or an undertaker might relocate to serve these towns, it was not the same.

At first, people returned weekly to Bruculinu to stock up on food items, visit friends and relatives or feel the pulse of the old neighborhood. They returned to be married or to have their children baptized in St. Joseph's Church on Suydam Street. As time passed, and their families grew and became more and more involved in local school and social activities, these visits became more and more sporadic.

The new suburban opulence also caused many to leave behind the rustic everyday food of the older generations. The younger children who had never lived in Bruculinu drifted away from our culture. They knew only a few words of Sicilian, and when speaking English they had what the older generation called "an out-o'-town accent."

E VENTUALLY, IT BECAME CLEAR that we, too, must move away. "Boy, da neighborhood's really gone downhill," my mother and aunts would say. Screams and other violent sounds seeped through our windows, and it was no longer safe to be on the street at night. As the old shops closed, familiar faces were replaced by those of strangers.

We moved not so far away to the nearby section of Cyprus Hills. The clean, quiet, tree-lined streets of this solid working-class neighborhood housed people of mixed European heritage. Grant Avenue was the last block of Brooklyn to border Queens. At the corner was the Jamaica Avenue el, and the passing of trains, now muffled by distance and trees, reminded us of our old apartment under the Myrtle Avenue el. But Grant Avenue was a vastly different place.

The apartment was certainly nicer, but these clean white walls held no history. They would never remind us of my grandmother, or my father, or Ziu Turiddu, or all of the others now passed away. And with the family scattered, the likelihood of building a rich new store of memories here was slim. We may still have been in Brooklyn, but this wasn't Bruculinu.

ONE DAY IN 1967, Papa Andrea came home with a prize. He fairly bounded through the door into the kitchen of our second-floor apartment. Spring's sunlight streamed through the café curtains. Although my grandfather was 95 years old, the sunlight played off his sparkling eyes and rosy cheeks showing the vitality of a much younger man.

Without taking off his jacket, he sat down at the table and gently placed the small brown paper bag containing the prize in front of him. Encircling it with his arms and with a beaming smile, he said to me in Sicilian, "Look, my boy! Look what I have!" He carefully opened the fold and pulled out a small cloth sack with Italian writing on it. The sack was sewn closed at the top. Dramatically, he took his folding knife out of his pocket, opened it, and with the deftness of a surgeon, snipped the thread. He reached in and, cradling a small handful of the contents in his palm, said, "You see, my boy? You see what it is? *Risu aburiu!*"

He sat there all day long scooping the grains of Arborio rice, letting them cascade over his hand into the bag, repeating over and over again, with a triumphant chuckle, "*Risu aburiu!*"

His prize was more than just rice. These ancient seeds had followed him from the mountains of Sicily across the sea to America, from the streets of Bruculinu, even to this new, quiet place. As each grain slipped through his fingers, it held a memory, a dream, a hope fulfilled or lost. The old man laughed because, now, in the twilight of his hour, this measure of rice showed him how bountiful his life had been.

301

BRUCULINU IS GONE NOW. I haven't visited in over 20 years, but even at that time the place was unrecognizable to me. Its true vitality was never physical, but rather spiritual. And the spirit of Bruculinu, America, is carried deep in the minds and hearts of all of us who experienced its streets, learned its lessons and lived its richness.

Recipes

THE FOLLOWING RECIPES are from the rustic cuisine of Polizzi Generosa in the Madonie Mountains of western Sicily. For the most part, they have been handed down to us by the early-twentieth-century immigrants from that ancient city.

Maccu

$\mathcal{D}$ried Fava Bean Puree

M *ACCU* IS AN ANCIENT SICILIAN PEASANT DISH, dating back millennia. In ages past, it was sometimes the only food found on the poorest of tables. Today, it is eaten as a soup course.

Dried fava beans come in two forms: peeled (yellow) and unpeeled (brown). The peeled are preferable for this recipe. When using the unpeeled ones, add an additional four ounces and peel them after soaking. Dried fava beans can be found in Italian and Middle Eastern grocery stores.

For 6 servings

- 1 pound dried peeled fava beans
- 8 cups spring water, for cooking
  Sea salt
- ⅓ cup chopped leaves and tender stems of wild fennel
  or bulb fennel
  Extra-virgin olive oil
  Black pepper

Put the fava beans in a colander and wash them under cold running water. Check for stones and other debris. Transfer to a large bowl, cover with cold water and soak overnight.

Drain the beans and put them in a heavy medium pot with 8 cups spring water and 1 teaspoon salt. Bring to a boil, reduce the heat to low and simmer for 1 hour, stirring frequently to prevent sticking.

Stir in the fennel and cook 30 minutes to 1 hour more, or until the beans can be mashed to a puree with a wooden spoon against the side of the pot. Mash all the beans in this manner. When the beans are cooked and mashed, taste for salt, adding more if necessary. Serve hot with a drizzle of oil and a grinding of black pepper.

Risu chi Favi Virdi

*R*ice with

Fresh Fava Beans

I N THE EARLY SPRING, fresh fava beans abound in the terraced mountain gardens of Sicily. They herald spring's renewal and are prepared in a soupy dish to warm the last of winter's chill.

Fresh fava beans grow in a brownish green pod. They are about seven inches long and pithy. Their season is throughout the spring and early summer, and they can be found in Italian and Middle Eastern grocery stores and in some supermarkets.

For 6 servings

1½ pounds fresh fava beans in the pod
    Sea salt
  1 pound long-grain rice
 ¼ cup chopped leaves of wild fennel or bulb fennel
 ⅓ cup extra-virgin olive oil
  1 cup grated imported pecorino cheese, preferably Locatelli
    Black pepper

Bring 7 cups water to a boil in a heavy medium pot. Meanwhile, shell the fava beans. Put the fava beans in the boiling water, cover and blanch for 2 minutes to loosen the skins. Using a slotted spoon, transfer them to a colander. Turn off the heat and reserve the cooking liquid in the pot, covered.

Cool the fava beans quickly under cold running water. Squeeze them out of their skins into a bowl, making a small cut in the skin if necessary.

Add ¼ teaspoon salt to the bean water and bring it to a boil over medium heat. Add the rice and bring back to a boil. Add the fava beans and the fennel. Reduce the heat to medium and cook at a tremble, stirring from time to time so the rice does not stick to the bottom of the pot and adding more water if necessary, until the rice is al dente, about 20 minutes.

Remove the pot from the heat and mix in the oil. Add the cheese and stir it well into the rice and beans. Taste and adjust the salt if necessary. Sprinkle the top with a good amount of freshly ground pepper. Cover and let stand for 3 minutes.

Serve the rice hot from the pot in which it was cooked.

Sparaci a Sciuscieddu

sparagus Soup

S *CIUSCIEDDU* DERIVES FROM THE SICILIAN VERB *susurrari,* to whisper. The term, brought over from Polizzi Generosa, refers to a number of dishes so hot that they must be blown on, or whispered over, to cool them sufficiently before eating.

A paste of grated pecorino cheese and eggs is stirred into the soup and warmed just long enough for the cheese to melt and for the eggs to thicken but not seize.

For 4 large servings

1	small onion, finely chopped
⅓	cup extra-virgin olive oil
1	pound asparagus, the thickest available
5	cups water
16	sprigs Italian parsley
	Sea salt
3	large eggs
1½	cups grated imported pecorino cheese, preferably Locatelli
	Black pepper

Put the onion and oil in a heavy 4-quart pot over medium-low heat and sauté the onion until it is a rich golden color, about 10 minutes.

CHAPTER XVII.

Cut away the thick fibrous ends of the asparagus and peel the thickest parts. Cut the asparagus into 1-inch pieces. Add to the pot, turning the pieces in the oil for 1 to 2 minutes. Do not let them brown. Add the water and parsley and season lightly with salt. Reduce the heat and simmer, covered, for about 12 minutes, or until the asparagus is soft.

Meanwhile, beat the eggs in a small bowl. Whisk in the grated cheese until the paste is the consistency of mayonnaise. Whisk the paste into the soup. It may be necessary to turn the heat back on to very low to melt the cheese, but do not allow the eggs to seize. Serve immediately with a grinding of black pepper.

Pasta chi Funci

Pasta with Mushrooms

THE MUSHROOMS IN THIS DISH are not sautéed but slowly stewed, producing a wonderfully deep, earthy flavor.

In the autumn, the woods around Polizzi Generosa abound with several varieties of extraordinary wild mushrooms. One type is called *funci 'i ferla*. They are large and round, resembling our cultivated portobello variety in taste, size and texture.

For 6 servings

1½   pounds portobello mushrooms
½   cup chopped Italian parsley
½   cup plus 2 tablespoons extra-virgin olive oil
1   tablespoon tomato paste dissolved in 1 cup water
    Sea salt
    Black pepper
1   pound linguine or spaghetti
¾   cup grated imported pecorino cheese, preferably Locatelli

Wipe the mushrooms clean, using as little cold water as possible to remove dirt. Trim the stems, discarding any that are dried out. Cut the caps and remaining stems into ½-inch pieces.

Put the mushrooms, parsley, ½ cup of the oil and the dissolved tomato paste in a heavy pot large enough to hold the mushrooms and, later, the cooked pasta. Season with salt and black pepper. Cover and cook at a gentle simmer for 50 minutes. If at any time the liquid evaporates and the mushrooms begin to crackle, add more water.

Fill a large pot with 6 quarts water. Add the remaining 2 table-spoons olive oil and 2 tablespoons salt and bring to a boil. When the mushrooms are almost done, put the pasta in the boiling water and cook until al dente. Drain and toss the pasta with the mushroom sauce in the pot in which it cooked. Add the cheese and taste for salt, adding more if desired. Continue to cook on low heat, uncovered, for 3 minutes, stirring gently with a wooden fork. To prevent the dish from cooling in the least, serve it from the pot.

Cappedda d'Ovu

Little Egg Hats

THIS DISH IS AS PLEASING TO THE EYE as it is to the palate. Also, the minor piece of kitchen magic used in its preparation brings a smile to the chef. Hard-boiled egg-white halves are stuffed and prepared in such a way as to resemble little hats floating in a pool of tomato sauce.

When served as part of a meal, this dish is accompanied by mashed potatoes. Arrange the potatoes in several small mounds around the edge of the plate, so they can be easily drawn into the sauce. When you serve *cappedda d'ovu* as a snack, stand half-slices of bread around the edge instead.

For 4 servings

8 large eggs
1 28-ounce can peeled Italian plum tomatoes
2 tablespoons extra-virgin olive oil, plus more for frying
2 garlic cloves, peeled and left whole
  Sea salt
1 tablespoon tomato paste dissolved in ¼ cup water
2 teaspoons sugar
1 sprig basil
  Black pepper
⅔ cup grated imported pecorino cheese, preferably Locatelli
4 sprigs Italian parsley, chopped

Put a medium pot of water on to boil. Pierce the large end of each of 6 eggs with a pin to prevent cracking. Boil the eggs for 10 minutes. When they are cooked, run them under cold water to release the shells. Peel the eggs, pat them dry and cut them in half the long way. Set aside.

Meanwhile, prepare the tomato sauce. Place a food mill fitted with the smallest-holed (¹⁄₁₆ inch) disk over a bowl. Mill the tomatoes with half their juices in order to remove the seeds, which can make the sauce bitter. Scrape the pulp from the bottom of the mill into the bowl.

Put the 2 tablespoons oil and the garlic in a heavy skillet large enough to later accommodate 12 egg halves in a single layer. Place over low heat and sauté the garlic until it is light golden. Remove and discard. Turn off the heat to avoid splattering and stir in the tomatoes. Season to taste with salt and add the dissolved tomato paste, sugar, basil and black pepper. Simmer for 15 minutes.

Put the hard-boiled egg yolks in a bowl. Add the 2 raw eggs, the cheese, parsley and black pepper. Beat into a smooth paste. Stuff an equal amount of the paste into each egg white, mounding the paste slightly.

Pour ½ inch of oil into another skillet, about half the diameter of the first. Place over low heat. When the oil is hot, place a comfortable number of egg halves into the skillet, white side down. After a few moments, push them gently with a spatula to make sure they haven't stuck to the pan. Fry until rich golden brown, about 5 minutes. Carefully turn the eggs over. The heat will cause the stuffing to expand, forming a "brim" around the egg "hat." Continue to fry until firm. Drain the egg hats on brown paper or paper towels, then place all the eggs in the large skillet, yolk side down, to absorb the flavor of the simmering sauce for 5 to 10 minutes. Plate and serve.

Gattò

Potato and
Eggplant Cake

GATTÒ IS DERIVED FROM THE FRENCH WORD for cake, *gâteau.* The cuisine of Polizzi Generosa includes several versions of this potato cake. In this one, the sharp flavor of the pecorino cheese in the potato crust stands up to the hearty richness of the veal *ragù*, eggplant and mozzarella in the filling.

Gattò is best served on its own, followed by a mixed green salad. Leftovers may be reheated wrapped in foil in a hot oven.

For 6 servings

2½ pounds eggplant
   Sea salt
   Extra-virgin olive oil
3 pounds russet, Yukon Gold or Yellow Finn potatoes
4 tablespoons (½ stick) unsalted butter, melted, plus more for
   greasing the pan
4 large eggs, beaten
1⅔ cups grated imported pecorino cheese, preferably Locatelli
4 sprigs Italian parsley, finely chopped
   Black pepper
1 tablespoon tomato paste
1 28-ounce can peeled Italian plum tomatoes
1 medium onion, finely chopped
¾ pound ground veal
2 teaspoons sugar
2 slices soppressata salami, ¼ inch thick, diced

6 ounces mozzarella, shredded
Unflavored fine dry bread crumbs, for lining the pan
and sprinkling on top

Cut each eggplant in half the long way. Using a small knife, poke many deep slits into the flesh. Sprinkle liberally with salt and place the eggplant halves, cut side down, against the sides of a colander. Place the colander in the sink or in a bowl to release the bitter liquid that will leach out. Let stand for 2 hours.

About 20 minutes before the eggplants are ready, preheat the oven to 375°F.

Rinse the salt off the eggplants under slowly running water and pat dry. Place on a baking sheet, cut side up, and drizzle oil over each half. Bake for 50 to 60 minutes, or until the flesh offers little resistance when prodded with a spoon. When the eggplant is cool enough to handle, peel away the skin. Chop the flesh into a fine pulp and spread it in a shallow layer on a platter to cool. Set aside.

Peel the potatoes and cut them into chunks of equal size. Put them in a pot of lightly salted cold water over medium-high heat. Boil until tender, 35 to 40 minutes, depending on the size of the pieces. Drain thoroughly and, using a potato masher or a fork, coarsely mash the potatoes with the butter. Let cool slightly and employ the same method to mash in the eggs, grated cheese, parsley and pepper to a smooth puree. (Do not use a machine, as overworking the potatoes will turn them starchy.) Transfer to a shallow bowl to cool. When the puree reaches room temperature, refrigerate until needed. It will be easier to handle when chilled.

In a small bowl, dissolve the tomato paste in ½ cup of the juice from the can of tomatoes. Discard the remaining liquid. Place a food mill fitted with the smallest-holed (1/16 inch) disk over a bowl. Mill the tomatoes in order to remove the seeds, which can make the sauce bitter. Scrape the pulp from the bottom of the mill into the bowl.

Put 3 tablespoons oil and the onion in a large skillet over

315

medium heat. Sauté until the onion is translucent, about 5 minutes. Increase the heat to high, add the veal and sauté until browned. Stir in the tomato-paste mixture and let it thicken for 1 to 2 minutes. Break up any large clumps of meat with a wooden spoon. Turn off the heat to avoid splattering and pour in the tomatoes. Stir in the sugar and season with salt and black pepper. Simmer, uncovered, over low heat, stirring occasionally, for 40 minutes.

Transfer the sauce to a large bowl. Using a slotted spoon, add the chopped eggplant, leaving behind any liquid that may have separated from it during cooling. Stir in the salami and let cool, then add the mozzarella.

Preheat the oven to 350°F, with a rack positioned in the upper third. Grease the sides and bottom of a 10-inch springform pan with butter and coat it generously with bread crumbs. Sprinkle an additional tablespoonful of crumbs on the bottom. Assemble the *gattò* just before baking. (If you do it too far in advance, liquid may leak through the potato crust.)

Use about two thirds of the chilled potato mixture to line the bottom and sides of the pan in an even layer, smoothing it with a spatula and making sure it is not too thick in the corners or too thin at the top edge. Using a slotted spoon, put the tomato mixture in the pan, leaving behind any liquid that falls through the holes. Completely cover the top with the remaining chilled potato mixture in an even layer. Seal the edges well by using a spatula to gently push the potato from the top edge of the pan into the potato of the top layer to enclose the filling. Sprinkle with more bread crumbs and drizzle with oil.

Bake for 50 minutes, or until golden brown.

Carefully run a knife around the edge of the sides to loosen them from the pan. Let the *gattò* rest for 10 minutes before removing the sides of the pan, then 5 minutes more before cutting and serving.

Capiddi d'Ancilu

ngel Hair

FOR MANY SICILIANS IN FORMER TIMES, *capiddi d'ancilu* was the closest thing to a sweet they knew. Some people from Bruculinu may still remember their mothers or grandmothers preparing this wholesome food as an after-school treat.

Capiddi d'ancilu is made from a finely cut omelette (supposedly resembling the blond tresses of an angel) sweetened with syrup and dusted with chopped nuts and cinnamon.

For 4 servings

1	cup sugar
½	cup spring water
¼	cup shelled raw whole hazelnuts (filberts)
¼	cup shelled raw whole almonds
1	tablespoon unsalted butter
4	large eggs, beaten
	Ground cinnamon, for dusting

Preheat the oven to 450°F.

Put the sugar and water in a small saucepan over low heat and bring to a boil. Let it boil for 5 minutes. Pour the syrup into a bowl, and let it cool for the remainder of the preparation time.

Toast the hazelnuts and almonds together for 10 minutes. Take care that the nuts do not burn. When they are cool enough to handle, rub them together to remove as much of the brown powdery skin from the hazelnuts as possible. Let the nuts cool completely.

Finely chop them in a food processor and put them in a bowl until needed.

Melt the butter in a 9-inch skillet or omelette pan over medium-low heat. When it stops foaming, pour in the beaten eggs. Cook gently until the bottom is golden, about 3 minutes. Do not let it brown. Flip the omelette and cook until golden on the other side, about 2 minutes. Remove from the pan and cut the omelette into strips as wide as the omelette is thick.

Dip the strips into the still warm syrup, coating them well. Arrange them in a mound on an oval serving dish and toss with the chopped nuts. Dust with ground cinnamon. Serve warm.

Acknowledgments

I WISH TO EXTEND MY SINCEREST THANKS to my agent, Martha Casselman, whose belief in this project, understanding and hard work have carried it from the earliest draft through publication; to my manager, Gary Quinn, who knew I had books to write before I did; to my editor, Rux Martin, whose love affair with this book has been sometimes stormy, sometimes fair, but who has always offered the utmost support and the clearest vision to bring the streets of Bruculinu to the heartland of America; to Susan Derecskey for her enthusiastic editing of the recipes; to David Nussbaum for his precise recipe testing; to Jayne Yaffe for her exquisite manuscript editing; to Susan McClellan for her elegant designs; to Michelle Hackwilder of the Brooklyn Historical Society and to my dear friend Andrea Balis for her time at the society's photo library; to Greg Gorman for his extraordinary author portrait; to Anthony Adler, Larry Gilbert, Phillip Goldfarb (my Brooklynite brother) and David Zarem for their good counsel.

I extend my deepest thanks to all those who graciously shared their kitchen secrets, especially Pino Agliata, Flo Braker, Enza Dolce, Carol Field, Adam Perry Lang, Santo Lipani, Russ Parsons and Donald Silvers, a fountain of culinary knowledge.

I extend my grateful appreciation to the long list of people who shared their own remembrances of Brooklyn, including my aunts Mae and Josephine Coco, Bert Armus, Julia Danile, Tony Guma, Charles Iadanza, Felicia LaBanca, Frances MacEwen, Frank Sivero, *fratimiu*, Frances Toto, Steve Toto, Donald Vilardi, Frances Vilardi and Al Viviano.

And, as always, my most special, heartfelt thanks to my wife, Carol, whose love and support are as steady as the beating of my own heart.

319

The Recipes by Category

Antipasto *(Sprogghiu Pitittu)*

Stuffed Olives *(Alivi Chini)* 285
Peppers Roasted in Ashes *(Pipi suttu Cinniri)* 268
Hearts of Artichoke Salad *(Nsalata 'i Trunzi 'i Cacuocciuli)* 217
Chickpea Fritter Sandwiches *(Pani e Panelli)* 194
Rice Balls with Butter *(Arancini al Burru)* 92
Fried Squid *(Calamari Fritti)* 70
Baked Stuffed Squid *(Calamari Chini 'o Furnu)* 72
Christmas Eve Salt Cod *(Cunigghiu)* 89

First Courses *(Primi Piatti)*

Dried Fava Bean Puree *(Maccu)* 304
Wheat Berry and Chickpea Porridge *(Cuccia)* 54
Asparagus Soup *(Sparaci a Sciuscieddu)* 308
Rice with Fresh Fava Beans *(Risu chi Favi Virdi)* 306
Macaroni with Beans *(Pasta chi Fasoli)* 18
Pasta with Chickpeas *(Pasta chi Ciciri)* 176
Pasta with Italian Green Beans *(Italieddi e Fasoleddi)* 270
Pasta with Mushrooms *(Pasta chi Funci)* 310
St. Joseph's Day Pasta *(Pasta chi Sardi)* 196
Anellini with Eggs and Cheese *(Aneddi cu l'Ovu e Tumazzu)* 119
Baked Macaroni *(Maccaruni 'o Furnu)* 287
Filled Crepes *(Manicuotti)* 56
Rice Bombe *(Tumala d'Andrea)* 220
Sicilian Pizza with Onions *(Scacciata cu Cipuddi)* 294

Second Courses *(Secunni Piatti)*

Sicilian-Style Omelette *('a Frocia)* 178
Little Egg Hats *(Cappedda d'Ovu)* 312

One-Course Meals *(Pasti Completi)*

Accompaniments *(Conturni)*

Stuffed Zucchini *(Cucuzzeddi Chini)* 226

Saint Joseph's Bread *(Pani 'i San Giuseppi)* 198

Desserts *(Cosi Duci)*

Angel Hair *(Capiddi d'Ancilu)* 317

Pudding of the Angels *(Budinu 'i Ancili)* 124

Marsala Biscotti *(Viscotta 'i Marsala)* 163

Orange Biscotti *(Viscotta 'i Aranci)* 259

Hazelnut Cookies *(Nucatuli)* 165

Ladyfingers *(Taralli)* 44

Filled Puffs *(Sfinci 'i San Giuseppi)* 202

Sweet Ricotta Turnovers *(Cassateddi)* 228

Christmas Pastry *(Cucciaddatu)* 106

Yuletide Wreath *(Struffuli)* 109

Cassata *(Cassata alla Siciliana)* 231

      Almond Paste *(Pasta Riali)*

      Soaking Syrup *(Sciroppu)*

      Sponge Cake *(Pan 'i Sponza)*

      Sugar Glaze *(Zuccaratura)*

Chocolate Nut Truffles *(Castagnoli)* 292

Prickly Pears *(Fucurinia)* 17

Lemon Ice *(Limunata)* 253

Strawberry Ice *(Granita 'i Fraguli)* 255

Cherry Ice *(Granita 'i Girasi)* 256

Cinnamon Gelato *(Gelatu 'i Cannedda)* 257

Strawberry Jam *(Cunserva 'i Fraguli)* 27

Black Coffee *(Café Niuru)* 46

Tangerine Liqueur *(Mannarina)* 76

The Sicilian Pantry

Anchovies

For these recipes, use anchovies packaged flat in olive oil in two-ounce cans or little jars. The best-quality ones are drier and require more delicate handling. Anchovies are also packed in salt. These must always be thoroughly rinsed and boned before use.

Bread Crumbs

Always use unflavored fine dry bread crumbs made from the crust and white of good Italian bread. To make these at home, keep leftover bread, uncovered or in a paper bag, in a dry place until it is very hard. Grate on the smallest holes of a box grater or in a food processor. Stored in a tightly closed container in a cool, dry place, bread crumbs have a long shelf life.

Capers

Capers are the flower buds of a shrub native to the Mediterranean. They are sun-dried and then packed in salt or pickled in vinegar brine. The pickled ones must be rinsed before use. The salt-cured ones, which have a subtler flavor, must be soaked in a small bowl of water and then rinsed to remove the excessive salt. Capers are graded according to size; the smallest, most expensive are called nonpareil. I have found the larger ones, however, to have more flavor.

Cheese

In order to reproduce the authentic flavors of Sicily, good-quality cheeses are essential.

Pecorino is the cheese most often used in these recipes. It is an aged, hard cheese made from ewe's milk, whitish to pale yellow in color. Pecorino romano is a style of pecorino made in the region around Rome. Locatelli is the brand name of the best-quality imported pecorino romano commonly available in this country. The name is printed clearly on the wax rind. Domestic romano cheese is also available, but it is made from a mixture of cow's and goat's or ewe's milk and lacks the intense flavor of the imported product.

When purchasing pecorino, buy it in a piece rather than grated. It is best from the center of the wheel with the wax rind attached at one end. The wax will help prevent the cheese from becoming too hard and dry. Stored double-wrapped in plastic in the refrigerator, pecorino will keep for several months.

Just before use, grate the cheese on a hand grater. A machine will not properly reduce the cheese to fine threads but rather chop it into tiny round pieces. This will affect the delicacy of its flavor.

Ricotta is the second cheese made from the milk of either ewes or cows. After the first cheese is formed, the remaining whey is re-cooked, *ri-cotta.* When it reaches a scalding temperature, the ricotta rises to the top. Ricotta should be pure white, creamy and fluffy, never grainy or yellow. Good-quality ricotta is available at Italian markets and specialty food stores. If the proper kind cannot be found, follow the simple recipe for making a ricotta-like cheese on page 202.

Ricotta salata is a salted, pressed ewe's milk ricotta. It is sometimes called hard ricotta, *ricotta dura,* and there is a Greek version, *myzithra.* Ricotta salata is available in several textures. The softer ones are creamier and less salty. All are best shredded on the largest hole of a box grater. Purchase ricotta salata in smaller quantities than pecorino, as it has a tendency to oxidize and turn brown. If the oxidized layer is thin, it may be pared away and the remainder of the cheese used.

Mozzarella is a delicately flavored, creamy, soft, white cheese. In most of Italy and Sicily, it is made from whole cow's milk. In this country, commercially produced mozzarella is often made from partially skimmed milk. It tends to be too sharp tasting and granular in texture for these recipes. Whole-milk mozzarella can be found at Italian groceries.

In recent years, a type of mozzarella made from water buffalo milk has become quite popular. *Buffala,* which comes packed in water or whey, is intended to be eaten uncooked and is not suitable for cooking. Fresh whole-milk mozzarella packed in water or whey is also available at Italian markets, specialty food stores and some large supermarkets. It can be made suitable for use in cooking by taking it out of the water and drying the surface. Wrap it in cheesecloth and aluminum foil. Refrigerate it for a couple of days to dry out and harden.

Cinnamon

We usually think of cinnamon as an ingredient in sweet rather than savory dishes. For most of the thousands of years it has been in use, however, this has not been the case. Cinnamon is an essential ingredient in curry as well as many other delights of the Levant and North Africa. It is via this trade route that it found its way into Sicilian cuisine.

As with all spices and dried herbs, store cinnamon in a tightly closed container in a cool, dark place. Renew it on a yearly basis.

Fennel

Wild fennel is a fernlike plant with bright green leaves that resemble dill leaves but with an aroma and flavor reminiscent of licorice. In this country, fennel grows wild as far north as southern New York, Kansas and the Pacific Northwest in backyards, vacant lots, on hillsides—just about anywhere there is a patch of earth. It is extremely tenacious. Its season is usually from February to July, when it begins to go to seed. If you are certain what this plant looks like, by all means forage it for use in these recipes. Wild fennel can be grown easily in your garden from seeds (see Mail-Order Sources, page 328), but be aware that it spreads like a weed.

Cultivated fennel, called bulb fennel or sweet anise, has a large edible bulb. The leaves have a less intense flavor than wild fennel, but they can be substituted in these recipes.

Saffron

Saffron is the yellow-orange stigmas from a small crocus; it is the most expensive spice in the world. Fortunately, a very small amount goes a long way. When a recipe calls for a pinch of saffron, it should be about 20 threads. Since saffron has such a strong flavor, I feel it is best to err on the light side. The flavor of saffron will begin to lose its intensity after six months, so buy it in small quantities. Good-quality saffron packaged in tiny containers is often available in Italian markets. Middle Eastern or East Indian markets are excellent sources for the freshest saffron, it being a common ingredient in those cuisines.

Tomatoes

For the tomato sauce recipes in this book, use imported canned peeled whole Italian tomatoes. The best are a variety called San Marzano. They are deep red, soft but not watery, and velvety to the touch. The flavor is sweet, rich and intense but not acidic. Remember that no matter how many happy peasants or Italian words there are on the label, if it doesn't say "Product of Italy" somewhere on the can, it is not Italian.

A Word about Food Mills

In most kitchens today, the food mill has fallen into disuse, replaced by the blender, food processor and other electric gadgets. None of these, however, can remove seeds from canned tomatoes or gently puree and strain like an old-fashioned food mill.

Use the type of food mill that has two or three interchangeable disks with holes of different sizes ranging from about ¹⁄₁₆ inch to ³⁄₁₆ inch. The holes in a mill with one fixed disk are generally too large to remove the tiny Italian tomato seeds. The process is fast and easy, less than 5 minutes for a can of tomatoes and much less time for other foods.

To mill tomatoes, install the smallest-holed disk and place the mill securely over a bowl. Pour in the tomatoes, and applying slight pressure, turn the handle clockwise about eight times. Then turn it counter-clockwise a couple of times to clear the disk. Repeat until all that is left in the top of the mill are the tomato seeds. Scrape into the milled tomatoes all of the pulp that has stuck to the bottom side of the mill.

Mail-Order Sources

For fine imported Italian and
Sicilian products, durum wheat
and chickpea flour:

Domingo's Italian Grocery
17548 Ventura Boulevard
Encino, California 91316
(818) 981-4466

For fine imported products, local
fresh cheeses, meat and sausage:

Iavarone Brothers
75-12 Metropolitan Avenue
Middle Village, New York 11379
(718) 326-0510

For excellent ricotta, mozzarella
and other fresh cheeses:

Caseificio Gioia
9469 Slauson Avenue
Pico Rivera, California 90660
(562) 942-2663

The Mozzarella Company
2944 Elm Street
Dallas, Texas 75226
(800) 798-2954
or (214) 741-4072

For rich, dark coffee:

**Graffeo Coffee Roasting
Company**
733 Columbus Avenue
San Francisco, California 94113
(415) 986-2420

For food mills and quality cook-
ware:

Let's Get Cookin'
4643 Lakeview Canyon Road
Westlake Village, California
91361
(818) 991-3940

For fennel and other garden seeds:

Thyme Garden
20546 Alsea Highway
Alsea, Oregon 97324
(541) 487-8671

Index